Contemporary Problems in Moral Theology

Contemporary Problems in Moral Theology

Charles E. Curran

Fides Publishers, Inc., Notre Dame, Ind.

Preface

The first five essays in this volume have appeared as separate studies of particular problems existing in moral theology today. These essays make no pretense of forming a systematic study, but rather illustrate the content questions and methodological problems in contemporary moral theology. The final essay, written specifically for this volume, synthesizes some methodological approaches mentioned in the earlier essays and offers approaches to the two most important questions facing the discipline today: methodology and the teaching function of the Church.

As a token of my gratitude I am dedicating this volume to the many people who have given me help and hope during the two years in which these essays were written.

I would like to thank the following publishers and periodicals for permission to use materials which first appeared in their publications: *Worship* for "The Sacrament of Penance Today"; Herder and Herder for parts of "The Natural Law and Contemporary Moral Theology" in *Contraception: Authority and Dissent*, ed. Charles E. Curran (New York, 1969); Corpus Books for parts of "The Natural Law and Contemporary Theology" in *Absolutes in Moral Theology?*, ed. Charles E. Curran (Washington, 1968); Joseph F. Wagner for "Sexuality and Sin: A Current Appraisal" in the *Homiletic and Pastoral Review; Continuum* for "Social Ethics and Method in Moral Theology," which was originally published there in a somewhat different form. "Moral Theology and Genetics: A Dialogue" was presented originally as an address at the Conference on Theology in the City of Man celebrating the Sesquicentennial anniversary of St. Louis University and appeared with some modifications in the *Journal of Ecumenical Studies*.

Contents

1 The Sacrament of Penance Today   1

2 Natural Law and Contemporary Moral Theology   97

3 Sexuality and Sin: A Current Appraisal   159

4 Moral Theology and Genetics: A Dialogue   189

5 Social Ethics and Method in Moral Theology   225

6 Afterword: Moral Theology Today   242

  Index   269

1

The Sacrament of Penance Today

It is a fact accepted by many people today in the Roman Catholic Church that the sacrament of penance as it currently exists in the sacramental life and discipline of the Church occupies a less important and even a marginal role in the lives of many Catholics. Most parish priests report that "the number of confessions is down quite a bit from what it used to be." Houses of religious women and seminaries where only a few years ago the canonical rule of weekly confession was practiced quite rigorously have now given up either in theory or at least in practice such a regimen. One is surprised at the number of Catholics both clerical and lay who will admit that they have not "been to confession" in the last year or two or three. Is such a lessening in the importance attached to confession by Christian people a good thing or not? How does one even try to evaluate this fact?

At the same time there are some changes taking place in the practice of the sacrament of penance in the life of the Church. Perhaps the most widespread change has occurred in the area of confession for children. Now in many parishes throughout our country and abroad, children are not receiving penance or going to confession before they receive the Eucharist at age seven. Sometimes confession is put off to the later grades in elementary school.[1] Another changing practice is the growing number of penance celebrations in which people gather together to hear the word of God, to examine their own life in accord with it, to admit their own sinfulness, to pray together for God's mercy and pardon, to change their hearts, to pardon one another, and to thank God in prayer and song for his mercy and forgiveness. At the present time the discipline of the Church demands that for a sacramental confession there must be the accusation of mortal sins according to number and species to the priest and the absolution given by the priest. Sometimes this private confession of sins takes place in conjunction with the penance celebration, but sometimes there is no individual confession.[2] The Second Vatican Council recognized that "the rite and formulas for the sacrament of penance are to be revised so that they give more luminous expression to both the nature and effect of the sacrament" (Constitution on the Liturgy, n. 72). A number of articles and books have appeared urging changes in the rite and format of the sacrament. In the meantime some priests are conducting penance services which do not include private confession of sins to a priest. Will this be an acceptable ritual of the sacrament in the future? What about at the present time? Is a pastor or priest justified in having such penance services without private confession? Are they truly sacramental?

The sacrament of penance thus raises many questions today. In the midst of this upheaval how can we come to a better understanding of the nature and role of the sacrament of penance and be in a position to judge the suggestions that are being made or even being put into practice today? The principle of sane renewal within the Church must try to come to grips with the problems of the present in the light of the needs of the present and also in the light of the best insights of the past. The writings on the sacrament of penance which have appeared in the last few years definitely follow a very legitimate principle of renewal.[3] Many of the basic notions of the sacrament of penance derive their meaning and importance from the Scriptures themselves so that an effort has been made to study these aspects primarily in the light of the Scriptures. Also within the last decades many historical studies have been done in the area of sacrament of penance. Historical studies are of great importance because they remind us that the present moment is not an absolute but a relative and historically conditioned period of time in which some aspects of the sacrament of penance now receive much greater emphasis than they did in the past, while other aspects of the sacrament which were very prominent in the past are not emphasized enough today. The historical changes and development underline the relativities in the present ritual and structure of the sacrament of penance and at the same time furnish important data for a better understanding and for the future restructuring of the sacrament.

Historians of the sacrament of penance mention three different stages in the evolution and development of the sacrament. The so-called public penance, which is better called solemn or canonical penance (there was never any universal norm calling for the public confession of one's sins), was in existence especially from the fourth to the sixth centuries and included three stages.[4] The first stage was the formal entry into the order of penitents by an official act through the imposition of the hands of the bishop. One should note, however, that the public aspect of this entry into the order of penitents was not primarily to cause humiliation to the penitent but rather to assure him of the prayers of intercession of the Church from whose members he had been somewhat removed because of his sin. The second phase was the expiation of his sin in the order of penitents. The penance required of the person was very harsh and even continued at times for the rest of his life. The final stage of this rite was the solemn reconciliation of the penitent to the community through the imposition of the hands of the bishop before the assembly of the faithful.

The second form of penance in the history of the Church has been called tariffed penance, which apparently originated with the Irish monks and spread to the continent during and after the seventh century. This type of penance took place in a much less solemn and public manner; the penitent merely mentioned his sin to the minister. Since this rite originated in monasteries, the ordinary minister of penance was the priest and not the bishop. The priest then imposed a satisfaction on the penitent in keeping with his particular sin and condition. This satisfaction or penance, if you will, was written down in books called the *Libri Paenitentiales*, hence the name of tariffed penance because in these books were set down in a casuistic manner the satisfaction which should be required for particular sins. Two other characteristics distinguished this form of penance from the earlier type. Penance previously had been given to the Christian only once like baptism itself, but now the Christian was able to receive the sacrament more frequently in the course of his life. A second important difference was that the satisfaction or expiation was reduced.

The third stage in the evolution of the sacrament of penance, called by some the modern period, begins at the end of the twelfth century and is highlighted in the decrees of the Council of Trent. The *Libri Paenitentalies* are no longer employed, and the individual priest becomes the judge of the penance to be given the penitent, thus emphasizing a role of the minister of the sacrament as judge. The satisfaction becomes much less harsh and important in the whole structure and understanding of the sacrament. Reconciliation takes place immediately, and the confession of sins itself takes on primary importance and even assumes a penitential value in itself. The telling of one's sins to the priest becomes in itself a penitential act as a humiliation of the person. The entire sacrament now is called confession after the aspect which has assumed the greatest importance in this period. This is fundamentally the structure of the sacrament of penance as it exists in the dicipline of the Church today.

The Pastoral Constitution on the Church in the Modern World took up one of Pope John's themes, the need to read the signs of the times, and incorporated this method into its approach to the questions of life in the world of the twentieth century. In attempts to renew the sacrament of penance, the fledgling science of religious sociology has also been trying to discover the signs of the times in the attitude of Catholics to the sacrament of penance—their problems, difficulties, and desires. Only a few of these studies have been made, but they are helpful in pinpointing some of the problems existing in the experience of contemporary Christians.[5] The more inductive methodology invoked by Vatican II does give a greater importance to the experience of Christian people, but this must be considered with the other elements that enter into the renewal of theology. But in the question of penance theologians from their scriptural, historical and systematic studies agree with the experience of many Catholics in criticizing the juridical preoccupation of the present format of the sacrament and the danger of a mechanical or even magical understanding of penance.[6]

Efforts to renew the sacrament of penance must see this renewal in terms of a better theological understanding of the meaning of the sacrament of penance which can be derived from many of the other renewals which have taken place in the Church but which owe much to a greater attention to the scriptural themes of the sacrament of penance, to the different stages and emphases in the historical development of the various rites of the sacrament, and to the experience of contemporary Christians. Yes, there is need for a change in the rite of the sacrament of penance, but true renewal will not come about merely by changing the rite itself. One must first have a better understanding of all the elements which fit into the sacrament of penance; and only in the light of a better and more complete understanding of the meaning of penance will it be possible for people to participate more meaningfully in this penitential celebration. A change of ritual in itself, although badly needed, is not sufficient, for rites and signs have to fulfill their function of pointing to a deeper reality. This study will emphasize the notions contributing to a deeper understanding of the sacrament of penance so that in this light one can better see the need for new rites and be better prepared to enter into the penitential celebration. A few years ago Karl Rahner published an essay emphasizing the ecclesial dimension of the sacrament of penance under the title of "Forgotten Truths Concerning Penance."[7] The present study does not pretend to give a full theology of the sacrament of penance but rather to bring to light some of the aspects which have in one way or another become forgotten truths about this sacrament.

A word of caution is in order. In many ways today the primary question facing contemporary theology and many Christians is the "God question." The death of God theology is now itself dead, but the problem of God remains as the most important problem in theology. In theology as well as in human life the God problem is perennially important even though it cannot enter fully into theological discussions of particular issues. In the theory and practice of the sacrament of penance the God question remains central because the heart of the sacramental encounter concerns the forgiveness and love of God in Christ offered to the repentant sinner. A number of the problems connected with contemporary man's evaluation of the sacrament of penance have their roots in the very basic question of God.

SIN

Penance as the sacrament of the "forgiveness of sin" obviously presupposes the existence and importance of sin. But does sin have any meaning for modern man? Is sin a vital reality for the twentieth century Christian? If there is no real importance attached to sin and sinfulness, then the sacrament of penance becomes meaningless. Maybe the sense of sin was just a morbid concept from the Middle Ages which man come of age has rightly put behind him.

There is a reluctance on the part of all of us to admit our sinfulness, but it seems that sin still retains an importance in the experience of man today. Technology and science have given man an awesome power over creation; knowledge has been increasing at an ever growing rate; man is continually finding out more about himself and his world. But sinfulness also marks the life of man as an individual and a society. In times of great scientific strides and progress man tends to forget his own limitations and sinfulness, but a meditative reflection on reality cannot help but uncover even in our modern world the existence and importance of sin.

Sin can simply be described for the present as a lack of love and an alienation from God and others. If we are honest with ourselves, we have to admit our own sinfulness.

Our own selfishness and unwillingness to go out of our way to help others are factors we cannot forget as much as we might like to. Are we willing to share what we have with the poor man? Are we willing to embrace the outcast and the forgotten? Are we primarily motivated by the demands of our neighbor in need or rather by our own selfish needs? Are we really willing to change the established structures of our society in which we hold privileged positions at the expense of others? If sin is the opposite of love, then there is quite a bit of sin in our lives, despite the fact that we become uncomfortable when we think about it.

But sin is not just an individual phenomenon. Sin shows its effects in our society as a whole and perhaps is most present in the fact that many of us are unwilling to admit our own sinfulness. A few years ago the death of God theology and the secular city theology tended to downplay the reality of sin. Charles West of Princeton Theological Seminary has described the two opposing viewpoints at the 1966 Conference on Church and Society sponsored by the World Council of Churches as the "theological technocrats" versus the "theological guerrillas."[8] The theological technocrats were those who celebrated the joys of the secular city in which man is becoming progressively more whole and more free. However, their opponents pointed out that while these people were finding salvation and freedom in the secular city, this same secular city society was imprisoning two-thirds of the world in hunger, misery and poverty. Today we can be thankful for the protest movements that have reminded us of the sins that are existing in our society. We must acknowledge that our sins both individually and collectively have been hurting many others.

How easy it is to forget our own sinfulness while at the same time condemning the sinfulness of others. A few years ago there was a television documentary on the Hitler regime in Germany. The final portion of the film showed the last days of the Third Reich and portrayed Hitler as a megalomaniac whose distorted pride and fury made him keep fighting to the bitter end despite all the human death and suffering caused by him. However, never once did the film even suggest that part of the responsibility might have been ours. What right did we as Christians have to demand an unconditional surrender? Perhaps we were just as responsible as Hitler in prolonging the carnage of war. Last year the Sunday Magazine section of the *New York Times* had an article on the end of the hippie movement which was called "The Death of Love." The hippie community was an attempt to have people live together in the bonds of love, but the experiment was unsuccessful precisely because people forgot the existence of sin. Sin ultimately entered the hippie community in the form of drugs, taking advantage of others, self-promotion and feuds. How often today many overly romantic people fail to realize the existence of sin in the world! On the surface it might seem that man has outgrown the reality of sin, but a moment's reflection reminds us of the existence of sin in our own lives and in our own world. Unfortunately, sin is alive and well in the twentieth century.

The Christian message has always realized the importance of sin; in fact, the Christian mystery does not make sense apart from the reality of sin. "It was a fundamental assertion of the kerygma that Jesus came into the world to save sinners, and that he in fact did so by his death."[9] According to the Matthean account (1:21) he was called Jesus precisely because he would save his people from their sins. The redemptive work of Christ Jesus has meaning only in terms of sin; the Paschal Mystery is ultimately the triumph over sin and death. Although his death showed forth the power of sin and the separation between sin and Christ

Jesus, the resurrection was the sign and promise of victory. The gospel message clearly sees the mission of Christ Jesus in terms of redemption and victory over sin. The early Church was aware of its call to continue this mission and free men from sin and bring them into the newness of life in Christ. Christian anthropology recognizes the limited and sinful nature of man; in fact, any view of man which does not give sufficient attention to his sinfulness cannot claim to be Christian.[10]

Despite the importance of sin in the Christian message, Catholic theology has been negligent in developing an adequate understanding of sin. Too often sin has been considered only in terms of the model of law and obedience which emphasizes sin as a specific external action. These actions were then thoroughly categorized and catalogued in lists. Sin as an external action viewed in the light of obedience to the law of God is a very inadequate model for understanding the reality of sin. A mechanical, individualistic, and actualistic concept of sin robbed sin of its real existential meaning for the Christian. Perhaps it is true that the world has lost the sense of sin, but even more unfortunate is the fact that Catholic Christians have lost a true understanding of sin.

A renewed understanding of sin should find its basic inspiration in the Scriptures but also make use of the insights of contemporary understandings of man and anthropology.[11] Both Scripture and contemporary understandings of man argue for a view of sin that follows the model of relationality. Man is a creature living in a multiplicity of relationships; sin is that which destroys these relationships. Perhaps the best illustration of the meaning of sin in the Scriptures is the account given in the first chapters of the book of Genesis. Modern scripture studies remind us that the Genesis account is not an historical account of two people but rather a reflective meditation many years later on the reality of sin. The Judaeo-Christian message makes no sense without an understanding of sin, and the authors here narrate in a very fanciful way their understanding of sin. Contemporary theologians can only marvel at the insight of the authors of Genesis.[12]

The covenant relationship between God and man characterizes the whole of the scriptural understanding of the relationship between God and man. The story of salvation is the story of God's loving choice of a people as his own. Sin is the refusal of man to accept the gift of God's love. Although man has spurned this gift, God is so faithful in his commitment that he sent his Son to restore the relationship of love and offer all mankind an opportunity to enter into his covenant relationship. The Christian believes that all men receive this same invitation in one way or another from God. Thus in Genesis sin is viewed not primarily as a particular external act or even as a particular act of disobedience seen in itself (these are aspects of the reality of sin but not the primary aspect) but rather as the refusal of man to accept his relationship of loving dependence on God. Man wanted to be like God—this was the temptation which was proposed to him. The fact that sin is to be seen in terms of a relationship is more evident in other details of this story. The author implies that God came down and walked with Adam and Eve in the evening in the cool of the garden—a very fanciful way of picturing the relationship of love between them. As a consequence of sin, however, Adam and Eve hid themselves when Yahweh came to walk with them in the garden. As a result of their sin Adam and Eve were expelled from the garden, a sign they had truly broken their relationship of loving dependence on God. Death, according to Genesis, is the penalty of sin; but such a penalty cannot be conceived as merely an arbitrary punishment for wrongdoing. Since sin itself is separation from the author of life, then death is the natural consequence of sin and not just an extrinsic penalty or punishment.

But sin also affects man's relationship with his fellow man. Genesis is lyrical in its description of the love union of Adam and Eve. Eve is the helpmate and companion that Adam was not able to find in the rest of creation; she is flesh of his flesh and bone of his bone. The love union of the two is described by the fact that they left all other persons and things to become one body. But sin deeply affected that union of love, as is portrayed in Adam's reaction to Yahweh after his sin. Adam, instead of defending and protecting his wife with whom he formed one body, now placed the blame on her—"It was the woman you put with me; she gave me the fruit, and I ate it" (Genesis 3:12). The very next chapter describes how the children of Adam and Eve killed one another. The author graphically makes his point: sin affects the relationships existing among men.

The Genesis narrative develops its meditative reflection on sin by illustrating that sin also affects man's relationship with the world. Before the "fall," Adam is portrayed as the king of all creation which exists in perfect subordination to man as is evidenced by the fact that Adam gave a name to all the animals. Sin brings discord into this marvelous harmony of the world. In that which is most characteristically masculine, man's relationship with the cosmos is changed through sin. From henceforth he will know suffering, sweat, and fatigue as he tries to work the fields to provide for his needs and those of his family. The remarkable harmony in which the world would have been as putty in his hands is shattered so that man will now know pain and suffering in work as he tries to eke out his existence against the forces of the world rather than in harmony with them. Sin's effect on man's relationship to the world is also graphically illustrated in the case of Eve, for she is affected in that which is most characteristically womanly—the bearing of children. As a result of sin she would now know the pains of childbirth and bring forth her children in pain and suffering. Thus the membranes of her own body would resist the process of childbirth and cause her pain rather than exist in perfect harmony with the birth process. One can only admire the theological acumen and literary genius which thus presents the reality of sin as affecting man's relationship to God, neighbor and the total cosmos.

The opening eleven chapters of Genesis and much of the Old Testament underline the dynamic aspect of sin especially in its cosmic dimension. In the last few years Catholic theology and catechetics have emphasized the concept of salvation history, but the opening chapters of Genesis are truly a history of sin. Man continues to fall into sin which then by incarnating itself in society and structures tends to grow and increase. The Old Testament frequently recalls the many saving interventions of God (e.g. Noah, Abraham, Moses, etc.); but despite all these saving interventions, the people fall back into the condition of sin. The Old Testament was very conscious of the cosmic aspect of sin which has been emphasized in the concept of the sin of the world developed by some contemporary theologians.[13] Sin affects man and incarnates itself in the structures, customs and institutions of his environment, and thus the reign of sin grows and increases. In such an environment the individual easily becomes contaminated by sin. There are many ways in which one can view the reality of sin, e.g., disobedience to the divine commands; but the model of multiple relationships from the viewpoint of the Scriptures and the best insights of contemporary understandings of man appears to be the most adequate.

In the Christian understanding of man, salvation or redemption is the gracious act of God freeing man from sin
and restoring him to the relationship of love. Catholic theology has always required man's free acceptance of this gift
of God's love which involves his change of heart and entrance
into a relationship of love with the Father through Christ
Jesus which affects all the relationships which constitute the
person. This gift of salvation, which some theologians today
call wholeness, is offered in one form or another to all mankind; but for the Christian it is made explicit in the gospel
message preached by the Church which continues the mission of Jesus in time and space. Does man ever overcome
his sinful condition? The answer is yes and no. Traditional
Catholic theology understands that when man accepts the
gracious gift of salvation he has now overcome his radical
separation from God, and man, but every human being in
this world falls short of the fullness of love in his relationships
with God and man. In this sense man is at the same time
justified and a sinner (*simul justus et peccator*). Thus conversion, justification, or salvation (whatever term is chosen
to describe this reality) is never perfect but always striving
for a greater wholeness. Also there is the possibility that
man might entirely break off his relationship of love with
God and neighbor and thus again separate himself in sinful
isolation. Human sinfulness and sin occupy an important
place in the Christian understanding of reality, so that if
one does not know or experience the reality of sin and sinfulness then the concept of conversion or penance is meaningless.

The above description corresponds to the traditional concept of mortal and venial sin, but the distinction is not
viewed primarily in terms of a particular action. Mortal sin
from the scriptural viewpoint is better interpreted in terms
of a relationship which affects not only the individual's
relationship with God but also his relationship with his

neighbors and the whole world, thus affecting the very core of the person. According to the Scriptures conversion is the process of passing from death to life, from darkness to light, from the old to the new, from flesh to the spirit, a change of heart animated by the gift of the life-giving Spirit.[14] Mortal sin is the opposite of this process and is described in the older categories as the passing from the state of grace to the state of sin. Contemporary theologians with this scriptural basis and borrowing insights from various philosophical viewpoints have lately described sin in terms of a fundamental option.[15] From a Thomistic viewpoint mortal sin is seen as the orientation of the person away from God as his last end with the substitution of another ultimate end, which in the last analysis is the person himself. From an existentialist perspective, mortal sin is the project of existence which overturns the foundational orientation and tendency of the life of the person. From a personalist understanding, sin is the breaking of the relationship of love with God and neighbor. All these different viewpoints emphasize the fact that mortal sin is not just an external action viewed in itself but rather a fundamental orientation of the person, a notion which corresponds with the biblical concept of a change of heart.

In the past moral theology distorted the concept of mortal sin by understanding sin primarily in terms of an external act, thereby viewing sin more as a thing than as a relationship. Catechisms and textbooks frequently classified the catalogues of actions which were mortal sins. Thus sin lost its intensely personal meaning, to say nothing of its social and cosmic dimension. If mortal sin is viewed as just an external act, then the existence of mortal sin appears to be much more frequent than in the concept of a relationship.

A more relational understanding of sin especially as specified in the theory of the fundamental option gives less importance to the external action itself. The external act in such a theory is essentially ambiguous, for it has meaning only insofar as it is revelatory of the human person and his relationships with others. Common sense and prudence have always accepted the reality that you cannot judge a person on the basis of just one short meeting or in the light of one particular action. One cannot judge the ability of an athlete by just seeing the results of one particular action. The sharp word that a person utters may have a variety of meanings. It could very well indicate an intense dislike for the person with whom he is talking, or it might only be indicative of impatience, a migraine headache or the failure to have had a second cup of coffee. Modern psychology also emphasizes the ambiguity of the external act. The full personal meaning of a particular act very often can never be truly known, for even the individual is not always that conscious of his personal motives. A particular act would involve mortal sin only if the act were expressive of this breaking of a fundamental relationship of love with God and neighbor.

Catholic theology has long recognized that man goes from "sin" to "grace" not by one action but by a long series of actions which form one process. Mortal sin must now be viewed in the same way. One does not change so fundamental a relationship just in one particular action, but ordinarily there is a process taking place over a period of time in which this relationship gradually becomes weakened and then is finally broken. This process must ultimately culminate in an action which involves the very existential core of the person and such actions are not frequent in our lives. In such an understanding it is impossible for a person to be in and out of mortal sin two or three times a week. The poor approach of the past has cheapened the very notion and concept of mortal sin which as a consequence has lost real meaning for many Catholics today. Mortal sin is not a common occurrence, and is generally the culmination of a development lasting over a period of time. Again, personal experience reminds us of how difficult and hard it is for us to change some of our basic human orientations. This experience in our relationships with others and with ourselves should reveal some understanding of the reality of our relationship with God.

The stress on the external act in the past definitely distorted the concept of mortal sin. In fairness even to the catechism requirements for mortal sin, it must be pointed out that they included other criteria in addition to the act itself. The threefold criteria for the existence of mortal sin included: grave matter, full knowledge, and full consent of the will. These three conditions if properly understood call for an almost total reaction from the depth of the person himself, a truly fundamental option or orientation. Unfortunately, theology and catechetics gave primary importance to the matter itself as the ultimate determining criterion of the existence of mortal sin. Such a concept even led to the conclusion that certain actions always involve grave matter.[16] The theory behind this insistence on the matter of the external action itself in its best possible interpretation was the presumption that grave or important matter will ordinarily involve the person in the very core of his existence, whereas light matter will ordinarily not evoke a total response on the part of the person. Today our knowledge of man and human relationships is such that it is difficult to place much importance on such presumptions especially because we now appreciate the difficulty involved in saying that any one action expresses the very depth of the personality. Once sin is viewed in terms of the fundamental relationship between the person and God which consists primarily in a basic orientation and not in individual actions, then even the presumptive nature of the older approach no longer retains great value or usefulness.

What then are the criteria for establishing the existence of mortal sin? In actuality there are no certain criteria by which one can establish the existence of mortal sin. Perhaps the best approach remains that found in the Scriptures. Man's relationship with God is known and manifested in his relationship with his neighbors. This is the gist of the so-called judgment scene in Matthew. "Lord, when did we see you hungry or thirsty, a stranger or naked, sick or in prison, and did not come to your help?" (Mt 25:44). John reminds us that we cannot love the God we do not see if we do not love our neighbor whom we do see. The Christian commandment joins together love of God and love of neighbor into a unity so that the best criterion of our love for God is precisely our love for our neighbor, but even this criterion fails to be very specific and remains difficult to apply accurately again because of the essential ambiguity of the external act. It always remains difficult to tell if one has broken this multiple relationship of love. Even the person himself in many cases cannot be aware of it in any reflexive way because of the very nature of this relationship and because of the difficulties of totally understanding one's own motives.

Some theologians conscious of the ambiguity of the external action viewed apart from the orientation of the person have tended to introduce other distinctions in the understanding of sin. For example, a threefold distinction is made: Mortal sin, serious sin, venial sin. Mortal sin is reserved for that which really separates man from love; whereas serious sin is an action viewed in itself which is of serious nature but by itself cannot indicate whether the relationship of love is broken or not.[17] Another theologian introduces such distinctions as sin, mortal sin, serious sin, subjectively non-serious sin, venial sin, light sin, subjectively no imputation of sin.[18] I do not believe that such distinctions are necessary or ultimately even that helpful from a theological or catechetical viewpoint. At best they tend to be only presumptions, and the danger always exists of making them into rigid categories. While such elaborate distinctions serve as a salutary reminder of the complexity and ambiguity of the reality of sin, they remain only approximations which tend in a somewhat simplistic way to analyze the relationship between God and man. It seems to be better to retain just the concepts of mortal sin and venial sin with the realization that mortal sin is the breaking of this multiple love relationship and thus involves a core decision of the whole person, whereas venial sin refers to the lessening of the relationship without involving a total break in that relationship. Naturally there are many degrees involved in the way in which this relationship can be affected without being severed.

However, there is a possible danger of dualism in the approach which sees sin primarily in terms of this fundamental relationship or option which involves the person in the very core of his being. In the past there was an overemphasis on the external act itself, but in the newer perspective there is the danger of not giving enough importance to the external act itself. Mortal sin should be viewed primarily in terms of intentionality, subjective involvement, and personalist categories; but there remains the danger of forgetting about the external act itself. Catholic theology in the last decade has embraced the more personalist categories of thought, but there is an inherent danger that such thought patterns will not pay enough attention to the social, political, and cosmic aspects of reality. The problems facing mankind today are of such social complexity that a narrowly personalist approach will not be able to cope with them.[19] The human act remains a very complex entity. In theology most problems arise not from positive error but from a failure to give the proper weight to all the elements involved.

The notion of mortal sin described above views the individual act insofar as it is an expression of the whole person existing in his fundamental relationships with God and neighbor. However, the complex external act can be viewed from other aspects; for example, one can consider the external act insofar as it affects the persons and the world itself independently of the personal intentionality and involvement of the person placing the act. When a deranged person maims another, there is very little subjective involvement of the core of his personhood in such an act, but such an action does have very drastic consequences on the unfortunate victim and on society itself. A highly scientific and technological society (which, however, is not to be canonized) appreciates the importance of the external act, as does a theology which sees man called to help create the new heaven and the new earth by his own actions. If one is going to reserve the word sin for the fundamental option of love, then perhaps it would be helpful to speak of the external act viewed in relationship to self, others and the cosmos apart from the intentionality of the person in terms of right or wrong. Thus one could say that certain actions (cruelty, indiscriminate warfare, etc.) are wrong without necessarily involving grave sin on the part of the person. An older Catholic theology did appreciate the problem by making the distinction between formal and material sin. Formal sin was precisely the external act insofar as it proceeded from the knowledge and will of the subject, whereas material sin was the act viewed in itself apart from the subjective involvement of the person in the act. One could even employ the term sin in a true but analogous way to describe the external act viewed in terms of its "objective" relationships, but perhaps the need to emphasize the reality of sin as the deeply personal orientation of one's life in terms of the primary relationships which constitute that existence would argue against using the term sin to describe this other aspect of the external act. No matter what terminology is chosen, an understanding of sin in terms of relationality and the fundamental option must avoid the danger of not paying sufficient attention to the external action viewed in its relationships to self, others, and the world apart from the intentionality of the agent. This problem in the understanding of sin points to the deeper philosophical problem involving a proper understanding of the relationship between subjective and objective. Theology today is striving to overcome a false dichotomy, but at times some distinctions such as those made above will be necessary.

Thus a better approach views mortal sin in terms of personal relationships, the involvement of the subject in his own orientation, and a process which gradually develops over the course of time. Such an understanding of sin has important practical and pastoral consequences. In practice one cannot speak of the act viewed in itself as mortal sin. There is no possible answer to the question: Is killing or lying or adultery or blasphemy a mortal sin? (It would be a legitimate question to ask if such an action were right or wrong.) In fact one cannot even have mortal sins. The plural form indicates that sin would be a thing, but if mortal sin is properly understood in terms of a broken relationship of love then it does not admit the plural usage. There are no definite criteria for determining the existence of mortal sin precisely because of the essential ambiguity of the external act. Mortal sin seen as the culmination of a gradual process resulting in the breaking of these fundamental relationships is obviously a rare occurrence in comparison with an older understanding of mortal sin.

The reality behind the concept of venial sin must also be viewed in terms of a condition of the person and his fundamental relationships with God, neighbor, and the world. Catholic teaching has maintained that the ordinary Christian cannot avoid the reality of venial sin in his life. This is another way of saying that man always remains, *simul justus et peccator* (justified and a sinner at the same time), for his relationship of love with God, neighbor, and the world is never perfect. The individual act of venial sin refers to an action which does not come from a core personal involvement in an orientation away from God but rather is expressive of a coolness or lack of full dedication in this relationship of love. In the theory of the fundamental option venial sin remains a peripheral action which does not involve the core decision of the person. In the Thomistic perspective venial sin involves an illogical act because while the person in the core of his being is still united to God as his ultimate end, this particular act is contrary to that orientation. However, the act remains on the periphery of man's self and does not change the reality of his orientation to God as his ultimate end. Venial sin illustrates the condition of man who constantly falls short of the total love union with God, neighbor and the world to which he is called. An emphasis in the past on particular acts has tended to see venial sin primarily in terms of particular acts of commission, whereas the realization of the sinful condition of man opens up the wider horizons of the human condition itself and also acts of omission as well as commission.

New approaches in moral theology have been criticized by some for doing away with the concept of sin; in fact, people have applied to some contemporary theologians the scriptural words: "Behold him who takes away the sins of the world." There is no doubt that an older theology and catechetics tended to develop a very warped notion of sin in the minds of many. The danger remains that in rejecting such inadequate notions the contemporary Catholic is at times tempted to forget the whole concept of sin. But the Christian message is robbed of its true meaning if one does not appreciate the reality of human sinfulness.

The loving gift of God in Christ to all of us presupposes the sinful condition of all mankind in which we would be imprisoned without the gracious gift of God's redeeming love.

No one can appreciate the great gift of God's love without an understanding of the reality of sin from which we have been freed by his gracious mercy and forgiveness. Mortal sin is a comparatively very rare occurrence in the Christian life, but this should only emphasize its importance and its true meaning as the breaking of our multiple relationships of love with God, neighbor and the world. The contemporary Christian also needs to be more conscious of his enduring sinful condition—the fact that even though he is united in love with God and neighbor, nevertheless, he constantly falls short of the love that is asked of him. Modern man in his superficial thinking at times does tend to forget the reality of sin. The history of theology furnishes many examples of theologies which have forgotten the existence of sin and its impact on our existence. The naive hopes of utopian dreams have been dashed against the reality of human sinfulness. Despite all the progress of science and technology men have not been able to overcome the basic human problems of selfishness, exploitation, self-interest, and the failure to accept responsibility for the neighbor in need. Many Catholics today have passed from a triumphalism of the Church to a triumphalism of the world. We are now very much aware of the sinfulness of the Church and the fact that a pilgrim Church is constantly in need of reform and renewal, but frequently we forget the reality of sin existing in the world itself with the suffering, hardship and frustration which that will entail. The perennial danger for man is to be lulled into forgetting the existence of sin. Then his whole life and his Christianity can become very comfortable. Is this not the problem with much of what passes for Christianity today?

The contemporary Christian needs to become more aware of the reality of sin—not in a morbid and scrupulous way, but in a manner that enables him to appreciate more the reality of God's loving gift, to understand his own continuing failure to respond totally to that gift, and to encourage him to join with the Risen Lord in the struggle against sin. Catholic theology has explained the sacramental system in terms of the extension of the Incarnation in time and space. The love of God for man and man's response become visible in the sacramental celebration. The reality of sin also becomes incarnated in time and space through the actions of men in the world, so that there are truly "sacraments of sin"—signs which make present the reality of sin in our human existence. Poverty, war, discrimination, alienation, institutional violence—these are all among the many sacraments of sin existing in our world. How easy it remains for the contemporary Christian to forget the existence of sin, but a thoughtful reflection on human existence today in the light of the scriptural message of love of God and neighbor, especially the neighbor in need, reveals the continuing presence of sin in our life and world. Since Christianity so joins together the love of God and neighbor that the love for neighbor becomes the sign and criterion for our love for God, so too our sinful condition is manifested above all in our relationships with our neighbor and the world. The inequities of our world, the fact that the rich people and nations exploit poor people and nations, the will for power and the subjection of the weak and the failure of men to accept their responsibilities for the world and others are all signs of the reality of sin. The social, political, cultural, economic, and even religious aspects of our human existence all contain elements that show forth the failure of men to live the gospel message of love of God and neighbor. Through the eyes of faith the conscientious Christian sees the sacraments of sin in our world. Just as the sacraments celebrate the loving gift of God to men so too the sacraments of sin constantly remind us of the reality of our failures to love. How can the Christian be complacent and uninvolved in the presence of sin in our lives and our world?

In the neo-Orthodox phase of Protestantism, sin was emphasized as reminding man of his boundaries and limitations so that he became more conscious of the need for God's merciful love. In the last few years, as exemplified to an extreme in the "death of God" theology, Protestant theology has stressed not the imperfections and the limitations of man but especially his power and his responsibility. Man come of age now must take responsibility for the shaping of his earthly existence. Today there seems to be a tendency to realize that the thinking of the last few years might have been too naively optimistic. A balanced theological perspective should keep in view both aspects of sin as it points up sinful man's need for God's loving mercy but also redeemed man's vocation to take responsibility and struggle against the forces of sin in his own heart and in the world. (Remember that this gift of redemption is offered to all mankind.) A proper understanding of sin is necessary for the contemporary Christian to appreciate the gift of God in Christ by which we have been saved from sin and death, for redemption is meaningless unless we can appreciate the gratuitous, loving gift of our redemption. The Christian message sees the reality of sin as manifesting itself primarily in the very death of Jesus who died because of the power of sin and death. Sin is so important an aspect of human existence and so strong that it brought about the death of Jesus, but his death and resurrection also marked the triumph and victory over sin and death.

The Christian now allied through baptism with the Paschal Mystery of Christ Jesus is called to overcome sin and death in his daily life and in the world through the same life-giving love whose greatest sacrament remains the Paschal Mystery of Christ Jesus. Sin still exists in our world and always will exist until the end of time, but the Christian cannot merely sit back and be content in the presence of sin. The Christian is called to cooperate in the redemptive work of Christ in overcoming the forces of sin and death in his own life and in the world. This will be a continual struggle which will never completely be successful and which will end in death, but a death which is also a share in the victory of Christ over sin and death itself. To forget the reality of sinfulness is to forget a very indispensable part of the Christian mystery. Only one who is conscious of sin and sinfulness can appreciate the greatness of the gift of redemption and the Christian vocation to struggle against and ultimately triumph over the reality of sin through a self-giving love which gives even unto death.

PENANCE

Mark's gospel narrative summarizes the teaching of Jesus: "There he proclaimed the Good News from God: 'The time has come,' he said, 'and the kingdom of God is close at hand. Repent, and believe the Good News'" (Mk 1:15). Repentance forms a central part of the message of Jesus, but this concept of repentance has to be properly understood. Repentance in the New Testament frequently translates the Greek word *metanoia*. The concept expressed by this word forms a very important reality in both the Old and the New Testaments, which was expressed in the Old Testament primarily by the word *shuv*.[20] Repentance or conversion thus means the change of heart by which the sinner accepts and embraces the good news of the loving gift of God. The moral message of repentance is the call to a change of heart, and this must remain the dominant theme of the sacrament of penance. This section will consider the important aspects of the biblical concept of repentance or conversion which must be present in the celebration of penance.

Conversion or repentance is above all the free gift of God to man, since such a change of heart remains outside the realm of man's possibilities without the initiative on God's part. Conversion is the result of God's mercy and forgiveness before it can be the result of man's efforts. Man is now capable of turning his heart to God because God has first graciously turned himself to man. The Old Testament indicates the connection by using the same word to denote God's turning to man and man's turning to God.[21] The basic message of the Scriptures is the continuously saving intervention of God in human history to free men from sin. This is the Good News proclaimed by the New Testament, for this gift in no way depends upon man's worthiness or his efforts. Man of himself can never overcome the separation and alienation which is the reality of sin. In many ways the Scriptures reinforce the fundamental message of the Good News—the fact that God in his love and mercy has first deigned to offer man the gift of love and the forgiveness of sin. For example, the insistence on the poor, sinners, and children as the privileged people in the reign of God only emphasizes the fact that this is primarily the merciful love of God which first offers this gift. The primary reaction of the recipient is joy and gratitude for the gift of God's love.

Conversion or repentance as God's loving gift also calls for a response on the part of man, the change of his heart, the acceptance of this relationship of love. Catholic theology has always stressed (perhaps sometimes too much) the response of man to the gift of God. This response as described by the concept of *metanoia* is a change of heart which is illustrated in many ways by the New Testament; the passing over from death to life, from darkness to light; the creation of the new man in Christ Jesus; the new life received from the life-giving Spirit of the risen Lord; the joyful return of the prodigal to the house of the Father. This change of heart affects all the multiple relationships in which man finds himself; in fact, this change of heart is known and manifested above all in man's relationships with his fellow man. The follower of Jesus is told that he should not offer his gift at the altar if he remembers that his brother has anything against him, but rather he should leave his gift, go and become reconciled with his brother and then return to offer his gift.

There is no true forgiveness of sin on God's part unless the Christian is willing to forgive his fellow man. Forgiveness cannot be a merely legal or juridical reality but involves a profound change of heart which must manifest itself in the manifold relationships of the Christian with others. The Christian is taught to pray: forgive us our sins as we forgive those who trespass against us. The parable of the debtor who was forgiven a huge debt by his master but then failed to forgive a very insignificant debt to a fellow servent serves as a continual reminder that forgiveness of sin involves a change of heart on our part. (Mt 18:23-35). The sacrament of penance then must concentrate on the need for a change of heart and not merely emphasize a juridical listing of sins. Even more importantly the forgiveness of sin can never remain just an isolated religious phenomenon apart from the daily life of the individual. One cannot profess love of God and close his heart to his neighbor and the world. Conversion involves multiple relationships (as does sin) so that one must avoid the danger of neglecting any one aspect of these relationships. In the past, Catholic practice suffered by so stressing sin in its relationship to God that we forgot about the relationship with our fellow man. The sacrament of penance had little connection with daily life. However, today there seems to be a danger in the opposite direction. People talk about the secularization of sin and conversion so that the whole reality is seen in terms of man's relationship with his fellow man, and thus the forgiveness of sin requires merely that we ask our brother for forgiveness without seeing much need to ask God for forgiveness. A proper understanding of the multiple and interconnected relationships of Christian love, sin, and forgiveness argues for the need to keep all the aspects in proper perspective. Forgiveness comes from both God and neighbor, and the penitent person must resolve to improve his relationships of love with God, neighbor, and the world.

Another important characteristic of conversion, which likewise corresponds to a proper understanding of sin, involves the need for continual growth and conversion. Through justification and first conversion man does change his heart and enter into a relationship of love union with God and neighbor, but this change of heart and relationship of love are never perfect. If the Christian compares his life with the moral message of Jesus, he must honestly admit that he continually falls short of the fullness of the Christian life. Continual conversion always remains the fundamental imperative for the pilgrim Christian who strives to respond more totally to the gift of the new life in Christ Jesus. The Christian should always have an uneasy conscience in the realization that sinfulness is still present in his own heart, in his relationships with others, and in the structures and institutions of his society. The uneasy conscience does not become the source of morbid fear and scrupulosity, for the Christian is always conscious of the mercy and forgiveness of God and his own imperfect response to this gift. The continued existence of sin and the Christian's incorporation into Christ's victory over sin and death form the basis for the Christian imperative of a continual growth and change of heart in relations with God, neighbor and the world. The Christian should never succumb to the temptation of being lulled into complacency by forgetting about the existence of sin. The sacrament of penance could be one way of making the Christian more conscious of his sinfulness, the mercy of God and the need for continual conversion.

PENANCE AS VIRTUE AND PENANCE AS SACRAMENT: SCHOLASTIC SYNTHESIS

The format of the sacrament of penance as we know it today has been in existence from about the end of the twelfth century, but the speculative questions about the sacramentality of penance and the inner constitution of the sacrament remained to be settled. The septenary number of the sacraments with penance in the fourth place had an established place in theology from the time of Peter Lombard.[22] However, before and after Lombard, the question centered on the mutual relationship of the acts of the penitent and the absolution of the priest. What is their mutual relationship and how do they bring about the forgiveness of sin which is the effect of the sacrament?

The three acts of the penitent (later declared to be such by the Council of Trent) are contrition, confession and satisfaction. Contrition, confession, and satisfaction can very easily be interpreted as a more detailed and explicit understanding of the fundamental *metanoia* or change of heart described in the Scriptures. From an anthropological perspective these three acts refer to the basic change of orientation which is required for true conversion and forgiveness of sin. Contrition is the sorrow of the heart, and is always the most important element in the process of conversion; but such a change of heart is not fully human until it is expressed on the lips and proclaimed to others and until man then puts this change of heart into practice and makes amends for his sinful actions of the past. The change of heart by its very nature tends to manifest itself on our lips and in our actions. Thus the teaching proposed by the medieval scholastics and later by the Council of Trent is in general continuity with the basic biblical teaching on conversion.

The problem arises in trying to assign the proper relationship between penance as a virtue and penance as a sacrament. At this time the divine and ecclesial aspect of the sacrament was seen in the sacramental absolution of the priest. What is required for the forgiveness of sin? What are the respective roles of the personal acts of the penitent and the absolution of the priest as the minister of the Church and of the divine action of forgiveness? Abelard (1142) attributes the forgiveness of sin to the acts of the penitent, whereas absolution merely declares in the forum of the Church what has already taken place. He cites the example of the ten lepers who were cured by Jesus and then sent to show themselves to the priests. Likewise he employs a comparison with Lazarus who was brought back to life by Jesus but remained bound by the winding clothes that others must remove.[23] Note that Abelard obviously did not know and appreciate the early history of the sacrament of penance with the greater role which was played by the Church. This failure to know and take into account different historical developments was one of the weak points in all scholastic thinking.

Peter Lombard in his influential *Sentences* developed the same idea as Abelard, but there was some opposition to this merely extrinsic functioning of absolution with regard to the forgiveness of sin.[24] Hugh of St. Victor distinguished a double aspect of sin: hardness of heart and the penalty of future damnation. Contrition and the acts of the penitent take away the first bond of sin, whereas the absolution of the Church removes the due penalty of future damnation.[25] Most of the theologians before Thomas Aquinas, including Albert the Great and the Franciscan masters, did not give enough importance to the absolution. Thomas Aquinas, according to the testimony of those who are in total agreement with him as well as those of other "schools" in the matter of penance, equitably solved the problem of the mutual relationship between the virtue of penance and the sacrament of penance or, as the problem can be stated in another way, the relationship between the acts of the penitent on the one hand, and the absolution of the priest on the other hand in bringing about the forgiveness of sin.[26] Thomas applied to the concept of the sacrament the Aristotelian notion of matter and form. The matter of the sacrament of penance consists of the three acts of the penitent, whereas the form is the absolution of the priest. The matter and form together bring about the efficient causality of this sacrament which results in the forgiveness of sin. This theory is closely connected with Thomas' concept of justification according to which Thomas sees three moments in the act of justification—the infusion of grace, the double act of the will away from creatures and towards God, and the remission of sins. Thomas affirms the indispensable unity between the gift of grace and the cooperative response of man's free will. These three aspects exercise a reciprocal causality on each other. Thus, in the question of penance, contrition can be both the effect of the sacrament and the cause of it. The acts of the penitent and the absolution work together as the efficient cause of the forgiveness of sin. Thomas talks about the sacramental sign as exercising an instrumental causality because the ultimate causality in the whole process belongs to God himself.[27]

But the problem of reconciling the acts of the penitent and the absolution of the priest is not solved that easily. Thomas with most of his predecessors and contemporaries readily admitted that in most cases the penitent person was already contrite and thus had his sins already forgiven before he came to the sacrament of penance. How can the absolution of the priest have any real effect when the person's sins are already forgiven since he has had the basic change of heart? Thomas responds by developing the notion of the sacrament *in voto* or in promise. For Thomas there can be no absolute separation between the virtue of penance or contrition and the sacrament of penance. Every true virtue of penance of its very nature leads to the sacramental encounter. Thus the sacrament itself is not limited to the here and now, but rather the sacrament takes into consideration the fact that the conversion of the penitent is a human act that develops over a period of time and has its own historicity. Thus in a very real way the sacrament begins to exist from the first act of the penitent and reaches its culmination in the sacramental rite itself even if the penitent has already made his fundamental change of heart and had his sins forgiven.[28] Some theologians reject this notion of the sacrament *in voto* as being untenable, but others praise it as a recognition of the historicity and temporality of human acts entering into the sacrament which thus is not totally restricted to the here and now.[29] This concept shows how the sacrament is more intimately tied up with the daily life of the person and also can serve as the basis for denying any kind of cleavage between liturgical piety and personal devotion.[30]

The school of Scotus and his followers did not totally accept the synthesis of Aquinas. They do not refer to the acts of the penitent as the strict matter of the sacrament of penance (Trent purposely left the question vague by referring to the acts of the penitent as the "quasi-matter" of the sacrament of penance) which constitute an essential part of the sacrament. The acts of the penitent are not part of the cause but only the necessary conditions for the effect of the sacrament. The Scotist teaching follows from his more voluntaristic approach to all theology. Basic to his teaching on the sacrament of penance is the understanding that there are two ways of justification requiring different dispositions on the part of the penitent. According to this view since God and the Church are operative in the sacrament, then a lesser disposition is needed by the penitent, for otherwise there would be no real value to the sacrament itself. The two ways of justification are a great sign of the mercy of God who in the sacramental way does not demand as much of a disposition on the part of the penitent. In a rather oversimplified way, the sacrament makes up for some deficiencies on the part of the person. Until the last decades the majority of theological and catechetical writing followed the Scotistic approach. For the forgiveness of sin outside the sacrament perfect contrition or love of God above all things and not merely the fear of punishment was required. Within the sacrament attrition was sufficient. In fairness to this school it must be pointed out that what they demanded for attrition was frequently in practice what Thomists would have called contrition.[31]

The Thomistic school with its realism has always demanded the same ultimate disposition of the person inside or outside the sacrament. It is significant that the renewal in the theological scholarship of the liturgical movement was based primarily on the Thomistic approach. Such influential sacramental theologians as Rahner, Schillebeeckx, Anciaux and deLetter were all operating from within the Thomistic viewpoint.[32] By stressing only the one way of justification this approach showed the unity in the liturgical and spiritual life of the Christian. There could be no separation between liturgical and personal or private piety. Thomas' approach which always demanded the same change of heart on the part of the person underscores the importance and the need for a personal response in the sacrament of penance. Unfortunately, the Scotistic approach is more liable to the charge of magic since it does require less of a disposition inside the sacrament. There is no doubt that exaggerations of the Scotistic viewpoint have had a very harmful effect on the theology and practice of the sacraments in the life of the Church leading to the dangers of magicalism and the separation of the liturgical life from the daily life of man in the world. Thomas Aquinas saw the necessity of viewing the acts of the penitent and the absolution of the priest as working together and not substituting for one another. Thomas solved the problem without diminishing the need and importance of both aspects in the forgiveness of sin. One can take issue with the concept of causality employed by Thomas, but his basic insight of uniting the acts of the penitent and the absolution of the priest without sacrificing the importance of either remains an important conrtibution to the theology of penance. However, Thomas did not develop the communitarian and ecclesial aspects of penance.

ECCLESIAL ASPECT OF PENANCE

The Council of Trent begins its teaching on the sacrament of penance by describing the necessity and institution of penance.[33] In general terms the function of the Church is to continue in time and space the mission of Jesus, which has as a very fundamental aspect the forgiveness of sin. The very fact that there would be an opportunity for those who have sinned grievously after baptism to become reconciled again with the merciful Father through Christ and the Church indicates the great mercy and forgiveness of God. An essential part of the Good News preached by Jesus was the gift of forgiveness of sin and the new life through his Spirit. From a theological perspective one can readily see how the Church which makes visible in time and space the mystery of Jesus would necessarily continue to make present his mercy and forgiveness for men.

The Scriptures testify to the power of Jesus in the forgiveness of sin. The core teaching of Jesus as an invitation to conversion and penance has already been mentioned. The Scriptures also contain a series of texts in which both in reality and in parable the forgiveness of sin is expressed. In parable form there is no more eloquent testimony of the mercy of God than the three parables in Luke 15—the parables of the shepherd who finds the one stray sheep, the woman who finds the lost coin, and above all the parable of the prodigal son. This last parable presents a very informative illustration of the meaning of sin and conversion. Above all the parable emphasizes the mercy and forgiveness of the Father rather than the attitude of the son so that some exegetes prefer to call it "the parable of the merciful father." One can notice details in this parable that could easily refer to the situation in the early Church of offering mercy and forgiveness even after baptism.[34] Other examples from the gospel are frequent: the woman taken in adultery, the good thief, the paralytic, the publican, etc. Another series of texts in the gospels affirm that Jesus himself expiates for the sins of the whole world and that he has the power to forgive sin. In this total scriptural and theological context it is only natural that the Scriptures say something about the continuation of this power to forgive sin and show forth the reconciling love of the Father in Christ Jesus. The Fathers of the Church especially referred back to the text in the 18th chapter of Matthew which in the context of the forgiveness of sin indicates that Jesus gives to his disciples the power of binding and loosing.[35] The second important New Testament text, which the Council of Trent refers to as the time in which Christ principally instituted the sacrament of penance, is found in John 20:22. Here the risen Lord who has overcome the forces of sin and death in his own resurrection through the power of the Spirit now confers on his disciples the gift of the same Spirit so that they have the power of forgiving sin.[36] Obviously many of the scriptural references to the forgiveness of sin refer to baptism, but other references apply to a forgiveness for sin after baptism.

The history of the Church bears out the fact that the Church was conscious of the fact that Jesus had conferred upon it the power of forgiving sins committed after baptism. It has already been pointed out that there has been a diversity of rituals and formats in which the Church has carried out its mission of making present the mercy and forgiveness of God. In the early Church there are references to the power of the Church in forgiving sins after baptism as early as the end of the first century in the *Didache*. However, in the early centuries there was among some a tendency to rigorism seen in the practice of allowing penance only once to a person in his lifetime and also in the attitude of some like Tertullian the Montanist who claimed there were certain grievous sins which the Church could not forgive. The testimony from the early centuries is very sketchy, but by the fourth and fifth centuries the process of solemn penance as described earlier had become quite common and universal.

In the present rite for the sacrament of penance, the function of the Church is seen primarily and almost exclusively in the role of the priest as minister. The priest pronounces the absolution and reconciles the penitent with the Church. Thanks to the Thomistic approach this should not be interpreted in a juridical or magical way, for there is no forgiveness of sin without the radical change of heart on the part of the sinner which is manifested in all his relationships. The sacrament of penance makes present and visible the mercy and forgiveness of God in Christ, but the sinner must accept such merciful love and change his heart. However, in the last few years theologians have realized that the present rite does not emphasize properly the full role of the Church. The whole Church enters into the absolution and into the reconciliation without denying the special function of the hierarchical priesthood. A number of elements have contributed to a better understanding of the role of the Church and the need to make this aspect more prominent in the sacramental format.

Salvation for the Christian has never been a merely individualistic affair, for from the very beginning God has chosen a people as his own. In the Old Testament salvation came explicitly through belonging to the chosen people, whereas in the New Testament the Church as the community of the saved is the new people of God. The ecclesiological renewal of the last decades has emphasized the communitarian nature of salvation in and through the Church as the people of God. The very basic Christian concepts are themselves communitarian and not merely individualistic. Christian love refers not only to the relationship between the individual and God, but also such love forms the basis of the fellowship among all those who confess God as their Father and Christ Jesus as their brother. The Christian commandment joins together love of God and love of neighbor in such a way that our love for the neighbor is the sign or sacrament of our love for God. The body of Christ which is the Church is animated by love which brings about the fellowship of all in the one Lord.[37] Sin is not merely an offense against God and our neighbor, but also an offense against the Church as the people of God gathered together in his love. Sin thus weakens and offends the very life of the Church and the *koinonia* of the faithful.[38] The ecclesial nature of love and sin argues also for the ecclesial nature of forgiveness. Like Christian love and sin, forgiveness is not merely an individualistic relationship with God, but embraces also the need to forgive our brothers. Forgiveness is not only communitarian in a general sense but also ecclesial for the same reasons that love and sin are also ecclesial realities.

What is the exact object of the power of forgiving sins which according to the gospels Jesus gave to his Church? The gospels refer to the power of binding and loosing and the power of forgiving and retaining. What does this mean? The most common interpretation of this power until the last few years has been that they refer to two distinct and alternative powers. The priest as the minister has to choose between these two powers of either loosing and remitting or binding and retaining. In this case the binding and retaining is either an authoritative declaration before God and the Church that the sinner is unworthy of absolution or that from the denial of absolution there follows a juridical obligation to return to the sacrament for obtaining forgiveness. However, in either hypothesis there remains the problem that binding-retaining is not really a positive and distinct act in itself, but only the negative of absolving. "All these difficulties arise ultimately from the same fact, viz. that, objectively speaking, a refusal of absolution, no matter how cleverly it may be explained, cannot be any more than the (in certain circumstances) obligatory omission and refusal of an act—no more than this can be said of the refusal of baptism (which does not involve any judicial decision on the part of the Church). Such a refusal cannot be an independent act with its own, new legal consequences, which is, after all, precisely what the above explanation must presuppose."[39]

Rahner and many others today argue that binding and loosing are to be seen as two distinct and successive acts in the total reaction of the Church to sin.[40] The concept of binding and loosing found in Matthew 18 appears to support this view. To bind means to put under the ban in the sense that the sinner by his action separates himself from the love that joins together the members of the Church (even if in the strict sense of the term he does not cease to be a member of the Church) so that the Church must now react in a visible way to this sin of her member. Loosing then is the reconciliation of the penitent sinner with the Church. The context in Matthew refers to excommunication from the community and this understanding was not unknown in Judaism at the time of Jesus. Rahner, who has done extensive historical work in the sacrament of penance, sees this scriptural understanding of binding and loosing as well illustrated in the format of the sacrament of penance in the early Church. Here the action of the Church is precisely this twofold action of placing one outside the visible community and then reconciling one with the community. This meaning is also in continuity with one of the meanings of the term in the Hebraic sense and thus shows a closer continuity with the Israelitic tradition. Rahner points out that one must not interpret this twofold action of excluding from the community and then reconciling with the community in the same sense as excommunication is understood in the Church today, for the concept of ecclesiastical excommunication comes from a different source. There is, nevertheless, a sense in which this more communitarian and ecclesial understanding of binding and loosing is still found in the life of the Church. The present discipline of the Church requires that one cannot fully participate in the Eucharistic banquet if he is conscious of mortal sin and has not been reconciled in the sacrament of penance. Thus there is a liturgical excommunication, if you wish, in which the person in mortal sin separates himself from the Eucharistic community and can only be brought back into full participation in the Eucharist through a previous reconciliation in the sacrament of penance. However, one could argue, as I would, that the law of the Church in this matter is rather of a disciplinary nature which does not necessarily reflect an essential theological or even doctrinal element.

In this interpretation binding and loosing have a very important ecclesial function which also follows from the ecclesial nature of sin itself. The first reaction of the Church is to make public and sacramentalize the fact that the sinner by his action separates himself not only from God but also from the Church which is the body of Christ or the people of God animated by his love. The solemn act of reconciliation or loosing indicates that the penitent sinner has now rejoined in a full manner the community which is the sign of his reconciliation with Christ and the Father.

This interpretation of the scriptural terms of binding-retaining and loosing-remitting is accepted by a number of theologians today but has not won the assent of all. There is a problem in the fact that in John the order is reversed so that remit comes before retain. Others also argue that the concept of putting under the ban and then reconciling one with the community does not fit in with our contemporary notion of the sacraments in general and penance in particular. What if there is just a placing under the ban or an exclusion from the community and not the final reconciliation with the Church, how can there be a sacrament in that case? Also there seems to be no positive act of the Church today in excluding one from the community. The only positive intervention of the Church takes place when the absolution of the priest is given.[41] It seems to me that many of these objections against the more ecclesial understanding of binding and loosing (i.e., placing one outside the community and then reconciling the penitent sinner with the community) are based on a rather narrow and juridical understanding of the sacrament as totally restricted to the here and now (remember that Thomas was willing to take into account the historicity and temporality of the human acts which enter into the sacrament and thus extend the sacrament in time and space) and also based on an understanding of penance seen only in its present format without taking into account the different formats that have existed in the past and can exist in the future. However, there do remain some valid reasons for interpreting the scriptural concepts of binding and loosing in other ways, but these would not necessarily exclude the communitarian notion of separation from and reconciliation with the community. Although Alszeghy would not accept Rahner's concept of reconciliation with the Church understood as taking away an excommunication, he would still maintain an ecclesial dimension in every grave sin and a re-union with the Church in every justification.[42]

There have been other interpretations of the meaning of binding-retaining and loosing-remitting. Some scholastic theologians such as Bonaventure and Suarez see binding and loosing as two aspects of the same power which at one and the same time looses from sin and binds to the satisfaction imposed. Again this interpretation seems to be almost totally dependent on the existing form of the sacrament and is an anachronism if read back as a proper interpretation of the New Testament. One other interpretation of the scriptural power of binding and loosing which remains very probable today is the signification of universal power or the fullness of power. Binding and loosing would thus be interpreted in the same way as other biblical expressions such as sitting and rising to signify a type of universality.[43] Even in this meaning the ecclesial concept could still be very prominent, for it would refer not only to the excluding from the community and the reconciliation but also to all the other actions which the Church employs (e.g., prayers) for the conversion of the sinner.[44] Thus there is a growing tendency today to see the biblical concepts of binding and loosing as well as the historical experiences of the older forms of penance as emphasizing the importance of the ecclesial community in the sacrament of penance.

One theological attempt to explain the ecclesial aspect of the sacrament, supported by many of the scriptural and historical reasons mentioned above, views the reconciliation with the Church as the *res et sacramentum* of the sacrament of penance. B. Xiberta in his book *Clavis Ecclesiae*[45] tried to explain the ecclesial and communitarian aspect of the sacrament of penance in terms of this theological notion. The concept of *res et sacramentum* first appeared in reaction to the teaching of Berengarius on the Eucharist, according to which there was no middle term between the material sign of bread and wine and the spiritual presence of the risen Christ with the believer. The defenders of the "real presence" felt the need for a third element of *res et sacramentum,* an element between the external sign of bread and wine (*sacramentum tantum*) and the ultimate reality of spiritual union with Christ (*res tantum*). This other element is the real presence of Christ under the species which is the *res* (reality) which is signified by the external sign of bread and is itself the *sacramentum* (sign) of the ultimate reality which is the spiritual union with Christ. This same notion was applied quite easily to the three sacraments which confer a character which was then described in terms of the *res et sacramentum.* In other sacraments such as penance an attempt was made to see the *res et sacramentum* in terms of the interior penance which was the ultimate disposition for the reception of the sacrament and its grace, but this presupposes a concept of dispositive causality which raises serious questions. In the present century theologians began to speak of the *res et sacramentum* as the ecclesial effect of the sacrament, a position adopted for the sacrament of penance by Xiberta in 1922 who argued from the Scriptures and history that peace with the Church was the sign and the pledge of peace with the Spirit. The immediate effect of the sacramental rite was the reconciliation with the Church which was in turn the sign of the ultimate *res*, the reconciliation with the Father through the life-giving Spirit of the Risen Lord.[46] There are some theologians today who have difficulty in accepting this precise theory. One problem concerns the very concept of *res et sacramentum* as necessarily applied to all the sacraments. A major theoretical difficulty is the exact relationship between the reconciliation with the Church and the reconciliation with God in Christ. Most contemporary theologians would still affirm the importance of the ecclesial aspect stressed by Xiberta and others even if some would not accept the strict theory of *res et sacramentum* as it is applied to reconciliation with the Church in the case of penance.[47]

In recent Catholic theology there has been a renewal in the understanding of ecclesiology which naturally brings into greater importance the ecclesial aspect of the life of the Christian. One of the major approaches to ecclesiology sees the Church in terms of the People of God. Another complementary approach sees the Church in terms of sacramentality, and especially in this understanding a much greater place is given to the ecclesial aspect of all the sacraments including penance. Thus contemporary ecclesiology reinforces the scriptural and historical data in understanding the ecclesial aspects of salvation and the life of the Christian.

In the very first paragraph, the Constitution on the Church refers to the Church as "a kind of sacrament or sign of intimate union with God, and of the unity of all mankind" (n. 1). Christ Jesus is the primordial sacrament of salvation and of the Father's love for man. The love and the mercy of the Father become visible and real for us in Christ Jesus who is the way, the truth and the life. We know and approach the Father through Christ, but the work of the risen Christ today in the world is carried on by his Spirit through the Church, and thus the Church is the sacrament, the sign that makes present to us the mystery of God's love for us in Christ Jesus. In every individual sacrament the mystery of the Church and of Christ become present, so that the sacraments are truly signs of the Church. The sacramental principle thus builds on the principle of the Incarnation so that in and through the sacramental celebration the Christian comes into contact with the mystery of the Church which mediates to him the mystery of Christ. In accord with the sacramental principle, the Church is not a mediator in the sense of an obstacle but rather the sign that makes present and visible the mystery of Christ, the primordial sacrament of the Father. Thus in becoming reconciled with the Church one does become reconciled with the risen Christ and the Father.[48]

In the sacrament of penance the ecclesial and communitarian element must be stressed more in the future. The entire Church and especially the community present at the celebration not only enters into the reconciliation but has a part to play in the prayer and worship of the celebration. In the present rite the ecclesial element is the absolution given by the priest. In its present form the absolution is in the indicative, but very often before the thirteenth century, the form of absolution was deprecative and not indicative. In fact, the term employed for the action of the Church was generally reconciliation and not absolution. The insistence on the *ex opere operato* efficacy of the sacraments against the Protestant reaction reinforced the need for an indicative formula for the absolution.[49] However, the deprecative form, that is, a prayer asking that God would grant the forgiveness of sin, is not merely an historical relic that must be explained away. The deprecative form of absolution helps to remind us of the ecclesial nature of the absolution and the fact that this is truly a prayer of the whole Church. The whole community in the celebration of the sacrament of penance prays for the penitent, and this prayer is heard by the heavenly Father. Thus in the early Church the constant prayers of the whole Church for the penitents had a truly sacramental aspect.

The mystery of redemption is an eternally actual act of the risen Lord which we come into contact with through the mystery of the Church and the sacraments.[50] The mystery of Christ is ultimately a twofold mystery of worship and sanctification. Christ is at one and the same time the gift of the Father's love for man and the perfect response of man to that love; in short, Christ is a mystery of saving worship. The Incarnation remains the great mystery of worship and sanctification. In the historical mission of Jesus his prayer and the offering of himself are infallibly heard by the Father who raises him in glorification and with him is the co-principle of the sending of the Spirit. The *ex opere operato* aspect of the sacraments consists precisely in the infallible connection between the worship of Christ and the response of the Father. The sacraments unite us with Christ in his twofold mystery: "As the mystery of worship which *ex opere operato* pleads for and brings the grace of redemption to the recipient, a sacrament stands in relation to Christ as the Son of his Father. As the mystery of grace that *ex opere operato* actually bestows the grace for which it prays upon the recipient, the sacrament stands in relationship to Christ as the co-principle of the Holy Spirit."[51] The Church and the individual must associate themselves with the prayer of worship of Christ which is infallibly heard by the Father. The twofold mystery of Christ—prayer or worship and the bestowal of love or grace—is present in every sacramental celebration, and there is need in the sacramental rite both for the form of request (deprecative) and the form of bestowal (indicative). The sacrament of penance needs a ritual that will emphasize the fact the whole Church and the individual are now praying to the Father in union with the worship of Christ Jesus which is infallibly heard by the Father who bestows the gift of his loving mercy and forgiveness.

In practice today there are many difficulties not only because the present format does not express the full twofold mystery of Christ and the Church in the sacrament of penance and the reconciliation with the community of the Church, but also because there is lacking in most pastoral situations today a truly existential realization of the Church as the community of the people of God. However, by stressing the need for the prayer of the whole Church joined with the minister and the penitent as well as the function and importance of reconciliation with the Church community, the Church can develop the proper understanding of itself as a community gathered around the risen Lord.

PENANCE AS JUDGMENT

According to the Council of Trent the sacrament of penance involves a judgment. In a solemn anathema the Council declares "If anyone says that the sacramental absolution of the priest is not a judicial act, but the mere ministry of announcing and declaring that sins are forgiven to the one confessing provided only he believes he is absolved, . . . let him be anathema" (*DS* 709).[52] This canon refers back to the more expository treatment of the sacrament of penance in the fourteenth session of the Council of Trent in which again the Council taught that the absolution was not merely an announcement or declaration but is like a judicial act in which the sentence is, as it were, pronounced by a judge (*DS* 1685). Notice in this exposition the fact that the Council fathers realized that the concept of judgment could be applied only analogously to the sacrament of penance. In other places Trent also makes reference to the sacrament of penance as a judgment. Since the nature of a judgment requires that it be carried out only on subjects, the priest then requires jurisdiction in order to absolve his penitents (*DS* 1686). Likewise the Council states that priests are unable to exercise this judgment unless they know the case, and thus there is the need for the penitent to confess his sins to the priest. Christ Jesus left his priests as rulers and judges to whom all mortal crimes would be brought in order that they might through the power of the keys pronounce the sentence of forgiveness or retention (*DS* 1679).

However, problems arise from the very use of the term judgment in the Council of Trent. Nowhere do the Fathers of Trent explicitly say what they mean by judgment, and in places they explicitly admit they are using it in an analogous fashion. In addition, the analogy with the criminal judicial process we know today suggests as many differences as it does similarities. The judge is primarily interested in the juridical order, whereas the sacrament of penance pertains to the intimate moral order of man's relationship with God, neighbor, the world, and the Church. The whole purpose of the sacramental rite of penance is the forgiveness of sin which is just the opposite of the judicial processes which take place in our courts. The "defendant" in the sacrament of penance in its present rite accuses himself of his sins in order to obtain pardon, whereas the defendant in criminal cases has lawyers to argue for his innocence. Thus there does exist a problem in the analogous application of the notion of a judicial act to the sacrament of penance.

Other complications also come to the fore. Most theologians specializing in the sacrament of penance point out the fact that since the time of Trent and afterwards, there has been an over-emphasis on the juridical aspects of penance. "It is the period of extreme juridization of the sacrament. The judicial act of the Council of Trent, which is seen only in opposition to the 'declarative' aspect, becomes a 'juridical sentence.' In this 'judgment,' the priest is the 'judge' who renders 'the sentence'; sin is 'an infraction'; the accusation and satisfaction appear as reparation of a 'legal transgression,' etc."[53] Such a severe but not uncommon complaint reminds us of the constant danger of juridicism in understanding the sacrament of penance. Another problem in terms of the Council of Trent itself is the fact that the Council was primarily talking about the format of the sacrament of penance as then known without a great knowledge of its evolving historical development. One must distinguish between the judicial aspect which belongs to the heart of the sacrament and the particular judicial aspects which might be more prevalent at a particular time in its historical development. Although the discipline of the Church does admit the existence of the sacrament of penance in certain cases in which there is no specific confession of mortal sins, the Council of Trent uses as one argument for the necessity of the specific confession of all mortal sins to the priest the fact that the priest is not able to exercise the judgment of penance without knowing the case (*DS* 1679).

The exaggerated juridicism attached to penance in the last few centuries is intimately linked with the juridicism and legalism of the notion of sin. Manuals of moral theology, for example, speak of the role of the priest as judge embracing the following: to know the case, to discern the disposition of the penitent, to impart a fitting satisfaction, to pronounce the judicial sentence (i.e., absolution) either absolutely or under condition.[54] These judicial functions of the priest are more difficult to understand and to carry out in light of a contemporary understanding of sin. The ultimate judgment described under the various functions of the priest as judge concerns the judgment about the proper disposition of the penitent, but it is precisely this judgment which a better understanding of sin makes practically impossible in many cases. If sin is viewed primarily and exclusively in terms of the external act, then such a judgment is comparatively easy; but if sin describes the multiple relationship involved in the fundamental option which takes place in the core of the personality, then this judgment about the proper state and disposition of the penitent cannot be made with any great certainty. The present format of the sacrament in which the penitent generally just lists a series of sins furnishes no adequate criteria for making such a judgment; in fact, as mentioned in the context of sin there are no precise and adequate criteria for making such a judgment about the disposition of the penitent. Sin remains primarily (but not exclusively) an action involving the core of the person which even the individual himself, let alone any outsider, cannot know adequately. Many prudent confessors realize this fact today and just leave the ultimate judgment in the hands of God. Even the theology manuals from their rather legalistic perspective still realized that all such judgments at best are presumptions and approximations. Ultimately the actions of the confessor which the theology manuals describe under the functions of the confessor as judge are beyond his ken. It seems that the theology manuals have insisted too much on the analogy with the law courts in determining what are the functions of the confessor as judge, but these functions really cannot be adequately carried out by the minister of the sacrament of penance.

In what sense then is the sacrament of penance a judgment? Following the principle of renewal in theology, it is first necessary to investigate the scriptural understanding of judgment and then the theological notion can be constructed in the light of the biblical data. In the course of theological development there have been two perennial dangers in the understanding of judgment: the temptation to legalism and juridicism and also the danger of seeing judgment primarily in terms of condemnation and fear. In the scriptural understanding judgment is the act by which justice is exercised.[55]

The judgment is thus salvific in the sense that its function is to restore the victim to his rights which necessarily also implies some repression of the guilty person. In the ancient world the function of the king was to give justice, and it was to him in this capacity that the poor and others appealed to help them vindicate their claims. The people of Israel, with their great faith in Yahweh, believed that he would come and restore to them justice, for as a people they understood that justice comes from Yahweh who will be faithful to his promise and bestow his justice and his peace upon the poor of Yahweh. For the people of Israel the judgment was an object of hope as exemplified in Ezekiel's speaking about the judgment of God as the time in which he will come to bring peace and liberation to his people (Ez 34:11-22). The psalmist frequently prays for the judgment of God. In the Roman rite at the beginning of the Eucharistic celebration, the priest and people formerly prayed together Psalm 43—*"Judica me Deus. . ."* Notice how this psalm looks upon the notion of judgment. "Defend me, take up my cause against people who have no pity; from the treacherous and cunning man rescue me, God." The judgment of God is thus the saving intervention of Yahweh on behalf of his people, and this justice of God will bring with it the hoped for salvation, peace, and light. The justice of God in this Old Testament understanding in no way stands opposed to his mercy; in fact, in the context of the covenant justice is frequently associated with *hesed* or merciful love. "Moderns often oppose justice and mercy; this antinomy holds a great place in the theology of a St. Anselm or of a St. Bernard. Biblical justice on the contrary is always mercy, and that is why the sinner longs for it as the sign of pardon."[56] There is, however, in the Old Testament a twofold aspect of the judgment and the justice of God. God is the judge-defender-avenger of his people Israel and the judge-adversary of the nations.[57] God became not only the avenger judge of the nations, but also of his own people to the extent that they were unfaithful to him. In prophetic speech the judgments of God were not so much his saving interventions as they were his punishments against an unfaithful people. In the contemporary Judaism of Jesus' time there existed a quite widespread understanding of the judgment as an apocalyptic and eschatological event, an understanding which undoubtedly influenced the New Testament writings.[58]

Although the Synoptics do not stress the notion of judgment in general, they do speak of the judgment of the last day. There is a rigorous condemnation for those who do not accept the gospel, but this judgment will definitely establish God's people. Johannine theology emphasizes that the judgment takes place now in the attitude of men to Jesus. Like the Synoptics, John too interprets the death of Jesus because of sin as the judgment upon the world. Paul speaks of a past judgment as well as a future judgment. The past judgment is that sentence of condemnation which has fallen upon all men because of their sin. No one can escape this judgment on his own efforts; man is freed from this condemnation by the death and resurrection of Jesus through which sin has been condemned and we have been saved. "Now therefore the justice of God reveals itself not as that which punishes but that which justifies and saves (Rom 3:21); all merit his Judgment, but all are justified gratuitously if only they believe in Christ Jesus (3:24ff.). For the believers, there is no longer a condemnation (8:1): God justifies them, who therefore would condemn them (8:34)? Under the ancient Law, the ministry of Moses was a ministry of condemnation, but that of the servants of the gospel is a ministry of grace (2 Co 3:9) and of reconciliation (5:19ff.). It is that which gives us full assurance on the day of judgment (1 Jn 4:17): the love of God for us is already manifested in Christ, so that we have nothing more to fear. The formidable menace of judgment hangs now only over the evil world; Jesus has come to free us from it."[59]

In the light of the problems connected with the notion of judgment in the sacrament of penance and in the light of the biblical understanding of judgment, one can better criticize and evaluate the various meanings that have been proposed for the judgment contained in the sacrament of penance. Some Catholic theologians have tended to deny the judicial aspect of absolution because such a concept seems opposed to the contemporary understanding of the sacrament of penance.[60] This is one possible explanation, but I believe it is possible to explain the judicial aspect of the absolution or reconciliation in such a way that one can be in general continuity with the past and also point out better the ecclesial aspect of the sacrament. Perhaps the most popular opinion, at least in the mind of Catholics, is that the judgment of absolution in this sacrament consists in the decision between two opposites; i.e., either to loose the penitent from his sins or to bind him. Such an interpretation, however, presupposes a concept of binding and loosing which appears to be unacceptable today. Likewise such an approach appears intimately tied up with a very juridical understanding of the sacrament of penance which does not take into consideration the difficulties involved in such a judgment or the meaning of judgment in the larger biblical and theological understandings. Even if the words themselves were capable of such an understanding, it would not seem that such an interpretation would distinguish the judicial nature of the absolution from the judicial nature of many other human acts. The judicial nature in this context refers to the choice between two opposites, but there are many human actions in which such a judgment must be made. Certainly there is an intellectual judgment made in such a case, but this is a judgment common to many human acts and not specific to the matter of absolution or reconciliation. In fact, such a judgment to a certain extent concerns the actions leading up to the absolution of the sacrament and not the absolution or reconciliation itself.

Another interpretation understands judgment in the sense of judiciousness—the granting of absolution is done judiciously and not capriciously. The priest cannot use this power arbitrarily in absolving those who are not disposed, etc. However, such a notion of judiciousness applies not to the absolution itself, but to the actions which precede the absolution; moreover, such judiciousness should be characteristic of every human action and not specifically characteristic of the penitential absolution.[61]

The differences between the judgment of absolution and the ordinary penal judgment of the courtroom are so great that one cannot adequately describe the judgment of absolution in terms of such a penal judgment of the courtroom in which the judge hears the evidence and pronounces sentence upon the defendant. The problem with many theological interpretations of penance arises from placing primary insistence on a juridical analogy from the actions of the judge in a law court. With the biblical renewal within the Church there has been a greater emphasis on the need for a development of the sacrament of penance within a truly biblical context. In 1953 P. Charles proposed a solution to the question of the judicial nature of the sacrament of penance which ingeniously tried to combine both a biblical basis and a law court analogy for the understanding of the judicial character of sacramental absolution.[62] The priest in the sacrament of penance is not a subordinate officer in the administration of justice, but rather takes the place of Christ, the supreme judge. "But the prerogative of the supreme judge, such as is reserved in our countries to the chief of state, the king or president as sovereign magistrate, is precisely not the power to punish but the faculty of granting pardon."[63] This represents the highest exercise of justice, for one is not acquitted in conformity with a code of laws, but rather one is pardoned by an act of benevolence and mercy which is the highest law. All must admit a point of comparison between the grace or amnesty granted by the chief of state and the pardon granted by the sacramental absolution, but here again there appear to be many more dissimilarities than similarities. Neither of these constitutes pardon in the same sense as the sacrament of penance. Such an action by the chief of state remains a very exceptional process and presupposes that a juridical process has already taken place. In the last analysis, the granting of clemency by the chief of state pertains not to judicial power, but to executive power. For these and other reasons the position proposed by Charles has not received wide based support.

How can one arrive at an adequate and satisfying understanding of the judicial nature of absolution? Since the Council of Trent did not explain its meaning and often insisted on the analogous use of the term, one must look outside the Council and its acts for any adequate solution. In such theological enterprises there looms the ever recurring danger of exclusivity. It would be too exclusive and hence inaccurate merely to consider the judicial character of absolution in terms of the court room analogy. One cannot neglect the aspects which cohere with the judicial reality, but it would be wrong to consider this aspect apart from the biblical and theological understanding of judgment. In the light of all these considerations one can conclude that the judicial nature of sacramental absolution means the public and authoritative declaration that divine forgiveness and mercy have now been given to the penitent.

The analogy from judicial reality has been well developed by G. B. Guzzetti who mentions that there have been many different forms of judgment.[64] A civil judgment refers to the public giving of rights in an authoritative manner. For example, if two people claim the same piece of property the judge ultimately decides that the property belongs to this particular person, and such a judgment is efficacious in the forum of society itself. The judgment publicly and efficaciously gives this right to this particular person, an action which cannot be done by a merely private individual. In a penal procedure the judge ascertains if the person is truly guilty and then publicly proclaims this and assigns the proper penalty. In other forms of judgment the judge ascertains if a certain action (a contract, a will) has juridical validity. The judgment of sacramental absolution does not correspond exactly to any of these three judgments, but these three judgments have something in common which they also share with the judgment of the penitential absolution. This common element is the public and authoritative nature of the ascertainment, the proclamation, or the execution which occurs in these diverse judgments. Thus the judicial character of absolution consists in the public proclamation of pardon or reconciliation belonging to this person like a judicial right which has consequences in the community.

Such an understanding of the judicial nature of absolution-reconciliation also coheres with the biblical and theological concepts involved.[65] The judgment of the sacrament of penance primarily consists in the authoritative proclamation of reconciliation and forgiveness of God—the basic biblical meaning of judgment. The judicial character of sacramental absolution participates in the theological understanding of God's judgment in Christ Jesus. The sacramental judgment looks back to the judgment of the cross and resurrection of Jesus and looks forward to the final judgment—a concept in keeping with the Thomistic realization that the sacraments are commemorative signs of the past, efficacious signs of the present and prophetic signs of the future.[66]

The judgment of absolution recalls the saving judgment of the death and resurrection of Jesus. The Paschal Mystery at one and the same time shows the power and force of sin and the victory of sin which puts to death him who came to give life, but at the same time signifies the ultimate victory of Christ through his redemptive death and resurrection. Sin as death is what separates man from the source of life, and thus the Paschal Mystery indicates the horrendous reality of sin and death from which we are freed through the loving gift of God in Christ. The sacrament of penance prolongs this "judgment" against the reality of sin as ultimate death and separation from the source of life. Sin must be unmasked in all its grim reality as the bearer of ultimate death, but this is only one part of the judgment. The judgment of the Paschal Mystery is ultimately the saving judgment of the victory of the resurrection over the power of sin and death. In the sacrament of penance, the penitent participates in this saving mystery precisely by joining himself to Christ in death to sin and selfishness and rises with him in the newness of life. Such participation on the part of the penitent involves *metanoia* or the change of heart which is the object of the kerygma of the early Church.[67]

The judgment of the penitential absolution also looks forward to the final judgment which indicates the final and complete victory of Jesus over the forces of sin and death. The Christian who now shares in the saving judgment of penance looks forward in hope to that final judgment in which the triumph over sin and death will be definitive. The Christian experiences in his own earthly pilgrimage the continual tension and struggle with his own sinfulness which is never completely overcome. The saving judgment of penance becomes a pledge and a promise of that future coming in the final judgment in which the work of salvation will be brought to its completion. The penitent receiving now the mercy and forgiveness of God in Christ is strengthened in exclaiming the Christian prayer of hope: "Come, Lord Jesus."

The theological understanding of the judgment of absolution, as the public and authoritative proclamation of pardon and reconciliation in the same manner as a judge publicly and authoritatively proclaims a right belonging to someone in society, involves a proper appreciation of the function and role of the Church. The Council of Trent spoke of the sacrament of penance as a judicial act to emphasize the ecclesial role and to distinguish the sacramental celebration from the mere ministry either of announcing the gospel or of declaring that sins are forgiven (*DS* 1685, 1709). Trent in these passages touches upon the function and role of the Church which now makes efficaciously present in the sacrament the saving judgment of God in Christ. The Church and its minister do not merely declare the saving Word of God as found in the Scriptures, but rather make that saving word now present and "incarnate" in the words of absolution and in the function of reconciliation.[68] The insistence of the Council of Trent on the judicial aspect of penance is theologically connected with an understanding of the Church as efficaciously continuing in time and space the mission of Jesus. This ecclesial aspect of judgment as the authoritative proclamation of pardon and reconciliation with the "rights" coming from it (a concept which without further explanation remains too juridical) reinforces the understanding of the ecclesial aspect of the sacrament which has been highlighted by contemporary theologians. Reconciliation with the Church and the Christian community in the sacrament of penance is intimately joined with reconciliation of the penitent sinner with the Father through Christ. In this way the public and authoritative intervention of the Church in reconciling the sinner mediates the return of the sinner to the house of the Father. The judicial character of the sacrament of penance rests on this authoritative and efficacious proclamation of the saving word of God's pardon now mediated to the penitent sinner and celebrated in the sacrament.

A correct understanding of the judgment in penance also emphasizes the essential worship aspect of every sacrament. All the sacraments are primarily signs of worship, but the worship aspect has never been highlighted in our conception of the sacrament of penance, a fact influenced by an inadequate realization of the judgment involved.[69] (In the present format the judgment consists in the words of absolution—"I absolve you.") Since the judgment of penance consists in the merciful and loving intervention of God in Christ in the forgiveness of sin, the first reaction of the penitent involves gratitude and thankfulness for the great gift of forgiveness and mercy. Penance truly becomes a celebration in which the individual penitent joins the whole worshipping Church in singing forth the praises of the merciful God who has shown such love to sinful men. Any renewal of the penitential rite needs to emphasize this aspect of worship by highlighting the gift of forgiveness and the grateful response of those who now share in this merciful love in the community of the Church. The mere formula of absolution does not fully express the greatness of the gift of forgiveness and reconciliation which the Church mediates to sinners. One conscious of the gratuitous love of the merciful Father, beautifully illustrated in the parable of the merciful Father in Luke 15 in which the initiative and forgiveness of the Father are stressed, participates in the penitential rite with the proper sentiments of thanks and praise. His participation is truly a hymn of praise to the merciful love of the Father who has offered his love and himself to men.

The worship aspect of penance intimately coheres with the joyful aspect of penance as the joyful return to the house of the Father. The gift of God in Christ and the response of the penitent sinner bring about the joyful encounter again illustrated in the parable of the merciful Father. Too often fear and darkness have replaced the joy and light so characteristic of the homecoming of the prodigal. A proper understanding of the judgment of the sacrament of penance thus brings to the fore the important aspects of worship and joy which must be a part of every penitential celebration. The saving judgment of God does not gloss over the horror and reality of sin, for the death of Jesus was the true judgment on sin itself; but the saving judgment of God in emphasizing the reality of sin also underscores even more the mercy and forgiveness of the Father. Unfortunately a too juridical understanding of the judgment involved in the sacrament of penance has distorted the real meaning of the sacrament. Judgment seen as the authoritative proclamation of the mercy and forgiveness of God in Christ to the penitent sinner as celebrated in reconciliation with the Church better coheres with the biblical and theological data while at the same time properly emphasizing the divine initiative, the worshipful response of the sinner, and the joyful aspect of the sacrament of reconciliation.

CONFESSION

The Council of Trent repeats the accepted theological notion that the matter or quasi-matter of the sacrament of penance consists in the acts of the penitent which are described as contrition, confession and satisfaction (*DS* 1673). These three actions describe with a greater specificity the basic concept of *metanoia* or change of heart which is the fundamental response of the penitent sinner. The importance of confession in the reality of conversion or penance is underscored in the Scriptures and theology. In James 5 we are admonished to confess our sins to one another. The context of the passage in Matthew 18, which ends with the conferring of the power of binding and loosing, contains an earlier admonition that the individuals should try to straighten out the matter between themselves before taking it to the whole community. In the Middle Ages the scholastics argued about the efficacy of confessing sins to one another and not to a priest. This was certainly regarded in practice as an ordinary way of obtaining peace after minor faults and an extraordinary way of obtaining pardon even for grave sin. Thomas Aquinas called such confession an incomplete sacrament, but later theologians under the influence of the Scotistic approach tended to deemphasize this aspect and emphasize the authoritative intervention of the Church through the absolution of the minister.[70] A proper understanding of sin also calls for a confession of guilt to the one we have offended by our sin. Since sin involves a multiplicity of relationships, conversion implies an admission of our guilt in terms of these multiple relationships. Too often in the recent past an overemphasis on the integral confession to the priest has made Catholics forget the need also to confess our sinfulness to one another and especially to the persons affected by our sinfulness. Like the basic concept of forgiveness, confession too becomes real only to the extent that it embraces our relationships with others and the world. Conversion itself is the process of passing from darkness to life, and confession is the public admission that we have done so. From a very human viewpoint there can be no reconciliation unless the offending party is first willing to admit his wrong to the other. Thus Scripture, theology, history and a consideration of human affairs show that confession forms an integral part of the change of heart and penance of the sinner.

The Council of Trent in its teaching has specified the notion of confession with regard to the specific confession of mortal sins to the priest in the sacrament of penance. According to Canon 7 of Session 14 of Trent, it is necessary by divine law to confess all and every mortal sin, even occult sins, those against the last two precepts of the decalogue, and the circumstances which change the species of sins, insofar as one can recall these with a due and diligent consideration (*DS* 1707). The chapter in Trent corresponding to this canon argues for such an integral confession from the fact that Christ Jesus left his priests as rulers and judges who are not able to make this judgment or to assign proper satisfaction unless the sins have been confessed to them in a detailed way and not just generically (*DS* 1679).

This teaching of the Council of Trent has been the focal point of the current debate about the restructuring of the format of penance and specifically about the need for the integral confession of sins as an essential part of the sacrament.[71] Some have argued that Trent requires such an integral confession of sins as a matter of divine law, and hence this in some way must always be a part of the ritual of penance for grave sins.[72] Others do not think that Trent stands in the way of a sacramental form of penance which does not include the integral confession of sins to a priest, but very often they do not really explain this position.[73] I do not think that the sacrament of penance does necessarily require an integral confession of sins to the priest, and there can be forms of the sacramental rite which do not include such integral confession; likewise, the Council of Trent does not prohibit such a development. What are the reasons for such a position?

Unfortunately, since the time of Trent, Catholic theology and practice have generally ignored the wider and fuller meaning of "confession" that had been an essential part of the Christian tradition. In the classical Latin usage *confiteri* signifies the recognition of a reality which can take place in two different domains. Concerning the truth, *confiteri* signifies a proclamation or declaration; and in this sense Christians spoke of confessing God or his name or confessing the faith. This confession was a public declaration and adhesion of their faith which was seen above all in the death of the martyr. Concerning the recognition of a fault, *confiteri* signifies the acknowledgment of that fault; and Christians generally made this usage clear by adding another word such as the confession of sins or the confession of my iniquity. The Scriptures, in this case the Old Testament, introduced into the Christian language a third sense of *confiteri*. As a translation of the Hebrew *hodeh*, confess meant to give praise or to give thanks. For example, the Latin version of Psalm 135 is: "Confitemini Domino quoniam bonus. . . ." which is now translated into English in one version as: "Give thanks to the Lord for He is good. . . ." Even in the Old Testament this concept of confession brought together the notion of sacrifices of praise and thanksgiving with the concept of the acknowledgment of one's faults. Man's sin was frequently the distress from which God had freed his people, and thus their confession was at one and the same time a recognition of the goodness of God their savior and a recognition of their own sinful condition which is in need of such help.[74]

Christian antiquity and the early Middle Ages continued to emphasize the primary aspect of confession as that of giving thanks and praise. Notice how this again coincides with the concept of judgment as the saving judgment of God's mercy and forgiveness and underlines the worship aspect of the sacrament of penance. For St. Augustine, his *Confessions* are not primarily revelations of his sinful life before his conversion but rather, as the very first line indicates, a hymn and sacrifice of praise and thanksgiving to God for his goodness and mercy.[75] The three meanings are joined in the Middle Ages to express the one reality as an act of faith and an acknowledgment of one's sinfulness in thanksgiving to the Father who, through his Incarnate Son and the Spirit they send, saves man and pardons him.[76] Unfortunately, a later theology so distinguished these three elements in the concept of confession that they became totally separated, and confession as the avowal of sin was considered primarily in juridical terms.[77]

Historians of the sacrament of penance have been quick to point out the over-emphasis on the aspect of confession in the understanding of penance ever since the twelfth century. The entire sacrament in our own day is identified primarily through the word confession, which is only one aspect of it. In fact, the difficulty in making one's confession to the priest took on some of the aspects of satisfaction itself. Not only did this aspect become predominant but it tended to be interpreted in a narrowly juridical way. The confession of sins was intimately connected with the confessor's role as judge. However, both the notion of judgment and the notion of sin are understood today in a much less juridical fashion. The detailed, or as the canons say, the integral confession of mortal sins obviously becomes less important and even less possible of attainment in the context of the contemporary understanding of sin and judgment.

History also can point out that the integral confession of mortal sins has not always been required in order to participate fully in the Eucharist. Zoltan Alszeghy, who argued that the proposals of Heggen for sacramental penance without specific confession of mortal sins cannot be reconciled with the teaching of Trent, willingly admits that in the first millennium of its existence the Church did not always require either absolution or integral confession of sins before full participation in the Eucharistic banquet.[78]

There have been a number of historical studies which have brought to light these different formats of the sacrament of penance which did not require integral confession of sins, but it is sufficient to cite just one example.[79] Louis Ligier has written a number of articles about the sacrament of penance in the Orient, especially in the period between the fourth and the ninth century, the period between the decline of the older penance form and the introduction of private penance.[80] During this time different liturgical rites of penance became a part of the official prayers of the Church—both in the Office and in the Mass. After describing these various rites, Ligier then poses the crucial problem about their sacramental value. The heart of the question is to ascertain "if the Oriental Churches recognize or would still recognize in these rites a sacramental efficacy or, if on the contrary, they would accord to them only the value proper to every *opus operantis. . . .*" The Orientals united to Rome no longer have these rites but only the sacramental rite of individual confession, but such other rites still exist among other Orientals. In fact, even in private confession among the Orientals there is no insistence on integral confession of sins, but rather a very generic admission that the penitent has sinned.[81] Ligier concludes: "As to the prayers and rites of penance which the Orient presents in the full Eucharistic liturgy, it is necessary to admit, it seems, that they enjoy a sacramental value."[82] It could be objected that these prayers and rites merely anticipate the purification which comes from the Eucharist itself, but these rites were precisely added to the Eucharist with a new and peculiar form which is undoubtedly penitential. Ligier's conclusion is not that the Latin Church abandon the individual confession with its integral auricular confession, but that the Latin Church retain both the individual and the communitarian rites of the sacrament of penance.[83]

Even the present canonical discipline indicates that the integral confession of mortal sins according to number and species is not an absolute demand of the sacrament itself.

Canonists speak of the integrity of the confessional as being formal or material. They realize there are some circumstances in which the penitent is excused from material integrity, that is, the enumeration of the number and species of all the mortal sins committed since the last confession. Canonists and theologians have generally listed a number of moral and physical reasons that render the integral and specific confession of mortal sins according to number and species impossible or unnecessary.[84] The law of the Church even allows for general absolution in certain cases in which there is no specific confession of sins. An Instruction of the Sacred Penitentiary of 1944 lays down the general principle that such general absolution without specific auricular confession is permitted when there is present "an altogether grave and urgent necessity proportionate to the gravity of the divine precept of the integrity of confession, for example, if penitents without any fault of their own, would be forced to lack for a long time sacramental grace and holy communion" (*DS* 3834).[85] This general absolution was given quite frequently in wartime with the provision that the sins be mentioned at the next confession. In addition, present Church discipline has extended the possibility of such general confessions to missionary lands in certain circumstances.[86] Thus even the current discipline of the Church points out that the requirement of the confession of mortal sins according to species and number is not so absolute as to allow no exceptions.

For some people the major stumbling block in changing the format of the sacrament of penance so that individual confession of mortal sins is not always required remains the teaching of the Council of Trent. Canon 7 of Session 14 taught that the confession of each and every mortal sin and the circumstances which change the species of such sins is required by divine law, and it declared an "anathema" against anybody denying this (*DS* 1707). Some have thus concluded that Trent has defined as an unalterable principle of Catholic dogma that the sacrament of penance requires the individual confession of all mortal sins according to their number and species. In the light of this problem Carl J. Peter has investigated the concept of anathema and of divine law as it was applied to auricular confession in the Council of Trent.[87] Peter follows the proposal of Fransen that the concepts of faith and heresy as employed in Trent have much broader meanings than divinely revealed truth and its denial. The fact that an anathema is attached to a certain teaching does not mean that such a teaching is proposed as divinely revealed. By the use of divine law Peter maintains that the Council of Trent meant much more than merely a disciplinary norm of the Church as some have maintained. Peter argues from his study of the Acts of the Council that integrity of confession is a divinely willed value but not an absolute value which must be present in every circumstance. Peter concludes that the teaching of Trent does not exclude a possible change in the liturgical rite which would involve "only generic confession and communal absolution coupled with the obligation of confessing specifically within a definite period of time."[88] Personally, in the light of all the other factors mentioned above, I see no reason to demand that specific confession be required afterwards. Likewise, in the light of both the different historical developments mentioned above and the overly juridical approach to penance since the Middle Ages, I see the value of integral confession in an even more relative way than Peter.

Confession remains an essential part of the sacrament of penance, but one must avoid interpreting such confession in the narrowly juridical sense of a mere listing of sins. The confession of sins is essentially an act of worship and an act of faith in the forgiving mercy of God in Christ by one who acknowledges his own sinfulness. Also the penitent sinner recognizes that he must not only confess his sin to God and the Church but also to his neighbor—especially when the neighbor has been harmed by his sin. History and theology both indicate that the Tridentine insistence on the specific confession of mortal sins according to number and species does not constitute an absolutely essential part of the sacrament of penance. In the light of a less juridical understanding of sin and judgment, the reasons for such a specific confession are also lessened. There are other more important values in the concept of penance so that there could be sacramental rites which do not expressly contain a specific confession of sins by the individual to the minister. In general I would hold for a plurality of formats for the sacrament of penance. There are theological and psychological values in the format of specific auricular confession, but there remains the need to develop other rites of the sacrament which emphasize more important values which are not present, or at least not evident, in the present rite for penance.

RELATIONSHIP BETWEEN EUCHARIST AND PENANCE

In the theological and ecclesiological circumstances existing until a few years ago there was a tendency to absolutize present structures and approaches as if they would not admit of any change. It should now be apparent that historically there have been a number of diverse formats of the sacrament of penance and that the specific confession of mortal sins does not necessarily have to be present in every sacramental rite of penance. Perhaps with some today there exists the opposite danger of paying no attention to former historical forms and trying to form a rite or liturgy based only on their understanding of the needs of the moment. This study has tried to employ an historical approach which avoids the extreme tendencies of either canonizing the past or paying no attention to the past. A knowledge of historical developments is most necessary in trying to devise new rites which must also take into consideration the needs of the present. A study of the relationship between penance and the Eucharist will also introduce another relativizing factor into these considerations.

The present discipline in the Church maintains that ordinarily no one conscious of mortal sin should receive "holy communion" without sacramental confession; but if there is a necessity and it is impossible to get to a confessor, one may receive communion having first made an act of perfect contrition.[89] Somewhat the same legislation exists for the priest celebrating the Eucharist with the added warning that he confess his sins as soon as possible, which is generally interpreted to mean within three days.[90] Even in the current legislation of the Church there is no absolute need for a person conscious of mortal sin to celebrate the sacrament of penance before participating fully in the Eucharistic banquet. This legislation also raises important historical and theological aspects of the question.

The relationship between penance and the Eucharist insofar as it concerns full participation in the Eucharist by one who has not been reconciled with the Church through sacramental penance also arose in the early Church. Cyril Vogel discusses this particular question in the light of the development of the sacrament of penance between the fourth and the sixth centuries.[91] Two particular characteristics of the penance at this time were the fact that such penance was offered to a person only once in the course of his life and the fact that the penance frequently involved very difficult expiation which might include such things as the necessity to quit the army or even the need to forego marital relations not merely for the duration of the expiation but for the entire future. In the light of these rigorous circumstances, it was only natural that sinners would hesitate to undergo canonical penance. Even bishops and Councils pointed out the dangers involved in a too hasty decision on the part of the young to enter the canonical penance. In these circumstances there was a natural tendency to put off penance until the time of death. Despite some rigoristic reaction this became a rather common custom, and the dying penitent was then reconciled without the arduous expiation which was required in the normal canonical penance. The Bishop of Arles, for example, even encouraged his people to prepare for this penance before death by their own personal effort. All Christians during their lifetime are capable of doing penance and mortifying themselves even if they are not in a position to participate in the canonical penance.[92] But then the crucial question concerns the participation of these people in the Eucharistic banquet. Vogel concludes: "It is therefore extremely probable that the faithful who on the exhortation of their pastors repented sincerely and tried to merit by their good works the penance on their death bed were admitted without reconciliation to the Eucharistic table."[93]

The question came up during the Council of Trent when the Council Fathers debated the requirement of sacramental penance before full participation in the Eucharist for those who were conscious of being guilty of mortal sin.[94] Cajetan and a number of other theologians such as John Fisher and Pope Hadrian VI maintained that there was no divine law which held that a person in mortal sin had to confess his sins before coming to the Eucharistic table. The Council Fathers were divided on this particular issue, and in their final redaction of the canon they left out anything which would or could indicate that this was a question of divine law.[94] The current canonical discipline is based on Trent and most commentators maintain it is not a matter of divine law.[95]

The historical and disciplinary aspects of the problem naturally focus attention on the theological understanding of the relationship between the Eucharist and the sacrament of penance. In a recent article studying this particular question J. M. R. Tillard concludes to "the central place of the Eucharist in the mystery of the pardon of God."[96] Tillard points out that the Council of Trent considered the Eucharist under two different aspects. Session XIII (1551) treated the Eucharist in terms of communion as the reception of the Body of the Lord; whereas Session XXII (1562) considered the Eucharistic sacrifice or the Mass. This second consideration constantly emphasizes the function of the Eucharist in the forgiveness of sin and the divine mystery of pardon. Particularly in reaction to their understanding of the reformers, the fathers of Trent wanted to underscore the efficacy of the Eucharist with regard to sin. The second chapter of this session insists on the propitiatory nature of the Eucharist by which God concedes grace and the gift of penance and forgives our crimes and even our great sins (*DS* 1743). The corresponding canon pronounces an anathema against anyone who would deny that the Eucharist is a propitiatory sacrifice for sins (*DS* 1753).

Contemporary theology no longer separates the different aspects of the Eucharist but considers the whole Eucharist as both sacrifice and sacrament. Communion cannot be separated from the entire Eucharistic banquet and sacrifice. The entire Eucharist as making present the Paschal Mystery of Christ is a participation in the redemptive aspect of this mystery by which we are freed from sin. According to Tillard the Eucharist and sacramental penance join together in the unique mystery of divine pardon of which, however, the Eucharist is the center.[97] There is only one pardon, but each of these two sacraments shows forth diverse aspects and modalities of the one mystery of pardon. Tillard does not believe that penance thus becomes a useless sacrament which is no longer necessary. The mystery of divine pardon is so great that there are a number of ways of expressing it and making it sacramentally present. Penance better brings out the aspect of penance as a conversion by which the sinner joyfully returns to the house of the Father. Tillard draws this practical conclusion from his study. The requirement of penance before the Eucharist for the person conscious of mortal sin results from a decision of the Church, for participation with a contrite heart at the Lord's Supper is in itself a source of pardon provided one has the intention of approaching in due time the sacrament of penance. His practical solution is to dissociate receiving the sacrament of penance from the participation in the Eucharist so that it is no longer a necessary condition for the latter. Then both sacraments would retain their proper identity and meaning. Tillard admits this is a delicate solution but no more difficult than some of the existing problems. Even if one disagrees with this practical solution, still no one can forget that the primary sacrament of pardon remains the Eucharist. Contemporary sacramental theology has emphasized that the Eucharist is the central sacrament and that all the other sacraments have their meaning in relation to it. Perhaps a too one-sided emphasis on the sacrament of penance has made us forget that the Eucharist remains the primary sacrament of forgiveness.

CONCLUSIONS

Sin, penance, or conversion and reconciliation are important realities in the life of the Christian today, but a poor understanding of these realities coupled with a magical and overly juridical approach to the sacrament of penance has caused many Catholics to forget or overlook these realities in our existence. The purpose of this study has been to bring to light the meaning of the mystery of sin and its forgiveness and the call for continual conversion in the life of the Christian. No attempt has been made to describe in concrete terms different formats for the sacrament of penance, since there are already in existence a number of such rites and penitential celebrations.[98] In addition there exists a danger of over-emphasizing the need for a change in the rite of penance. Such changes are absolutely necessary, but even more important is the understanding of the reality involved. Any ritual ultimately faces the more important question of meaning and significance, which also explains the concentration in this study on a better understanding of the mystery of sin and reconciliation.

Sin has to be seen not in terms of mere laws but in terms of multiple relationships so that conversion or repentance also involves multiple relationships. To limit forgiveness to man's relationship to God or to restrict it merely to reconciliation with my neighbor and the world would be an overly exclusive approach. The sacramental celebration of forgiveness stresses the gratuitousness of God's saving intervention and the grateful thanks and praise of the Church and the penitent for his great love. The whole Church as the community gathered together into the Risen Lord joins in this mystery of worship and sanctification. Reconciliation with God in Christ remains intimately connected with and signified in man's reconciliation with the community of the Church. The penitent constantly remembers his own sinfulness and the need for continual conversion. Since sin affects not only man's heart but his whole life, his Church, and his society, the penitent sinner is called to struggle against the power of sin in all these areas. Conversion, like sin itself, cannot be limited to the heart of the individual. Sacramental celebrations do not take the Christian out of his daily life but unite the whole life of the Christian in the one mystery of conversion or repentance. In the light of this broader understanding of the sacramental mystery of repentance, the present rite of the sacrament appears to be inadequate and insufficient. In general, the very complexity of the reality of sin and repentance calls for a plurality of sacramental formats.

The study has not discussed the sacrament of penance as it exists vis-à-vis the different realities of venial and mortal sin. The sacrament does exist primarily in terms of those who have broken their multiple relationship of love. However, the sacrament of penance also has meaning in terms of what was traditionally called venial sin which is the sinful condition of man always falling short in his efforts to give himself to God, others, and the world. Since Catholic tradition has maintained there are numerous ways in which this daily conversion takes place and in which venial sin is forgiven, obviously it would be wrong to limit this just to a sacramental celebration. The Christian who honestly becomes more aware of his own sinfulness also becomes more aware of the constant call to change his heart and his multiple relationships. The call to conversion is constant, and the Christian open to the *kairos* will find many opportunities to overcome his own sinfulness in his everyday life. There should also exist penitential prayers and formats even in familial settings which are not strictly sacramental. However, since this continual conversion forms so important a part of the Christian life, it is fitting that the Christian celebrates this in a sacramental way; but there should be a plurality of formats in which this takes place. In the last few years there has been much literature on the subject of the confession of devotion which refers to the sacrament of penance for one who is not conscious of having broken his relationship of love with God and neighbor.[99] At times there seems to be the danger of justifying this in terms of spiritual direction or psychological benefits for the individual. However, the ultimate reason for it can only be found in man's celebrating and entering more deeply into the mystery of merciful forgiveness and conversion which forms such an essential part of the Christian life. These celebrations would be very appropriate both in connection with different liturgical seasons of the year and in connection with the work of specific groups or communities in the Church.

The reality of mortal sin is much rarer than an older theology believed. In this connection one must see the full reality of conversion and forgiveness in terms of baptism, penance, and the Eucharist. Here too there can and should be a plurality of different sacramental rites. From what has been said it follows that the sacrament of penance does not necessarily need a specific auricular confession of one's "mortal sins" to the minister. There is a need to develop a plurality of rites which in their entirety try to express and celebrate the full mystery of forgiveness and conversion. One could also accept Tillard's suggestions and not require penance as a preparation for participation in the Eucharist, although I personally would prefer to see penance usually (but not always) in terms of a rite of reconciliation which obviously emphasizes the reconciliation with the community before one fully participates in the Eucharistic banquet.

On a pastoral level there are pressing problems in the present which cannot wait for a future solution. The fact that Catholics are "not going to confession" as often as they did in the past is not in itself alarming, but unfortunately there also seems to be in theory and practice a tendency to forget the reality of sin and the call for repentance in the life of the Christian. Many pastors realize the problems existing with the present format of the sacrament of penance and are experimenting with other formats to give a better appreciation and understanding of the meaning of sin and conversion. At times within communal penance services there is individual confession of "mortal sins according to number and species," but at other times there is not.[100] How does a theologian react to this fact existing in the Church today? Are these rites without individual confession truly sacramental? I believe they are.

This question raises the whole problem of liturgical experimentation. There are both convincing theological and pastoral reasons for changes in the rite of the sacrament of penance. The Constitution on the Liturgy of Vatican II reminds all that the regulation of the liturgy "depends solely on the authority of the Church, that is, on the Apostolic See and, as laws may determine, on the bishop. . . . Therefore absolutely no other person, not even a priest, may add, remove, or change anything in the liturgy on his own authority" (n. 22).

One of the problems has been the lack of experimentation in the sacrament of penance under the guidance and auspices of the hierarchy in general and especially in our own country. Experimentation is vitally needed because one cannot construct a liturgy totally in an *a priori* way. Experimentation is a practical recognition that one's approach both to theology and liturgy cannot be totally deductive, for the experience of Christian people must enter into the discussion. At the same time one cannot merely construct a liturgical rite on the basis of personal experience, since a knowledge of theology, liturgy, and history is also essential. There is a need for constant experimentation in these and other areas, and the failure to have such experimentation points to a deeper source of conflict and tension—the opposing theological methodologies and attitudes which are at work. Apparently the hierarchy still sees no real need for such experimentation, but meanwhile many people have felt the need to experiment on their own.

A realistic understanding and historical precedents, however, remind us that even with the best type of controlled and guided experimentation there will not always be a smooth transition in the whole process of change and development. Those who expect such a smooth transition operate with a worldview and a theological and ecclesiological methodology which tend to play down the emphasis on historicity, growth, and change. Newer forms and rites do not necessarily come from the top down; in fact, the history of the sacrament of penance indicates that new forms came into existence without the approval and even in the face of positive condemnation by the hierarchy. In 589 at the Third Synod of Toledo the Bishops of Spain sharply condemned the practice of allowing penance more than once in the lifetime of the person.[101] When new forms of penance were making their appearance, there was a negative reaction at times on the part of the hierarchy. In describing the Carolingian period Palmer admits that attempts were made without total success by some of the reform Councils to revive public penance and to outlaw the Celtic penitential handbooks.[102] Carra de Vaux Saint-Cyr recognizes the same unsuccessful effort on the part of the Carolingian reform to put down the new forms of penance. "Apparently the effort to restore the old rite smacked of undue concern for tradition."[103] There was not, however, massive opposition to the new forms on the part of Rome.

Change and growth necessarily imply a certain tension which cannot be totally eliminated by enforcing the regulation that there can be no change in the sacramental rite unless it is first approved by the hierarchy. Note that this does not give free rein to people to do whatever they want, for one must be guided by principles of sound theology, liturgy, and pastoral prudence. Catholic theology has consistently maintained that disciplinary laws must always be interpreted and applied in the light of the higher laws. In this particular case the theological and pastoral considerations could in some cases take precedence over the present disciplinary legislation, which is what traditional theology allows for in its understanding of *epikeia*.[104] The Church legislation in this matter has an importance for public order and the good of the Church. One cannot merely ignore such legislation, but on the other hand one cannot absolutize such present norms. The disciplinary aspect is only one consideration and not the ultimate consideration. The responsible theologian, however, also has an obligation to show, if possible, the continuity with the current norms and thus to ease the tensions as much as possible, realizing that he can never do away with the tensions completely. Even within the context of the present legislation, one can argue for the sacramental format which does not include the specific confession of mortal sins according to number and species.

The legislation today requires the confession of sins according to their number and species only for mortal sins, but this is not required if there are no mortal sins. It has been pointed out that the reality of mortal sin is much less common today than it was thought to be in the past. In the vast majority of cases there is no need for such integral confession according to number and species. The demand for material integrity itself is not an absolute, and more exceptions have been made in this matter in recent years, especially in mission countries. The Instruction of the Sacred Penitentiary of March 25, 1944, lays down the very sane theological principle that one is not held by the law of materially integral confession if some other altogether grave and urgent necessity arises which is proportionate to the gravity of the divine precept to make an integral confession. Since today theologians are more aware of the elasticity of "that divine precept" and since there are weighty theological and pastoral reasons calling for a change, then one does not need as grave a necessity today to justify the lack of a formally integral confession. The fact that people have failed to participate in the sacrament and now tend to forget the importance of the reality of sin and the redemptive mystery of forgiveness is sufficient reason in some circumstances to forego the present requirement of specific confession. Even in the past, theologians were most lenient in particular cases about foregoing the need for material integrity.

Within the context of the present discipline one can also point out the centrality of the Eucharist as the sacrament of forgiveness and the fact that according to many theologians, including Cardinal Cajetan, the requirement of penance before full participation in the Eucharist is only a requirement of Church law. Again one could argue that in certain circumstances there might be proportionate reasons for not having first celebrated the sacrament of penance with integral confession of sins.

Thus even in the context of the current discipline of the Church one could argue that communal celebrations without individual confession of sins could be truly sacramental celebrations. Naturally the priest celebrating these rites must exercise pastoral prudence in the way in which he introduces these rites and educates his people. Likewise one must caution against expecting that a mere change of rite either now or in the future is going to solve all the problems connected with the sacrament of penance. Many of the problems raised by the sacrament of penance center on the more fundamental question of the existence of God, the reality of sin, and the redemptive and forgiving love of God in Christ. The purpose of this study has been to develop a better understanding of the mystery of forgiveness and repentance. The Eucharist and the daily life of the individual furnish opportunities to participate in the Christian mystery of forgiveness and repentance, but the sacrament of penance remains one very important way which badly needs both a better understanding and new formats that will make Christians more aware of the reality of sin and of their participation through the community of the Church in the mystery of redemptive conversion.

NOTES

1.
For a theological explanation of such a practice with pertinent bibliography, see Gerard S. Sloyan, "The Age of First Confession," *Proceedings of the Catholic Theological Society of America*, XXII (1967), 201-213; F. J. Buckley, S.J., "What Age for First Confession?" *Irish Ecclesiastical Record*, CVII (1967), 221-252; W. M. Jones, "First Confession at Seven?" *Clergy Review*, LIII (1968), 613-618.

2.
P. J. Mars and F. J. Heggen have compiled several services of penance for adults in F. J. Heggen, *Confession and the Service of Penance* (London: Sheed and Ward, 1967), pp. 119-176. The same translation has been published in this country by the University of Notre Dame Press. Also see G. M. Nessim, O.P., "Liturgies communautaires et catéchèse du sacrament de pénitence," *Paroisse et Liturgie*, XLIX (1967), 122-146.

3.
P. J. Jossua, D. Duliscouet and B. D. Marliangeas, "Bulletin de Théologie: Crise et redécouverte du sacrement de pénitence," *Revue des Sciences Philosophiques et Théologiques*, LII (1968), 119-142, review much of the recent theological literature on the subject. C. Dumont, S.J., reviews recent books on penance, sin, and conversion in a special bibliographical summary in *Nouvelle Revue Théologique*, XC (1968), 715-726.

4.
The best historical works on the sacrament of penance available in English include: Paul F. Palmer, S.J., *Sacraments and Forgiveness* (Westminster, Md.: Newman Press, 1959); Bernard Poschmann, *Penance and the Anointing of the Sick,* tr. Francis Courtney (New York: Herder and Herder, 1964). This later work is a translation of *Busse und Letzte Ölung* which summarizes much of Poschmann's earlier historical work as found in *Paenitentia Secunda; Die abendländische Kirchenbusse im Ausgang des christlichen Albertums; Die abendländische Kirchenbusse im frühen Mittelalter.* Poschmann, however, does not seem to give enough importance to the difference between the canonical penance and the tariffed penance introduced by the Irish monks. Paul Anciaux, *The Sacrament of Penance* (New York: Sheed and Ward, 1962). See also Anciaux's more detailed historical study, *La théologie de pénitence au XIIe siècle* (Louvain: Publications Universitaries de Louvain, 1949). Paulus Galtier, S.I., *De Paenitentia: Tractatus Dogmatico-Historicus* (Rome: Pontifical Gregorian University, 1956). In this section I have followed closely Cyrille Vogel, *Le pécheur et la pénitence dans L'Église ancienne* (Paris: Éditions du Cerf, 1966). In this historical connection one should also note Karl Rahner, S.J., *La penitenza della Chiesa* (Rome: Edizioni Paoline, 1964) which brings together six historical studies on penance in the early Church and other systematic studies on penance which Rahner published separately over a number of years.

5.
The latest study of the attitude of Catholics toward penance is "Les chrétiens parlent de la confession," *La Vie Spirituelle,* CXIX (1968), 375-500. Other investigations of this type are mentioned by Jossua, *et al., Revue des Sciences Philosophiques et Théologiques,* LII (1968), 119-120.

6.
Zoltan Alszeghy, S.I., "L'aggiornamento del sacramento della penitenza," *La Civiltà Cattolica*, CXIX (1968), 140. Alszeghy, professor at the Gregorian University in Rome, has published his class notes on penance, *De Paenitentia Christiana* (Rome: Pontifical Gregorian University, 1962), and other articles on penance.
7.
Karl Rahner, *Theological Investigations*, II (Baltimore: Helicon Press, 1963), 135-174.
8.
Charles West employed this description in a paper read at the 1967 meeting of the American Society of Christian ethics.
9.
Jerome Murphy-O'Connor, O.P., "Sin and Community in the New Testament," in *Sin and Repentance*, ed. Denis O'Callaghan (Staten Island: Alba House, 1967), p. 18.
10.
Roger Lincoln Shinn, *Man: The New Humanism* (Philadelphia: Westminster Press, 1968), pp. 145-164.
11.
Ph. Delhaye *et al.*, *Théologie du péché* (Tournai: Desclée et Cie, 1960), which has been published in English by Desclée in a number of small volumes the most important of which is Albert Gelin and Albert Descamps, *Sin in the Bible* (New York: Desclée, 1965). *Il Peccato,* ed. Pietro Palazzini (Rome: Edizioni Ares, 1959), a 928-page volume which has appeared in English in three smaller volumes published by Scepter.
12.
Stanislaus Lyonnet, S.J., *De Peccato et Redemptione,* Vol. I (Rome: Pontifical Biblical Institute, 1957).

13.
Piet Schoonenberg, S.J., *Man and Sin* (Notre Dame, Ind.: University of Notre Dame Press, 1965), pp. 98-123.

14.
Bernard Häring, "Conversion," in *Pastoral Treatment of Sin* (New York: Desclée, 1968), pp. 87-176.

15.
John W. Glazer, S.J., "Transition Between Grace and Sin: Fresh Perspectives," *Theological Studies*, XXIX (1968), 260-274, summarizes some of the recent literature on the fundamental option especially from a more existentialist viewpoint. Other articles on the subject with appropriate bibliographies include: M. Flick, S.J., and Z. Alszeghy, S.J., "L'opzione fondamentale della vita morale e la grazia," *Gregorianum*, XLI (1960), 593-619; Pierre Fransen, S.J., "Toward a Psychology of Divine Grace," *Lumen Vitae*, XII (1957), 203-232. The approach adopted in this study tries to do justice at one and the same time to the subjectivity of the individual person and his relationships with God, neighbor, and the world. The core decision or option of the human person is seen primarily in terms of these multiple relationships. The denial or lack of emphasis on transcendence in some contemporary theological writing tends to over-emphasize the relationship to man and the world at the expense of man's relationship to God. It is true that an older theology pretended to know too much about this relationship, but a theological vision of man must always consider this most important aspect of human existence and unceasingly try to give a better understanding and appreciation of it. For a somewhat "updated traditional Thomistic" approach to the question, see F. Bourassa, S.I., "Le péché offense de Dieu," *Gregorianum*, XLIX (1968), 563-574.

16.
Anton Meinrad Meier, *Das Peccatum Mortale ex Toto Genere Suo: Entstehung und Interpretation des Begriffes* (Regensburg: Verlag Friedrich Pustet, 1966).

17.
Heggen, pp. 70-77.

18.
Kevin F. O'Shea, "The Reality of Sin: A Theological and Pastoral Critique," *Theological Studies*, XXIX (1968), 241-259.

19.
Johannes B. Metz, "The Church's Social Function in the Light of a Political Theology," *Concilium*, XXXVI (June 1968), 2-18. Metz incorporates this article and others developing the same theme in his book *Theology of the World* (New York: Herder and Herder, 1969).

20.
"Pénitence-Conversion," in *Vocabulaire de Théologie Biblique*, ed. Xavier Leon-Dufour (Paris: Éditions du Cerf, 1962), pp. 788-790; Jean Giblet, "Les sens de la conversion dans l'Ancien Testament," *La Maison-Dieu*, XC (1967), 79-92; from a Protestant perspective, see *The Ecumenical Review*, XIX (July 1967) which number is totally devoted to the question of conversion.

21.
John Power, S.M.A., "The Call to Penance in the Old Testament," in *Sin and Repentance*, pp. 1-17.

22.
Poschmann, p. 162.

23.
Patrologiae Cursus Completus, series latina, ed. J. P. Migne, 178 (Paris, 1855), 440ff. Hereafter cited as *PL*.

24.
Sententiae, IV, d. 18, c. 4

25.
PL 176, 551, 564ff.

26.
Poschmann writes of the "great and epoch-making achieve-
ment of Aquinas' teaching on penance," but also acknowledges "very considerable difficulties confronted the arguments on which he had based the unity of the sacrament and
personal penance" (pp. 178-179). Bruno Carra de Vaux
Saint-Cyr, O.P., "Theologia del sacramento della penitenza:
riflessioni e suggerimenti," *Sacra Doctrina,* XLVI (1967),
178-203, praises Thomas' theory as being good theology and
good anthropology lacking only a communitarian emphasis
which is stressed in contemporary theology. This article
based on the Thomistic treatment of penance summarizes in
this matter the thesis of his book, *Revenir à Dieu: Pénitence,
conversion, confession* (Paris: Éditions du Cerf, 1967).

27.
Summa Theologiae III[a], q. 86, a. 6; *IV Sent.,* d.22, q. 2, a. 1.
Note that Thomas' treatment of penance in the *Summa* is
incomplete. For a summary of the Thomistic approach see
Poschmann, pp. 168-171, and Carra de Vaux Saint-Cyr.

28.
IV Sent., d.22, q.2, a.1.; *Supplementum,* q.10, a.1; *De Veritate,*
q.28, a.8, ad 2. *Contra Gentiles* IV, 72; *Summa* III[a], q.90, a.2.

29.
Poschmann, pp. 175-176; Carra de Vaux Saint-Cyr, *Sacra
Doctrina,* XLVI (1967), 190ff.

30.
Karl Rahner, S.J., "Personal and Sacramental Piety," *Theological Investigations,* II, 109-134; E. Schillebeeckx, O.P.,

Christ the Sacrament of the Encounter with God (New York: Sheed and Ward, 1963), pp. 192-216.

31.

The following works summarize well the different positions of the two schools and their respective understandings of contrition and attrition in the forgiveness of sins. From the Thomistic perspective, P. de Vooght, O.S.B., "La justification dans le sacrement de pénitence," *Ephemerides Theologicae Lovanienses*, V (1928), 225-226; de Vooght, "A propos de la causalité du sacrement de pénitence," *Ephemerides Theologicae Lovanienses*, VIII (1930), 663-675; de Vooght, "La théologie de la pénitence," *Ephemerides Theologicae Lovanienses*, XXV (1949), 77-82; H. Dondaine, O.P., *L'attrition suffisante*, Bibliothèque Thomiste, XXV (Paris, 1943); P. de Letter, S.J., "Two Concepts of Attrition and Contrition," *Theological Studies*, XI (1950), 3-33; de Letter, "Vi clavium ex attrito fit contritus," *Theological Studies*, XVI (1955), 424-432. From the Scotistic perspective, P. Galtier, S.J., "Amour de Dieu et attrition," *Gregorianum*, IX (1928), 373-416; Galtier, *De Paenitentia*, pp. 341-365.

32.

J. P. Jossua *et al.*, *Revue des Sciences Philosophiques et Théologiques*, CII (1968), 127-133, maintain that the renewal in the theology of penance stems from Thomistic and kerygmatic influences.

33.

Enchiridion Symbolorum Definitionum et Declarationum, ed. H. Denzinger, A. Schoenmetzer, 32nd ed. (Barcelona: Herder, 1963), 1668. Hereafter referred to as *DS*.

34.

Salvatore Garofalo, "Il Peccato nei vangeli," *Il Peccato*, pp. 69-94.

35.
Rahner, *Theological Investigations*, II, 140.

36.
These texts are explained at greater length in the standard texts and in the following works already mentioned: Alszeghy, Anciaux, Galtier, Palmer, Poschmann, and Rahner. From the viewpoint of a more contemporary manual of theology, see M. Schmaus, *Katholische Dogmatik*, IV/1 (München: Verlag Max Huber, 1957), §264.

37.
Alszeghy, S.I., "Carità ecclesiale nella penitenza cristiana," *Gregorianum*, XLIV (1963), 5-31.

38.
Murphy-O'Connor, *Sin and Repentance*, pp. 18-50.

39.
Rahner, *Theological Investigations*, II, 141.

40.
Foremost among those who have proposed such an approach are: B. Poschmann, "Die innere Struktur des Busssakramentes," *Müncher Theologische Zeitschrift*, I, n. 3 (1950), 12-30; M. Schmaus, "Reich Gottes und Busssakrament," *Müncher Theologische Zeitschrift*, I, n. 1 (1950), 20-36; C. Dumont, "La réconciliation avec l'Église et la nécessite de l'aveu sacramentel," *Nouvelle Revue Théologique*, LXXXI (1959), 577-597. For a summary of the literature with a more complete bibliography and emphasis on the catechetical implications, see Ludwig Lehmeier, S.V.D., *The Ecclesial Dimension of the Sacrament of Penance from a Catechetical Point of View* (Cebu City, P. I.: San Carlos Publications, 1967), which was written as a dissertation at the Catholic University of America.

41.
G. B. Guzzetti, *Trattato di Teologia Dogmatica,* III/2 *La Penitenza* (Rome: Marietti, 1966). Guzzetti rejects the opinion of Rahner for the reasons mentioned and opts for the opinion that binding and loosing is a scriptural formula signifying the universality of power.

42.
Alszeghy, *Gregorianum,* XLIV (1963), 9.

43.
Guzzetti, pp. 55-56.

44.
Alszeghy, *De Paenitentia Christiana,* pp. 45-48.

45.
Bartholomew Xiberta, *Clavis Ecclesiae* (Rome, 1922).

46.
Paul F. Palmer, S.J., "The Theology of Res and Sacramentum," *Proceedings of the Catholic Theological Society of America,* XIV (1959), 122-127.

47.
Examples of those who would deny the applicability of a strict *res et sacramentum* theory to the reconciliation with the Church in the sacrament of penance, but still uphold the importance of ecclesial reconciliation include: Alszeghy, *Gregorianum,* XLIV (1963), 5-31; J. P. Jossua *et al., Revue des Sciences Philosophiques et Théologiques,* LII (1968), 132-133. For a very negative critique of reconciliation with the Church as the *res et sacramentum* of penance by one who admits that the theory has won widespread favor and been accepted by many eminent theologians, see Clarence McAuliffe, S.J., "Penance and Reconciliation with the Church," *Theological Studies,* XXVI (1965), 1-39.

48.
For the theological development of the Church as sacrament, see Karl Rahner, *The Church and the Sacraments* (New York: Herder and Herder, 1963); E. Schillebeeckx, O.P., *Christ the Sacrament of the Encounter with God* (New York: Sheed and Ward, 1963); Otto Semmelroth, S.J., *Church and Sacrament* (Notre Dame, Ind.: Fides Publishers, 1965).

49.
Palmer, *Sacraments and Forgiveness,* pp. 175-178 and 209-212.

50.
This paragraph summarizes the sacramental theory proposed by Schillebeeckx in *Christ the Sacrament of the Encounter with God.*

51.
Schillebeeckx, p. 71.

52.
Other studies on the ecclesial and communitarian aspects of penance include: P. Anciaux, "Privatbeichte und gemeinschaftliche Bussfeier," *Theologie der Gegenwart,* X (1967), 15-21; B. Carra de Vaux Saint-Cyr, O.P., "Le mystère de la pénitence: réconciliation avec Dieu, réconciliation avec l'Église," *La Maison-Dieu,* XC (1967), 132-154; Michael Hurley, "Penance: Sacrament of Reconciliation," *Sin and Repentance,* pp. 109-126; E. Lodi, "Le celebrazioni del sacramento della penitenza, esercizio privilegiato della esperienza ecclesiale del cristiano," *Sacra Doctrina,* XLVI (1967), 217-236; R.-L. Oechslin, O.P., "Dimension ecclesiale de la pénitence," *La Vie Spirituelle,* CXVII (1967), 551-565; G. Rossino, "Verso una confessione communitaria," *Perfice Munus,* XLII (1967), 336-342; O. Semmelroth, S.J., "Structuren und Perspectiven in Busssakrament," *Busse und*

Beichte, ed. L. Bertsch (Frankfurt: J. Knecht, 1967), pp. 68-88; Mariano Valkovic, "Aspetto ecclesiale del sacramento della penitenza," *Studia Moralia,* V (1967), 201-214.

53.
Jossua *et al., Revue des Sciences Philosophiques et Théologiques,* XLII (1967), 123.

54.
Marcellinus Zalba, S.I., *Theologia Moralis Summa,* III: *De Sacramentis; De Delictis et Poenis* (Madrid: Biblioteca de Autores Cristianos, 1958), 288ff.

55.
E. Beaucamp, O.F.M., and J.-P. Relles, "La justice et la Bible," *La Vie Spirituelle,* CXVII (1967), 289-310.

56.
Beaucamp-Relles, *La Vie Spirituelle,* CXVII (1967), 298.

57.
John L. McKenzie, S.J., *Vital Concepts of the Bible* (Wilkes-Barre: Dimension Books, 1967), pp. 43-44.

58.
Augustin George, S.M., "The Judgment of God," *Concilium,* XLI (January 1969), 9-23.

59.
"Jugement," *Vocabulaire de Théologie Biblique,* p. 511.

60.
Klaus Mörsdorf, "Der hoheitliche Charakter der sacramentalen Lossprechung," *Trier Theologische Zeitschrift,* LVII (1948), 335-348; Mörsdorf, "Der Rechscharakter der iurisdictio fori interni," *Müncher Theologische Zeitschrift,* VIII (1957), 161-173. Somewhat in the same vein is Otto Semmelroth, "Das Busssakrament als Gericht," *Scholastik,* XXXVII (1962), 530-549.

61.
For a summary of this and other interpretations of the judicial nature of penance, see Guzzetti, pp. 60-68.

62.
P. Charles, S.I., "Doctrine et pastorale du sacrement de Pénitence," *Nouvelle Revue Théologique*, LXXV (1943), 449-470.

63.
Ibid., p. 462.

64.
Guzzetti, pp. 66-68.

65.
I fundamentally agree with the concept of judgment proposed by Guzzetti, but his methodological approach is one-sided, since he considers the judicial aspect of penance only from the analogy of the judicial process in justice and fails to consider the scriptural, theological, and ecclesiological aspects of judgment.

66.
Summa Theologiae III[a], q.60, a.3, in corp.

67.
Schmaus (§265) develops the judicial aspect of penance in the light of a theological understanding of judgment. Although Schmaus does mention the resurrection, he arrives at too negative a connotation attached to the judgment in penance by emphasizing the judgment of the Cross against sin. However, his methodological approach of seeing judgment from a theological perspective has overcome the dangers of a purely juridical approach to the judgment of penance. For a summary, but no critique of Schmaus' position, see Patrick J. Hamell, "Penance and Judgment," *The Furrow*, XVIII (1967), 322-329.

68.
The teaching of Trent should not be understood as denying the efficacy of the Word of God, but rather it emphasizes the role of the Church in making the Word of God present in the sacramental rite.

69.
For example, in the rightly acclaimed work by Anciaux, the worship aspect of the sacrament is mentioned only briefly and near the end (*The Sacrament of Penance*, pp. 160-162).

70.
Walter Kasper, "Confession Outside the Confessional," *Concilium*, XXIV (April 1967), 31-42; Karl Rahner, "Laienbeichte," *Lexikon für Theologie und Kirche*, VI, 741ff.; A. Teetaert, *La confession aux laïques dans l'Eglise latine depuis le VIIIe jusqu'au XIVe siècle* (Paris: J. Gabalda, 1926).

71.
Carl J. Peter, "Auricular Confession and the Council of Trent," *Proceedings of the Catholic Theological Society of America*, XXII (1967), 185-188.

72.
Francis J. Connell, C.SS.R., "Common Confession Rite," *American Ecclesiastical Review*, CLVI (1967), 409-412. Z. Alszeghy, S.J., "Problemi dogmatici della celebrazione penitenziale communitaria," *Gregorianum*, XLVIII (1967), 578, objects to the proposals of sacramental communitarian penance proposed by Heggen because they are not reconcilable with the Council of Trent.

73.
Heggen does not explain how his proposal is reconcilable with Trent. Bernard Häring, C.SS.R., *Shalom: Peace: The Sacrament of Reconciliation* (New York: Farrar, Straus and Giroux, 1968), pp. 91-98, assumes by his terminology that

the present discipline on integral confession is merely Church law.

74.
J. Leclercq, O.S.B., "La confession: louange de Dieu," *La Vie Spirituelle*, CXVIII (1968), 253-265.

75.
J. Ratzinger, "Originalität und Überlieferung in Augustinus Begriff der 'confessio'," *Revue des Études Augustiniennes*, III (1957), 375-392.

76.
Leclercq, *La Vie Spirituelle*, CXVIII (1968), 260-263. Also Leclercq, "Confession et louange de Dieu chez Saint Bernard," *La Vie Spirituelle*, CXX (1969), 588-605.

77.
Thomas Aquinas II^a, II^{ae}, q.3, a.1, ad lum, recalls the three meanings of confession and assigns three distinct virtues corresponding to those three meanings. Faith corresponds to the confession of faith; worship corresponds to the confession of praise and thanks; penance corresponds to the confession of sins.

78.
Alszeghy, *Civiltà Cattolica*, CXIX (1968), 146-147. In this article Alszeghy still speaks in terms of the "definition" and the "dogma" of Trent, and sees the only possibilities for sacramental rites of penance without specific confession of sins either in terms of including a promise or *votum* of such integral confession of sins or as justified by grave reasons excusing from formal integrity. Alszeghy thus appears to me to give too much importance to the divine-law teaching of Trent on the specific confession of mortal sins.

79.
For a summary consideration of the different penitential rites inserted into the Mass in the Roman rite, see J. Jung-

mann, "De actu paenitentiali infra Missam inserto conspectus historicus," *Ephemerides Liturgicae,* LXXX (1966), 257-264.

80.
Louis Ligier, S.J., "Pénitence et Eucharistie en Orient: théologie sur une interférence de prières et de rites," *Orientalia Christiana Periodica,* XXIX (1963), 5-78; Ligier, "Dimension personelle et dimension communautaire de la pénitence en Orient," *La Maison-Dieu,* XC (1967), 155-187; Ligier, "Le sacrement de pénitence selon la tradition orientale," *Nouvelle Revue Théologique,* LXXXIX (1967), 940-967.

81.
Phillipe de Regis, S.J., "Confession and Spiritual Direction in the Oriental Church," in Carra de Vaux Saint-Cyr, O.P., and others, *The Sacrament of Penance* (Glen Rock, N.J.: Paulist Press, 1966), pp. 79-95. These articles originally appeared in *Lumière et Vie,* XIII, no. 70 (1964).

82.
Ligier, *La Maison-Dieu,* XC (1967), 182.

83.
Ibid., pp. 186-187; *Nouvelle Revue Théologique,* LXXXIX (1967), 967.

84.
Eduardus F. Regatillo, S.I., *Ius Sacramentarium,* 3rd ed. (Santander: Sal Terrae, 1960), pp. 370-373; Häring, pp. 91-110.

85.
For a complete English translation of the Instruction of the Sacred Penitentiary of March 25, 1944, see T. Lincoln Bouscaren, S.J., *Canon Law Digest,* III (Milwaukee: Bruce Publishing Co., 1954), 377-379.

86.
James E. Auth, "The Necessity of Integrity in the Sacrament of Penance," a dissertation for the degree of licentiate in Canon Law at The Catholic University of America, 1969, pp. 39-49.

87.
Peter, *Proceedings of the Catholic Theological Society of America,* XXII (1967), 185-200.

88.
Peter, p. 200.

89.
Canon 856. Note that here and elsewhere in this study the currently accepted canonical terminology is sometimes employed even though contemporary theology would prefer different formulations.

90.
Canon 807; Regatillo, pp. 85-86 and 199-200.

91.
Vogel, pp. 47-49.

92.
Vogel, pp. 45-46.

93.
Vogel, p. 48.

94.
DS 1647, 1661; Peter, pp. 195-196; J. M. R. Tillard, O.P., "Pénitence et eucharistie," *La Maison-Dieu,* XC (1967), 120-125.

95.
Regatillo, p. 200.

96.
Tillard, p. 130.

97.
Tillard, pp. 126-131.

98.
In addition to those mentioned in note 2, see A.-M. Roguet, O.P., "Les célébrations communautaires de la pénitence," *La Vie Spirituelle,* CXVI (1967), 188-202; Michel Caloni, "Apprendre a celebrer la pénitence," *La Maison-Dieu,* XC (1967), 223-235.

99.
For a summary and an evaluation of the recent literature on devotional confession, see John F. Dedek, "The Theology of Devotional Confession," *Proceedings of the Catholic Theological Society of America,* XXII (1967), 215-222.

100.
For a report on experimentation in Montreal, see "Good-bye to the Confessional?" *Herder Correspondence,* VI (1969), 200-205.

101.
Palmer, p. 126.

102.
Palmer, p. 152; specifically on the Council of Chalon, p. 156.

103.
M.-B. Carra de Vaux Saint-Cyr, O.P., "The Sacrament of Penance: An Historical Outline," *The Sacrament of Penance,* p. 41.

104.
Edouard Hamel, S.J., "La vertu d'épikie," *Sciences Ecclésiastiques,* XIII (1961), 35-56.

2

Natural Law and Contemporary Moral Theology

Pope Paul's encyclical *Humanae Vitae* explicitly employs a natural law methodology to arrive at its particular moral conclusions on the licit means of regulating births. The encyclical admits that the teaching on marriage is a "teaching founded on natural law, illuminated and enriched by divine revelation" (*H. V.* n. 4). The papal letter then reaffirms that "the teaching authority of the Church is competent to interpret even the natural moral law" (*H.V.* n. 4). Recently, Catholic moral theologians have been reappraising the notion of natural law.[1] The sharp response to the papal letter indicates there is a great divergence between the natural law methodology employed in the encyclical and the methodology suggested by recent studies in moral theology. The natural law approach employed in the encyclical raises two important questions for moral theology: the place of natural law in the total understanding of Christian ethics, the concept of natural law itself.

I. NATURAL LAW IN THE TOTAL CHRISTIAN PERSPECTIVE

The recent papal pronouncement realizes that natural law forms only a part of the total horizon of moral theology. The Apostles and their successors have been constituted "as guardians and authentic interpreters of all the moral law, not only, that is, of the law of the Gospel, but also of the natural law, which is also an expression of the will of God" (*H.V.* n. 4). The encyclical admits there is a source of ethical wisdom and knowledge for the Christian apart from the explicit revelation of the Scriptures, so that Christians and the Church do learn ethical wisdom from non-Christians and the world.

There have been many theologians especially in the more strict Protestant tradition who would tend to deny any source of ethical wisdom and knowledge which Christians share with all mankind.[2] Such theologians based their position on the uniqueness and self-sufficiency of the scriptural revelation, the doctrine of justification, and an emphasis on sin as corrupting whatever exists outside the unique revelation of Jesus Christ.[3] However, contemporary Protestant theologians generally maintain the existence of some ethical wisdom apart from the explicit revelation of God in the Scriptures and in Christ Jesus, even though they may avoid the term natural law.[4] Protestant theologians in the last few decades have employed such concepts as the orders of creation (Brunner), the divine mandates (Bonhoeffer), love and justice (Reinhold Niebuhr), love transforming justice (Ramsey), common ground morality (Bennett), and other similar approaches. This question is discussed in greater detail in Chapter Five.

The natural law theory as implied in the encyclical has the theological merit of recognizing a source of ethical wisdom for the Christian apart from the explicit revelation of God in Christ Jesus. This recognition remains a most important and lasting contribution of Catholic thought in the area of theological ethics. The difficult question for Christian theology centers on the relationship between the natural law and the distinctively Christian element in the understanding of the moral life of the Christian. The same basic question has been proposed in other terms. H. Richard Niebuhr describes five different models of the relationship between Christ and culture.[5] An older Catholic theology spoke about the relationship between nature and grace, between the natural and the supernatural. Niebuhr has described the typical Catholic solution to the question of Christ and culture in terms of "both-and"—both culture and Christ.[6] Such an approach corresponds with an unnuanced understanding of the relationship between nature and grace. The two are neither opposed nor identical; but they exist side by side. Grace adds something to nature without in any way destroying it. A simplistic view of the supernatural sees it as something added to the natural. But the natural retains its own finality and integrity as the substratum to which the supernatural is added.[7]

In such a perspective the natural tends to be seen as something absolute and sufficient in itself to which the supernatural is added. The natural law thus exists as a self-contained entity to which the law of the gospel or revelation is then added. *Humanae Vitae* seems to accept such a "both-and" understanding of the relationship between natural law and the gospel or revelation. "All the moral law" is explained as "not only, that is, of the law of the Gospel, but also of the natural law, which is also an expression of the will of God . . ." (*H.V.* n. 4). The papal letter calls for an anthropology based on "an integral vision of man and his vocation, not only of his earthly and natural, but also his supernatural and eternal, vocation" (*H.V.* n. 7). The "both-and" relationship appears again in paragraph 8 which refers to "the entire moral law, both natural and evangelical."

Not only the wording of the encyclical but the methodology presupposed in the argumentation employs a "both-and" understanding of the relationship of natural law and evangelical law. Msgr. Lambruschini, who explained the encyclical at a press conference, said that purposely no mention was made of scriptural arguments, but the entire reasoning was based on natural law.[8] Bernard Häring has criticized the encyclical because it does not even mention the admonition of St. Paul that husband and wife should "not refuse each other except by mutual consent, and then only for an agreed time, to leave yourselves free for prayer; then come together again in case Satan should take advantage of your weakness to tempt you" (1 Cor 7:5).[9] The Pastoral Constitution on the Church in the Modern World did take heed of Paul's admonition. "But where the intimacy of married life is broken off, it is not rare for its faithfulness to be imperiled and its quality of fruitfulness ruined" (n. 51). However, the primary criticism is not the fact that there is no reference to any particular scriptural text, but the underlying understanding that the natural law is something totally integral in itself to which the evangelical or supernatural law is added.

Christian ethics cannot absolutize the realm of the natural as something completely self-contained and unaffected by any relationships to the evangelical or supernatural. Christian theology derives its perspective from the Christian faith commitment. The Christian views reality in the light of the total horizon of the Christian faith commitment—creation, sin, incarnation, redemption, and parousia. Natural law itself is thus Christocentric.[10] The doctrine of creation forms the theological basis for natural law, and Christ as logos is the one in whom all things are created and through whom all things are to be returned to the Father. Natural law theory has taken seriously the implications of the incarnation through which God has joined himself to the human, the worldly, and the historical. However, nature and creation form only a part of the total Christian view. The reality of "the natural" must always be seen in the light of sin, redemption, and the parousia. Nature and creation are relativized by the transforming Christian themes of redemption and final resurrection destiny of all creation. The natural law theory is theologically based on the Christian truths of creation and incarnation, but these aspects are not independent and unrelated to the full horizon of the Christian view of reality. The Christian situates natural law in the context of the total history of salvation which transforms and criticizes what is only "the natural." Thus in the total Christian perspective there is a place for the "natural," but the natural remains provisional and relativized by the entire history of salvation.

The full Christian view of reality also takes account of the existence of sin and its effects on human existence. However, the natural law theory as illustrated in *Humanae Vitae* does not seem to give sufficient importance to the reality and effect of human sinfulness. In section III under "Pastoral Directives" the papal letter speaks about the compassion of Christ and the Church for sinners. "But she [the Church] cannot renounce the teaching of the law which is, in reality, that law proper to a human life restored to its original truth and conducted by the Spirit of God" (*H.V.* n. 19). The implication remains that the disruptive force of sin has already been overcome by the grace of God. Such an approach has definite affinities with a simplistic view of sin as depriving man of the supernatural gift of grace, but not affecting the substratum of nature. However, in the total Christian horizon the disrupting influence of sin colors all human reality.

Humanae Vitae does recognize some effects of sin in man. Sin affects the will of man, but the help of God will strengthen the good will of man (*H.V.* n. 20). Sin affects the instincts of man, but ascetical practices will enable the reason and will of man to achieve self-mastery (*H.V.* n. 21). Sinfulness also makes itself felt in some aspects of the social environment, "which leads to sense excitation and unbridled customs, as well as every form of pornography and licentious performances" (*H.V.* n. 22). But no mention is made of the fact that sin affects reason itself and the very nature on which natural law theory is based. Sin relativizes and affects all reality. How often has reason been used to justify human prejudice and arrogance! Natural law has been appealed to in the denials of human dignity and of religious liberty. The just war theory has been employed to justify wars in which one's own nation was involved.[11] History shows the effect of sin in the very abuses which have accompanied natural law thinking.

Recently, I have proposed the need for a theory of compromise in moral theology precisely because of the existence of sin in the world.[12] The surd brought about by human sinfulness is so oppressive that occasionally man cannot overcome it immediately. The presence of sin may force a person to do something he would not do if there were no sin present. Thus in sin-filled situations (notice all the examples of such situations in the current literature) the Christian may be forced to adopt a line of action which he would abhor if sin were not present. A theory of compromise does not give man a blank check to shirk his Christian responsibilities. However, there are situations in which the value sacrificed is not proportionate to the demand asked of the Christian. Protestant theology has often adopted a similar approach by saying that in some circumstances the Christian is forced to do something sinful. The sinner reluctantly performs the deed and asks God for mercy and forgiveness.[13] At times Protestant theology has overemphasized the reality of sin, but Catholic theology at times has not paid enough attention to the reality of sin.

The recent papal encyclical presupposes a natural law concept that fails to indicate the relative and provisional character of natural law in the total Christian perspective. Critics have rightly objected to a theory which tends to absolutize what is only relative and provisional. Take, for example, the teaching in Catholic theology on the right of private property. The modern popes have approached the question of private property in a much more absolute way than Thomas Aquinas. The differences of approach are instructive for the moral theologian. The popes, especially Leo XIII, stressed private property as the right of every man stemming from the dignity of the human person, his rational nature, his labor, his need to provide for himself and his family, and his need to overcome the uncertainties of life.[14] Thomas gave greater importance to the social function of all property and the reality of human sinfulness. Perhaps Thomas was influenced by the often-cited opinion of Isidore of Seville that according to the natural law all things should be held in common.[15] Thomas ultimately sees the sin of man as the reason for the existence of private property. Society would not have peace and order unless everyone possessed his own goods. Likewise, Thomas pointed out that earthly goods are not properly cared for if they are held in common.[16] Thomas maintained there would be no need for private property in the world of original justice.

There are other indications that private property is not as absolute a right of man as proposed in some papal encyclicals. With his understanding of a more absolute right of private property, Leo XIII spoke of the obligation of the rich to share their goods with the poor as an obligation of charity and not justice.[17] However, a very respectable and long tradition in the medieval Church maintained that the rich had an obligation in justice to share their goods with the poor.[18] Even in our own day one can ask if private property is the best way to protect the dignity and freedom of the human person. The great inequalities existing in society today at the very least must modify and limit the concept of the right of private property. In our historical circumstances man is much more conscious of the social aspect of property than was Leo XIII.[19] The teaching on private property well illustrates the dangers of a natural law approach that is not relativized by the whole reality of salvation history.

The natural law theory suggested in, and employed by, the encyclical *Humanae Vitae* has the advantage of affirming the existence of a source of ethical wisdom apart from the explicit revelation of God in Christ in the Scriptures. However, such a concept of natural law tends to absolutize what the full Christian vision sees as relative and provisional in the light of the entire history of salvation.

II. A CRITIQUE OF NATURAL LAW

The debate over the condemnation of artificial contraception in *Humanae Vitae* indicates a basic dissatisfaction with the natural law methodology employed in the encyclical. The encyclical uses a notion of natural law which has generally been found in the classical textbooks and manuals of moral theology, but precisely this concept of natural law is subject to severe negative criticism. This section will point out three major weaknesses in that concept of natural law: (1) a tendency to accept natural law as a monolithic philosophical system with an agreed upon body of ethical content which is the source for most, if not all, of Catholic moral teaching; (2) the danger of physicism which identifies the human act with the physical or biological structure of the act; (3) a classicist worldview and methodology.

NOT A MONOLITHIC PHILOSOPHICAL SYSTEM

The first defect will only be summarized here, since it is treated at greater length elsewhere. Natural law remains a very ambiguous term.[20] The first section of this study used the concept of natural as distinguished from supernatural; in addition, it has been pointed out that the word nature had over twenty different meanings in Catholic thinking before Thomas Aquinas. The word law is also ambiguous, since it tends to have a very legalistic meaning for most people today; whereas for Thomas law was an ordering of reason. Natural law ethics has often been described as a legalistic ethic, that is, an ethic based on norms and laws; but in reality for Thomas natural law is a deliberative ethic which arrives at decision not primarily by the application of laws, but by the deliberation of reason. Many thinkers in the course of history have employed the term natural law, but frequently they defined natural law in different ways. Thinkers employing different natural law approaches have arrived at different conclusions on particular moral topics. Natural law in the history of thought does not refer to a monolithic theory, but tends to be a more generic term which includes a number of different approaches to moral problems. There is no such thing as *the* natural law as a monolithic philosophical system with an agreed upon body of ethical content existing from the beginning of time.

Many erroneously believe that Catholic theology is committed to a particular natural law approach to moral problems. In practice, however, the vast majority of Catholic teaching on particular moral questions came into existence even before Thomas Aquinas enunciated his theory. Likewise, contemporary Catholic theology recognizes the need for a pluralism of philosophical approaches in the Christian's quest for a better understanding of man and his reality. There is no longer "one Catholic philosophy."

THE DANGER OF PHYSICISM

Ethical theory constantly vacillates between two polarities —naturalism and idealism. Naturalism sees man in perfect continuity with the nature about him. Nature shapes and even determines man. Idealism views man completely apart from nature and sees man as completely surpassing nature. Even Thomistic philosophy, the main Catholic proponent of natural law theory, knows an ambivalence between nature and reason.

The Thomistic natural law concept vacillates at times between the order of nature and the order of reason.[21] The general Thomistic thrust is towards the predominance of reason in natural law theory. However, there is in Thomas a definite tendency to identify the demands of natural law with physical and biological processes. Thomas, too, is a historical person conditioned by the circumstances and influences of his own time. These influences help explain the tendency (but not the predominant tendency) in Thomas to identify the human action with the physical and biological structure of the human act. A major influence is Ulpian, a Roman lawyer who died in 228.

Ulpian and Thomas. Ulpian defined the natural law as that which nature teaches all the animals. Ulpian distinguished the natural law from the *ius gentium*. The *ius naturale* is that which is common to all animals, whereas the *ius gentium* is that which is proper to men.[22] Albert the Great rejected Ulpian's definition of the natural law, but Thomas accepted it, and even showed a preference for such a definition.[23] In the *Commentary on the Sentences*, for example, Thomas maintains that the most strict definition of natural law is the one proposed by Ulpian: *ius naturae est quod natura omnia animalia docuit.*[24]

In his *Commentary on the Nichomachean Ethics*, Thomas again shows a preference for Ulpian's definition. Aristotle had proposed a twofold division of *iustum naturale* and *iustum legale*, but Ulpian proposed the threefold distinction of *ius naturale, ius gentium* and *ius civile.* Thomas solves the apparent dilemma by saying that the Roman law concepts of *ius naturale* and *ius gentium* both belong under the Aristotelian category of *iustum naturale.* Man has a double nature. The *ius naturale* rules that which is proper to both man and the animals, such as the union of the sexes and the education of offspring; whereas the *ius gentium* governs the rational part of man which is proper to man alone and embraces such things as fidelity to contracts.[25]

In the *Summa Theologiae* Thomas cites Ulpian's definition on a number of occasions.[26] In the classification of natural law again Thomas shows a preference for Ulpian's definition. Thomas accepts the division proposed by Isidore of Seville, according to which the *ius gentium* belongs to the category of human law and not to the category of divine law. Thomas uses Ulpian's definition to explain Isidore's division. The natural law pertains to the divine law because it is common to man and to all the animals.[27] In a sense, the *ius gentium* does pertain to the category of human law because man uses his reason to deduce the conclusions of the *ius gentium.*

Thomas thus employs Ulpian's definition of natural law as opposed to what reason deduces (the *ius gentium*) to defend the division of law proposed by Isidore. The same question receives somewhat the same treatment later in the *Summa.*[28] The texts definitely show that Thomas knew and even accepted the definition of natural law proposed by Ulpian.

Ulpian's Concept of Natural Law. Ulpian is important for the understanding of natural law morality. The natural law for Ulpian is defined in terms of those actions which are common to man and all the animals. There results from this the definite danger of identifying the human action with a mere animal or biological process. "Nature" and "natural" in Ulpian's meaning are distinguished from that which is specifically human and derived by reason. Traditional theology has in the past definitely employed the words "natural" and "nature" as synonymous with animal or biological processes and not as denoting human actions in accord with the rational nature of man.

Moral theology textbooks even speak of sins according to nature. The manuals generally divide the sins against the sixth commandment into two categories—the sins against nature (*peccata contra naturam*) and sins in accord with nature (*peccata secundum naturam*). "Nature" is thus used in Ulpian's sense, as that which is common to man and all the animals. In matters of sexuality (and Ulpian himself uses the example of the sexual union as an illustration of the natural law), man shares with the animal world the fact of the sexual union whereby male seed is deposited in the vas of the female. Sins against nature, therefore, are those acts in which the animal or biological process is not observed—pollution, sodomy, bestiality, and contraception. Sins according to nature are those acts in which the proper biological process is observed but something is lacking in the sphere which belongs only to rational men. These include fornication, adultery, incest, rape, and sacrilege.[29]

The classification of sins against chastity furnishes concrete proof that "nature" has been used in Catholic theology to refer to animal processes without any intervention of human reason. Many theologians have rightly criticized the approach to marriage sexuality used by Catholic natural law theoreticians because such an approach concentrated primarily on the biological components of the act of intercourse. The personal aspects of the sexual union received comparatively scant attention in many of the manuals of moral theology. Ulpian's influence has made it easier for Catholic natural law thinking to identify the human act simply with the physical structure of the act.

Ulpian's Anthropology. Ulpian's understanding of the natural law logically leads to disastrous consequences in the anthropological understanding of man. The distinction between two parts in man—that which is common to man and all the animals, and that which is proper to man—results in a two-layer version of man. A top layer of rationality is merely added to an already constituted bottom layer of animality. The union between the two layers is merely extrinsic—the one lies on top of the other. The animal layer retains its own finalities and tendencies, independent of the demands of rationality. Thus man may not interfere in the animal processes and finalities. Note that the results of such an anthropology are most evident in the area of sexuality.

A proper understanding of man should start with that which is proper to man. Rationality does not just lie on top of animality, but rationality characterizes and guides the whole person. Animal processes and finalities are not untouchable. Man's whole vocation, we have come to see, is to bring order and intelligence into the world, and to shape animal and biological finalities toward a truly human purpose. Ulpian's concept of natural law logically falsifies the understanding of man and tends to canonize the finalities and processes which man shares with the animal world.

A better anthropology would see the distinctive in man as guiding and directing the totality of his being. For Thomas rationality constituted what is distinctive and characteristic in man. Modern philosophers differ from Thomas on what is distinctively human. Phenomenologists tend to view man as a symbolic person; while personalists look upon man as an incarnate spirit, a "thou" in relation to other "you's." However, all would agree in rejecting a notion of man that sees animality existing in man and that retains animal finalities and tendencies without any intervention of the specifically human part of man.

I am not asserting that Thomas always identified human actions with animal processes or the physical structure of the act. In fact, the general outlines of the hylomorphic theory, by speaking of material and formal components of reality, try to avoid any physicism or biologism. Nevertheless, the adoption of Ulpian's understanding of "nature" and "natural" logically leads to the identification of the human act itself with animal processes and with the mere physical structure of the act. Such a distorted view of the human act becomes especially prevalent in the area of medical morals, for in medical morality one can more easily conceive a moral human action solely in terms of the physical structure of that action.

Likewise, Ulpian's notion of nature easily leads to a morality based on the finality of a faculty independent of any considerations of the total human person or the total human community. One must, of course, avoid the opposite danger of paying no attention to the physical structure of the act or to external actions in themselves. However, Catholic theology in its natural law approach has suffered from an oversimple identification of the human action with an animal process or finality.

Marriage and Sexuality. Ulpian's understanding of natural law logically has had another deleterious effect on Catholic moral theology. Until the last decade magisterial pronouncements frequently spoke of the primary and secondary ends of marriage.[30] The latest statements of Pope Paul, and the Pastoral Constitution on the Church in the Modern World (*Gaudium et Spes*), happily avoid this terminology.[31] However, such a distinction has obviously influenced Catholic teaching on marriage and sexuality. Many people have questioned the distinction as being contradicted by the experience of married couples.

The distinction logically follows from Ulpian's concept of the natural law and man, although I do not claim that Ulpian is the source of such a distinction. "Primary" is that which is common to man and all the animals. Ulpian, and Thomas in citing Ulpian, use the union of the sexes and the procreation and education of offspring as examples of that which is common to man and all the animals. "Secondary" is that which is proper to man. Since only men and not animals have sexual intercourse as a sign and expression of love, the love union aspect of sexuality remains proper to man and therefore secondary. The former teaching on the ends of marriage is logically connected with Ulpian's understanding of man and natural law. Thus the teaching of Ulpian on natural law has a logical connection with the inadequate understanding of a human action as identified with an animal process.

A More Primitive Attitude. Another historical factor based on the conditions of a primitive culture has also influenced the tendency to make the processes of nature inviolable. Stoic philosophy well illustrates a more general historical factor that tends to identify the human action with its physical or natural structure. One should avoid too many generalizations about the Stoics because Stoic philosophy included a number of different thinkers who covered a comparatively long span of years. In addition, Stoic philosophers invoked the natural law to justify practices that contemporary natural law theoreticians brand as immoral.[32] However, there is a common thrust to the ethical doctrine proposed by the Stoics.

Nature: Norm or Servant. Ethics considers man and his actions. Man wants to find happiness. What actions should man perform to find his happiness and fulfillment? A more primitive and less technical society will come to conclusions different from those reached by a more technically and scientifically developed society. Primitive man soon realizes that he finds his happiness in conforming himself to the patterns of nature.

Primitive man remains almost helpless when confronted with the forces of nature. The forces of nature are so strong that man is even tempted to bow down and adore. He realizes the futility in trying to fight them. His happiness will come only by adjusting himself.

Nature divides the day into light and dark. When darkness descends, there is little or nothing that man can do except sleep. When the hot sun is beating down near the equator, he will find happiness only by avoiding work and overexposure in the sun. In colder climates, man will be happy only when he uses clothing and shelter to protect himself from nature. If he wants to be happy, he will stay under some form of shelter and avoid the rain and snow. If there is a mountain in his path, the wise man will walk around the mountain rather than suffer the ardors of trying to scale the peak. For man living in a primitive society (in the sense of non-scientific and non-technical), happiness is found in conforming himself to nature.

Stoic philosophy built on this understanding of man living in a non-technical society. As Greeks, the Stoics believed in an intelligible world. They made the universe as a whole—the cosmos—their principle of intelligibility. Stoic philosophy held that reason governed the order of nature. Man's happiness consisted in conforming himself to reason, that is, in conforming himself to the order of nature. Reason rather easily became identified with the order of nature. The primary norm of morality, therefore, was conformity to nature.[33]

We who live in a scientific and technological society will have a different view of man and his happiness. Modern man does not find his happiness in conforming to nature. The whole ethos and genius of modern society is different. Contemporary man makes nature conform to him rather than vice-versa. Through electricity man can change night into day. There are very few things that modern man cannot do at night now that it is illuminated by electricity.

Contemporary man uses artificial heat in the winter and air conditioning in the summer to bring nature into conformity with his needs and desires. Nature did not provide man with wings to fly; in fact, the law of gravity seems to forbid man to fly. However, science has produced the jet plane and the rocket, which propel man at great speeds around the globe and even into the vast universe. When a mountain looms up as an obstacle, modern man either levels the mountain with bulldozers or tunnels under the terrain. Modern man could never tolerate a theory which equates human happiness with conformity to nature. Contemporary man interferes with the processes of nature to make nature conform to man.

These few paragraphs have not attempted to prove the influence of Stoic philosophy on St. Thomas. Rather, Stoic philosophy was used to illustrate how the conditions existing in a nontechnological society will influence the philosophical understanding of man and ethics. Thomas too lived in an agrarian, nonscientific world. The nontechnological worldview would be more prone to identify the human act with the physical process of nature itself.

Reality or Facticity. A more primitive society also tends to view reality in terms of the physical and the sensible. The child, unlike the adult, sees reality primarily in terms of externals. The tendency to identify the human action with the physical structure would definitely be greater in a more primitive society. For example, the importance that Catholic theology has attached to masturbatory activity, especially the overemphasis since the sixteenth century, seems to come from viewing it purely in terms of the physiological and biological aspects of the act. Modern psychology, however, does not place very great importance on such activity.

Theologians must incorporate the findings of modern science in trying to evaluate the human act of masturbation. To view it solely in terms of the physical structure of the act distorts the total reality of this human action. Contemporary theologians cannot merely repeat what older theologians have said. Today we know much more about the reality of the human act of masturbation than, say, St. Alphonsus or any other moral theologian living before the present century.[34]

It would be erroneous to say that Catholic theology has identified the human act with the brute facticity of natural processes or just the physical structure of the act itself. In the vast majority of cases, moral theology has always distinguished between the physical structure of the action and the morality of the action. The moral act of murder differs from the physical act of killing. The physical act of taking another's property does not always involve the moral act of stealing. However, in some areas of morality (for example, contraception, sterilization, direct effect) the moral act has been considered the same as the physical structure of the act itself.

The Morality of Lying. Another area in which Catholic theologians are moving away from a description of the human act in purely physical or natural terms is lying. The contemporary theological understanding of lying serves as a salutary warning to the natural law concept found in the manuals of theology because the morality of lying cannot be determined merely by examining the faculty of speech and its finality, apart from the totality of the human person speaking and the community in which he speaks.

The manuals of moral theology traditionally define lying as *locutio contra mentem.* The faculty of speech exists to express what is in the mind. When human speech does not reflect what is in the mind there is a perversion of the faculty. The perverted faculty argument is based on the finality of the faculty of speech looked at in itself. Accordingly, a lie exists when the verbal utterance does not correspond with what is in the mind. Theologians then had to face the problem created by the fact that at times the speaker simply could not speak the truth to his hearer or questioner (for example, in the case of a committed secret). A casuistry of mental reservations arose to deal with such situations.[35]

Today most contemporary Catholic theologians accept the distinction between a lie and a falsehood. A falsehood involves an untruth in the sense that the external word contradicts what is in the mind. However, the malice of lying does not consist in the perversion of the faculty of speech or the lack of conformity between the word spoken and what is in the mind. The malice of lying consists in the harm done to society and the human community through the breakdown of mutual trust and honesty. Thus, some theologians distinguish between a lie as the denial of truth which is due to the other and falsehood which is a spoken word not in conformity with what is in the mind.

The distinction between lying and falsehood obviates the rather contrived casuistry associated with broad and strict mental reservations.[36] But what does the more contemporary understanding of lying indicate? The new definition denies the validity of the perverted faculty argument. It is not sufficient merely to examine the faculty of speech and determine morality solely from the purpose of the faculty in itself. Likewise, the malice of lying does not reside in the lack of "physical" conformity between word and thought.

To view the faculty of speech apart from the total human situation of man in society seems to give a distorted view of lying. The faculty of speech must be seen and judged in a human context. Man can interfere with the physical purpose of the faculty for a higher human need and good. Perhaps in a similar vein, the notion of "direct" in the principle of the double effect cannot be judged merely from the sole immediate effect of the physical action itself, apart from the whole human context in which the act is placed. The morality must be viewed in a total human context, and not merely judged according to the physical act itself and the natural effect of the act seen in itself apart from the whole context.

The influence of Ulpian and the view of primitive man tend to identify the total human action with the natural or biological process. A better understanding of such historically and culturally limited views of man should help the ethician in evaluating the theory of natural law as understood in *Humanae Vitae*. I have not proved that the human act never corresponds with the physical structure of the act. However, I think it is clear that an ethician must be very cautious that older and inadequate views of men and reality do not influence his contemporary moral judgments. It does seem that the definition of Ulpian and the general views of a more primitive society have a logical connection with what seem to be erroneous conclusions of the natural law theory of the manuals.

A CHANGED WORLDVIEW

A third major weakness with the theory of natural law presupposed in the Encyclical stems from the classicist worldview which is behind such a theory of natural law. Bernard Lonergan maintains that the classicist worldview has been replaced by a more historically conscious worldview.[37] In the same vein, John Courtney Murray claimed that the two different theories on Church and State represent two different methodologies and worldviews.[38] And today, other more radical Catholic thinkers are calling for a change from a substantive to a process metaphysics.[39] At the least, all these indications point to an admission by respected Catholic scholars that the so-called classical worldview has ceased to exist.

The following paragraphs will briefly sketch the differences in the two approaches to viewing reality. There are many dangers inherent in doing this. There is really no such thing as *the* classical worldview or *the* historically conscious worldview—there are many different types of historical mindedness. By arguing in favor of an historically conscious worldview, I by no means intend to endorse all the theories and opinions that might be included under such a heading.

Since this section of the chapter will argue against a classical worldview, a reader might conclude that I am denying to past thinkers the possibility of any valid insights into the meaning of man and reality. Such a conclusion is far from true. There are even those (for example, Lonergan and Murray) who would argue that a moderate historically conscious methodology is in continuity with the best of Thomistic thought. We must never forget that some of the inadequacies in the classical worldview stem from the poor interpretation of St. Thomas by many of his so-called followers.

Two Views of Reality. The classicist worldview emphasizes the static, the immutable, the eternal, and the unchanging. The Greek column symbolizes this very well. There is no movement or dynamism about a Doric or Ionic column; the simple Greek column avoids all frills and baroque trimmings. The stately Greek column gives the impression of solidity, eternity, and immutability. Its majestic and sober lines emphasize an order and harmony which appear to last forever. This classical worldview speaks in terms of substances and essences. Time and history are "accidents" which do not really change the constitution of reality itself. Essences remain unchangeable and can only go through accidental changes in the course of time. Growth, dynamism, and progress therefore receive little attention.

The Platonic world of ideas well illustrates this classical worldview. Everything is essentially spelled out from all eternity, for the immutable essences, the universals, exist in the world of ideas. Everything in this world of ours is a participation or an accidental modification of the subsistent ideas. Man comes to know truth and reality by abstracting from the accidents of time and place, and arriving at immutable and unchangeable essences. Such knowledge based on immutable essences is bound to attain the ultimate in certitude.

The more historically conscious worldview emphasizes the changing, developing, evolving, and historical. Time and history are more than mere accidents that do not really change essential reality. Individual and particular differences receive much more attention from a correspondingly more historically conscious methodology. The classical worldview is interested in the essence of man, which is true at all times in history and in all civilizations and circumstances. A historically minded worldview emphasizes the individual traits that characterize him. Modern man does differ quite a bit from primitive man precisely because of the historical and individual traits that he has.

In the more historical worldview the world is not static but evolving. Progress, growth, and change mark the world and all reality. Cold, chaste, objective order and harmony are not characteristic of this view. Blurring, motion, and subjective feeling are its corresponding features, as in the difference between modern art and classical art. Modern art emphasizes feeling and motion rather than harmony and balance. It is not as "objective" as classical art. The artist imposes himself and his emotions on the object.

Perhaps modern art is telling the theologian that the older distinction between the objective and the subjective is no longer completely adequate. Music also illustrates the change that has occurred in our understanding of the world and reality. Classical measure and rhythm is gone; free rhythm and feeling mean very much to the modern ear. What is meaningful music to the ear of the modern is only cacophony for the classicist. Changes in art and music illustrate the meaning of the different worldviews and also show graphically that the classical worldview is gone.

Two Methodologies. The two worldviews created two different theological methodologies. The classicist methodology tends to be abstract, *a priori,* and deductive. It wants to cut through the concrete circumstances to arrive at the abstract essence which is always true, and then works with these abstract and universal essences. In the area of moral theology, for example, the first principles of morality are established, and then other universal norms of conduct are deduced from these.

The more historical methodology tends to be concrete, *a posteriori,* and inductive. The historical approach does not brush by the accidental circumstances to arrive at the immutable essences. The concrete, the particular, and the individual are important for telling us something about reality itself. Principles are not deduced from other principles. Rather, modern man observes and experiences and then tentatively proceeds to his conclusions in a more inductive manner. Note that the historical consciousness as a methodology is an abstraction, but an abstraction or theory that tries to give more importance to particular, concrete, historical reality.

As we have noted above, John Courtney Murray claims that the different views on Church and State flow from the two different methodologies employed.[40] The older theory of the union of Church and State flows from a classicist methodology. It begins with the notion of a society. The definition of a society comes from an abstract and somewhat *a priori* notion of what such a society should be. The older theory then maintains that there are two perfect societies, and deduces their mutual duties and responsibilities, including their duties and obligations vis-à-vis one another. The theory concludes that the *cura religionis,* as it was then understood, belongs to the State. The State has the obligation of promoting the true faith.

What happens when the older theory runs headlong into a *de facto* situation in which the separation of Church and State is a historical fact? The older solution lies in a distinction between thesis and hypothesis, which roughly corresponds to the ideal order which should exist and the actual order which can be tolerated because of the presence of certain accidental historical circumstances. Notice the abstract and a-historical characteristics of such a theory.

The newer theory of Church and State as proposed by Murray employs a more historically conscious methodology. Murray does not begin with an abstract definition of society and then deduce the obligations and rights of Church and State. Rather, Murray begins from a notion of the State derived from his observations of them in contemporary society. The modern State is a limited, constitutional form of government.

Its limited role contrasts with the more absolute and all-embracing role of the State in an earlier society. It does not interfere in matters that belong to the private life of individuals, such as the worship of God. Murray's theory has no need for a distinction between thesis and hypothesis, since he begins with the concrete historical reality. His conclusions then will be in harmony with the present historical situation.[41] Using a historical methodology, he can even admit that in the nineteenth century the older opinion might have been true, but in the present historical circumstances separation of Church and State is required.[42]

A classicist mentality is horrified at the thought that something could be right in one century and wrong in another. Note, however, that the historical methodology employed by Murray and Lonergan insists on a continuity in history and rejects any atomistic existentialism which sees only the uniqueness of the present situation without any connection with what has gone before or with what will follow in history.

A New Catholic Perspective. Theologians and philosophers are not alone in speaking of the changed perspective. In the documents of Vatican II the bishops do not officially adopt any worldview or methodology. But Vatican II definitely portrays reality in terms of a more historical worldview, and also employs a historically conscious methodology. The fact that the council has chosen to call itself a "pastoral" council is most significant; but "pastoral" must not be understood in opposition to "doctrinal." Rather, pastoral indicates a concern for the Christian faith not as truths to be learned but as a life to be lived.

The pastoral orientation of the council reflects a historical worldview. The bishops at the council also acknowledged that the Church has profited by the history and development of humanity. History reveals more about man, and opens new roads to truth. The Catholic Church must constantly engage in an exchange with the contemporary world.[43]

Gaudium et Spes frequently speaks of the need to know the signs of the times. The introductory statement of this constitution asserts the need for the Church to know them and interpret them in the light of the Gospel (n.4). The five chapters of the second section of the constitution begin with an attempt to read the signs of the times. The attention given to what was often in the past dismissed as accidental differences of time and history shows a more historical approach to reality. The constitution does not begin with abstract and universal ideas of Church, society, state, community, and common good, but rather by scrutinizing the signs of the times. *Gaudium et Spes* thus serves as an excellent illustration of the change in emphasis in Church documents from a classicist methodology to a more historically conscious approach.

The teachings on the Church as contained in the Constitution on the Church (*Lumen Gentium*) and the other documents of Vatican II also reflect a more historical approach and understanding. Previously Catholics pictured the Church as a perfect society having all the answers, and as the one bulwark of security in a changing world. However, *Lumen Gentium* speaks often and eloquently of the pilgrim Church. The charge of triumphalism rang true in the conciliar halls of Vatican II. A pilgrim Church, however, does not pretend to have all the answers.

A pilgrim Church is ever on the march towards its goal of perfect union with Christ the spouse. A pilgrim Church is constantly striving, probing, falling, rising, and trying again. A pilgrim is one who is constantly on the road and does not know there the security of his own home. So too the pilgrim Church is a church always in need of reform (*ecclesia semper reformanda*). Change, development, growth, struggle and tension mark the Church of Christ in this world. The notion of the pilgrim Church, even in language, differs very much from the perfect society of the theological manuals.

The conciliar documents underscore the need for the Catholic Church to engage in dialogue—dialogue with other Christians, dialogue with Jews, dialogue with other non-Christians, dialogue with the world. Dialogue is not monologue. Dialogue presupposes that Catholics can learn from all these others. The call for dialogue supposes the historical and pilgrim nature of the Church, which does not possess all the answers but is open in the search for truth. The need for ongoing dialogue and ongoing search for truth contrasts sharply with the classicist view of reality and truth.

Lumen Gentium rebuilds ecclesiology on the notion of the Church as the people of God and points out the various functions and services which exist in the Church (Chapter 2). Hierarchy is one form of service which exists in it. Another office is prophecy. The prophetic function exists independently of the hierarchy (n.12). The hierarchical Church can learn, and has learned, from the prophetic voice in the Church. History reminds us that in the Church change usually occurs from underneath. Vatican Council II brought to fruition the work of the prophets in the biblical, liturgical, catechetical and ecumenical movements.

Thank God for Pope John and the bishops at Vatican II, we can say, but there never would have been a Vatican II if it were not for the prophets who went before. Many of them were rejected when they first proposed their teaching, but such has always been the lot of the prophet. The pilgrim Church, with the prophetic office, will always know the tension of trying to do the truth in love. The Church sorely needs to develop an older notion of the discernment of the Spirit, so that the individual himself and the total Church will be more open and ready to hear its true voice while rejecting the utterances of false prophets.[44]

The Church portrayed in Vatican II is a pilgrim Church which does not have all the answers but is constantly striving to grow in wisdom and age and grace. Thus the conciliar documents reflect a more historical view of the Church, and even employ a historically conscious methodology.

Theological Consequences

A historical worldview and a more historically conscious methodology will have important consequences when applied to the field of moral theology, for the manuals of moral theology today definitely reflect the classicist approach. In fact, there is a crisis in moral theology today precisely because such theology seems out of touch with modern man's understanding of reality. Of course I do not claim that everything modern man says about reality is correct, but then not everything in the classicist worldview was correct.

Sin infects the reality we know, and the Christian thinker can never simply accept as is whatever happens to be in vogue. However, the God of creation and redemption has called us to carry on his mission in time and space. The Christian, then, is always called upon to view all things in the light of the gospel message, but whatever insights we may gain into reality and the world of creation can help us in our life.

Change and Development. The first important consequence of this new worldview and methodology affects our attitude towards change and development. The classical worldview, as we have seen, had little room for change. Only accidental changes could occur in a reality that was already constituted and known in its essence. Naturally such a view rejected any form of evolutionary theory because it was most difficult to explain evolution in such a system. On the other hand, the new worldview emphasizes the need for change. Change and growth do not affect merely the accidental constitution and knowledge of reality.

Man thirsts for truth and is constantly trying to find it. He is never satisfied with the knowledge he has at any given moment. Modern man realizes how incomplete this is, and he is continually probing to find out more about reality. The growth and progress of modern society demonstrate that development is absolutely necessary. The classicist methodology, on the other hand, claims a comparatively absolute and complete knowledge. Change naturally becomes a threat to the person who thinks that he already possesses truth. Of course, modern man recognizes that not all change is good and salutary. There will be mistakes on the way, but the greatest error would be not to try at all.

Let us take as an example the dogmatic truth about the nature of Christ. The early christological councils proposed the formula of one person and two natures in Christ, a formula that is not present in the Scriptures. At the time there was an agonizing decision to go beyond the language of the Scriptures. But why does change have to stop in the fifth century? Might there not be an even better understanding of the natures and person of Christ today? Modern man might have different—and better—insights into the reality of Christ. Who can say that the fifth century was the final point in the development of our understanding?

When the classical worldview does speak of development, it places much emphasis on the fact that the truth always remains the same but it is expressed in different ways at different times. The same essential truth wears different clothing in different settings. However, does not the truth itself change and develop? There is more involved than just a different way of stating the same essential reality. Even in such sacrosanct dogmatic teachings there is room for real change and development.

The historical worldview realizes the constant need for growth and development, and also accepts the fact that mistakes and errors will always accompany such growth. But the attitude existing towards theology on the part of many priests in this country epitomizes the older worldview. (Perhaps such a mentality on the part of priests has been an obstacle in the path of Church renewal.) As seminarians, they learned all the truths of the Christian faith. There was no need, in this view, to continue study after ordination, since the priest already possessed a certain knowledge of all the truths of the Christian faith.

Such an attitude also characterized the way in which theology was taught. Very little outside reading was done. The student simply memorized the notes of the professor which contained this certain knowledge. But the new methodology will bring with it a greater appreciation of the need for change and development in all aspects of the life and teaching of the Church.

Theology and Induction. Theology must adopt a more inductive methodology. Note that I am not advocating a unilaterally inductive and *a posteriori* approach for theology. However, in the past theology has attached too much importance to a deductive and somewhat *a priori* methodology. (Of course, as we shall see, with a more inductive approach moral theology can never again claim the kind of certitude it once did. At best, in some areas of conduct the ethician will be able to say that something clearly appears to be such and such at the present time.)

The classical methodology was a closed system, whereas a more historically conscious methodology proposes an open and heuristic approach. It will always remain open to new data and experience. Nothing is ever completely solved and closed, for an inductive methodology is more tentative and probing.

An inductive approach recognizes the existence of mistakes and errors, and even incorporates the necessary mechanism to overcome them. The building and manufacture of the Edsel automobile illustrates the possibility of error in a more inductive approach. Obviously, elaborate and expensive tests were run beforehand to see if there was a market for a car in the class of the projected Edsel. The decision to market the car was made on the best possible evidence. However, experience proved that the Edsel was a failure. A few years later, after similar exhaustive testing, the same company produced the Mustang, which has been a great success.

Theology, of course, is not the same as the other sciences. Progress and growth are much more evident in the area of the empirical sciences. However, the historicity of the gospel message and the historicity of man and the world demand a more historical approach in theology and the integration of a more inductive methodology. A more inductive approach in theology, especially in moral theology, will have to depend more on the experience of Christian people and all men of good will. The morality of particular actions cannot be judged apart from human experience. History seems to show that the changes which have occurred in Catholic morality have come about through the experience of all the people of the community. The fact that older norms did not come to grips with reality was first noticed in the experience of people.

Changes have occurred in the areas of usury, religious liberty, the right to silence, the role of love as a motive for marital relations, and other areas.[45] Certainly the rigorism of the earlier theologians on the place of procreation in marriage and marital intercourse has been modified by the experience of Christian people—for example, they held that marriage relations without the express purpose of procreation was at least venially sinful. And when the older theory of Church and State did not fit in with the historical circumstances of our day, John Courtney Murray showed that the living experience of people in the United States was more than just a toleration of an imperfect reality. In each case, experience showed the inadequacy of the older theory.

The older casuistry of mental reservation never set well with the experience of Christian people. The dissatisfaction with such casuistry played an important part in the understanding of lying now accepted by most contemporary theologians. Of course, just as theological methodology can never become totally inductive (the theologian always begins with the revelation of God in Christ), so too experience can never become the only factor in the formation of the Christian ethic. However, experience has a very important role to play. Since the experience of Christian people and all men of good will is a source of moral knowledge, an ethician cannot simply spell out in advance everything that must be done by the individual. Contemporary theology should enlarge upon and develop the concept of prudence which was an important experiential factor in the thought of Aquinas.

The Empirical Approach. Since a more historical methodology emphasizes the individual and the particular and employs a more inductive approach to knowing reality, Catholic theology will have to work much closer with the empirical and social sciences. It is these sciences that help man to pursue his goal and guide his development. A classicist approach which emphasized universals and essences was content with an almost exclusively deductive approach.

The Catholic Church in America today still reflects the fact that an older worldview did not appreciate or understand the need for the empirical and social sciences. The Catholic Church is probably the only very large corporation in America—I am here using "church" in the sense of a sociological entity and its administration—which does not have a research and development arm. How long could other corporations stay in existence without devoting huge sums to research and development? Heretofore, the Catholic Church has not realized the importance of change and growth.

Perhaps the crisis the Church faces today stems from a clinging to older forms of life when newer forms are required. However, without research and experimentation, who can determine which new forms are needed? The answers are not all spelled out in the nature of things.

Certitude. As we have already seen, a changed theological methodology must necessarily result in a different attitude towards certitude. The classicist methodology aimed at absolute certitude. It was much easier come by in the classical approach, for this method cut through and disregarded individual, particular differences to arrive at immutable, abstract essences. In a deductive approach the conclusion follows by a logical connection from the premise. Provided the logic is correct, the conclusion is just as certain as the premise. Since circumstances cannot change the essences or universals, one can assert that the conclusion is now and always will be absolutely certain. There is no room for any change. A deductive methodology can be much more certain than an inductive approach.

The penchant for absolute certitude characterized the philosophical system which supports the concept of natural law as found in theology manuals. Science, in this view, was defined as certain knowledge of the thing in its causes. Science, therefore, was opposed to opinion and theory. However, modern science does not aim at such certitude. Science today sees no opposition between science and opinion; in fact, scientific opinion and scientific theory form an essential part of the scientific vocabulary.

Absolute certitude actually would be the great enemy of the progress and growth that characterize modern life. Once absolute certitude is reached, there is no sense in continuing research except to clear up a few peripheral matters.[46] In the Thomistic framework there was really no room for progress in scientific fields. And there was little or no room for development within the sciences, so conceived, because the first principles of the science itself were already known. The revolutionary approaches within the modern sciences show the fallacy in the Thomistic understanding of science.[47]

A more historically conscious methodology does not pretend to have or even to aim at absolute certitude. Since time, history, and individual differences are important, they cannot be dismissed as mere accidents which do not affect essential truth. This approach does not emphasize abstract essences, but concrete phenomena. Conclusions are based on the observations and experience gleaned in a more inductive approach. Such an approach can never strive for absolute certitude.

Modern science views reality in this more historical manner and consequently employs this more inductive approach. The progress of scientific and technical mankind demands a continuing search for an ever better way. Even the Volkswagen is constantly being improved, and may be quite different in ten years. An inductive methodology can never cease its working. It constantly runs new experiments and observations, for modern science aims at the best for the present time, but realizes that new progress must be made for the future.

Positive Law. A more historically conscious approach and a greater emphasis on the person attribute a much changed and reduced role to positive law. Canon law exists primarily to preserve order and harmony in the society of the people of God, and not to serve as a guide for the life of the individual Christian.[48] Nor are civil laws primarily a guide for man's moral conduct. Civil law as such is not primarily interested in the true, the good, and the beautiful. Civil law has the very limited aim of preserving the public order.[49]

Society functions better not when law dictates to everyone what is to be done, but rather when law tries to create the climate in which individuals and smaller groups within the society can exercise their creativity and development for the good of the total community.[50] No longer is society under a master plan minutely controlled by the rules of the society. Rather, modern society's progress and growth come from the initiative of people within the society. Thus, the more historically minded worldview has a different perspective on the meaning and role of law in human life. Natural and human laws are no longer seen as detailed plans which guide and direct all human activity.

The Nature of Reality. A classicist worldview tends to see reality in terms of substances and natures which exist in themselves apart from any relations with other substances and natures. Every substance has its own nature or principle of operation. Within every acorn, for example, there is a nature which directs the acorn into becoming an oak tree. The acorn will not become a maple tree or an elm tree because it has the nature of an oak tree. The growth and "activity" of the thing is determined by the nature inscribed in it. Growth is the intrinsic unfolding of the nature within the substance.

Notice how such a view of reality affects morality. Human action depends upon the human nature. Human action is its intrinsic unfolding in man. Nature, therefore, tells what actions are to be done and what actions are to be avoided. To determine the morality of an action, one must study its nature. The above description, although a caricature of Thomas' teaching, does represent the approach to morality of the kind of unilaterally substantialist view of reality generally assumed in the manuals.

The contemporary view sees reality more in terms of relations than of substances and natures. Man is not thought of as a being totally constituted in himself, whose life is the unfolding of the nature he already possesses. There seemingly can be no real human growth and history when future development is already determined by what is present here and now. This is the point of difference between a naturalist view and a historicist view.[51]

According to a more contemporary, relational view, reality does not consist of separate substances existing completely independent of each other. Reality can be understood only in terms of the relations that exist among the individual beings. A particular being can never be adequately considered in itself, apart from its relations with other beings and the fullness of being. An emphasis on relations rather than substances surely cannot be foreign to Catholic thinking, since theologians have spoken of the persons of the Trinity as relations.

Human experience also reminds us of the importance of relationship even in constituting ourselves as human persons. A relational understanding of reality will never see morality solely in terms of the individual substance or nature. Morality depends primarily not on the substance viewed in itself but on the individual seen in relationship to other beings. Unfortunately, the so-called traditional natural law approach frequently derives its conclusions from the nature of a faculty or the physical causality of an action seen only in itself and not in relationship with the total person and the entire community.

A brief defense of Aristotle is necessary here to avoid false impressions. Aristotle did not have a static view of reality. Nature itself was a principle of operation that tended toward a goal, but the goal was specific rather than individual. The emphasis was on the species of oak tree, that is, and not on the individual oak as such. But Aristotle did not conceive of man as he did of lesser life.

As an acute observer of the human scene, he realized that most men do not achieve their goal of happiness and self-fulfillment. Man, he thought, does not possess an intrinsic dynamism which necessarily achieves its goal. Man's happiness, consequently, depends not on an intrinsic tending to perfection according to the demands of his nature, but rather his happiness depends on extrinsic circumstances.

Man has no intrinsic orientation (a nature) necessarily bringing about his perfection; rather, according to Aristotle, he depends more on the contingent and the accidental. Man needs freedom, health, wealth, friends, and luck to find his fulfillment.[52] Notice that Aristotle himself constructed a theory of man that answers some of the strictures made against textbook natural law theories today.

The classicist worldview of the manuals tends to arrange the world in a very detailed pattern. The function of man is to correspond to this structure (the "natural law") as minutely outlined. Man puts together the different pieces of human behavior much like he puts together the pieces of a jigsaw puzzle. He finds the objective pieces already existing and just fits them together. The more historically minded worldview, on the other hand, sees man as creating and shaping the plan of the world. Man does not merely respect the intrinsic nature and finalities of the individual pieces of the pattern. Rather, man interferes to form new pieces and new patterns.

A different worldview, as we have seen, affects our understanding of reality. The older stressed the objectivity of reality. In this view truth consists in the mind's grasp of the reality itself. A clear distinction exists between the object and the subject. Meaning exists in the objective reality, and the subject perceives the meaning already present in reality. Modern thought and culture stress more the creative aspects (both intellectual and affective) of the subject. Modern art reveals the feelings and emotions of the subject rather than portraying an objective picture of reality. The modern cinema confronts the viewer with a very subjective view of reality that calls for imagination and perceptivity on the part of the viewer. Catholic theologians are now speaking in somewhat similar terms of a transcendental methodology in theology.

Karl Rahner has observed that natural law should be approached in this way.[53] A transcendental methodology talks about the conditions and structure in the subject necessary for it to come to know reality, for this very structure is part of the knowing process. Bernard Lonergan speaks about meaning in much the same way.[54] Man's meaning can change such basic realities as community, family, state, etc. Meaning involves more than just the apprehension of the objective reality as something "out there."

A note of caution is necessary. Although Lonergan, for example, espouses a more historical consciousness and a transcendental method, at the same time he strongly proclaims a critical realism in epistemology. Lonergan definitely holds for propositions and objective truth, and truth as a correspondence. However, for Lonergan human knowing is a dynamic structure; intentionality and meaning pertain to that objectivity. He reacts against a "naive realism" or a "picture book" type of objectivity.

The problem in the past was that the objectivity of knowledge was identified with the analogy of the objectivity of the sense of sight. "Objective" is that which I see out there. Such a concept of objectivity is false because it identifies objectivity with just one of the properties of one of the operations involved in human knowing. Lonergan rejects both a naive realism and idealism.[55] It seems, however, that the objectivity talked about in manuals of moral theology is often a naive, picture-book objectivity.

The concept of natural law presupposed in Catholic theology manuals definitely reflects a classicist worldview, which sees a very precise and well-defined pattern existing for the world and man's moral behavior. This ordering and pattern is called the natural law. Natural law reigns in the area of the necessary.

Within the area marked out by the pattern showing the absolute and the necessary is the contingent and the changing. Just as natural law governs the life of man in the area of the principles common to all men, so positive law, both civil and ecclesiastical, governs the life of man in the contingent and the changing circumstances of life. The plan for the world is thus worked out in great detail in the mind of the creator, and man's whole purpose is to conform himself to the divine plan as made known in the natural and positive laws. (Despite the classical worldview of his day, in his system Thomas did leave room for the virtue of prudence and the creativity of the individual. However, the place later assigned to prudence in textbooks was drastically reduced, and thus Thomas' teaching was distorted.)

But a more historically minded worldview does not look upon reality as a plan whose features are sketched in quite particular detail according to an unchanging pattern. Modern man's moral existence does not primarily call for conformity to such a detailed and unchanging plan. He looks upon existence as a vocation to find the meaning of human existence creatively in his own life and experience. The meaning of human life is not already given in some pre-existing pattern or plan.

A historically conscious methodology must avoid the pitfall of a total relativism which occasionally creeps into Christianity in various forms of cultural Christianity. Man needs to understand the ontological foundations of historical development; the Christian needs to understand all things in the light of the uniqueness of the once-for-all event of Christ

Jesus. Both contemporary Protestant (for example, Macquarrie, Ogden) and Catholic (Rahner, Lonergan) scholars are addressing themselves to this problem.

Perhaps the characterization of the two worldviews in this chapter tends to be oversimplified. For one thing, the points of difference between them have been delineated without any attempt to show the similarities. The differences in many areas of morality—for example, the understanding and living of the evangelical norm of love and forgiveness—would be minimal. The reasoning developed in this section has prescinded, as well, from the question of growth and development in human values and morals. However, in the modern world of science and technology, characterized by instant communication, rapid transportation, and changing sociological patterns, it is clear that man needs a more historical worldview and a more historically conscious methodology than the person who lived in a comparatively static and closed society.

III. "PHYSICISM" AND A CLASSICIST METHODOLOGY IN THE ENCYCLICAL

The encyclical on the regulation of birth employs a natural law methodology which tends to identify the moral action with the physical and biological structure of the act. The core practical conclusion of the letter states: "We must once again declare that the direct interruption of the generative process already begun, and above all directly willed and procured abortion, even if for therapeutic reasons, are to be absolutely excluded as licit means of regulating birth" (*H.V.* n. 14). "Equally to be excluded . . . is direct sterilization. . . . Similarly excluded is every action which, either in anticipation of the conjugal act, or in its accomplishment, or in the development of its natural consequences, proposes, whether as an end or as a means, to render procreation impossible" (*H.V.* n. 14). The footnotes in this particular paragraph refer to the Roman Catechism and the utterances of more recent popes. Reference is made to the Address of Pius XII to the Italian Catholic Union of Midwives in which direct steriliza- tion is defined as "that which aims at making procreation impossible as both means and end" (n. 13, *AAS* 43 [1951], 838). The concept of direct is thus described in terms of the physical structure and causality of the act itself.

The moral conclusion of the encyclical forbidding any interference with the conjugal act is based on the "intimate structure of the conjugal act" (*H.V.* n. 12). The "design of God" is written into the very nature of the conjugal act; man is merely "the minister of the design established by the Creator" (*H.V.* n. 13). The encyclical acknowledges that "it is licit to take into account the natural rhythms immanent in the generative functions." Recourse to the infecund periods is licit, whereas artificial contraception "as the use of means directly contrary to fecundation is condemned as being always illicit" (*H.V.* n. 16). "In reality there are essential differences between the two cases; in the former, the married couple make legitimate use of a natural disposition; in the latter, they impede the development of natural processes" (*H.V.* n. 16). The natural law theory employed in the en- cyclical thus identifies the moral and human action with the physical structure of the conjugal act itself.

Humanae Vitae in its methodology well illustrates a classi- cist approach. The papal letter admits that "changes which have taken place are in fact noteworthy and of varied kinds" (*H.V.* n. 2). These changes give rise to new questions. How- ever, the changing historical circumstances have not affected the answer or the method employed in arriving at concrete conclusions on implementing responsible parenthood. The primary reason for rejecting the majority report of the Papal

Commission was "because certain criteria of solutions had emerged which departed from the moral teaching on marriage proposed with constant firmness by the teaching authority of the Church" (*H.V.* n. 6).

The encyclical specifically acknowledges the fact that there are new signs of the times, but one wonders if sufficient attention has really been paid to such changes. The footnotes to the encyclical are significant even if the footnote references alone do not constitute a conclusive argument. The references are only to random scriptural texts, one citation of Thomas Aquinas, and references to earlier pronouncements of the hierarchical magisterium. A more inductive approach would be inclined to give more importance and documentation to the signs of the times. The footnote references contain no indication of any type of dialogue with other Christians, non-Christians and the modern sciences. When the letter does mention social consequences of the use of contraception, no documentation is given for what appear to be unproven assumptions. Since the methodology describes the human act in physical terms, the practical moral conclusion is the absolute condemnation of means of artificial birth control. The encyclical thus betrays an epistemology that has been rejected by many Catholic theologians and philosophers today.

IV. DIFFERENT APPROACHES WITH DIFFERENT CONCLUSIONS

Natural law theory has traditionally upheld two values that are of great importance for moral theology: (1) the existence of a source of ethical wisdom and knowledge which the Christian shares with all mankind; (2) the fact that morality cannot be merely the subjective whim of an individual or group of individuals. However, one can defend these important values for moral theology without necessarily endorsing the particular understanding of natural law presupposed in the encyclical. In the last few years Catholic thinkers have been developing and employing different philosophical approaches to an understanding of morality. One could claim that such approaches are modifications of natural law theory because they retain the two important values mentioned above. Others would prefer to abandon the term natural law since such a concept is very ambiguous. There is no monolithic philosophical system called the natural law, and also the term has been somewhat discredited because of the tendency among some to understand natural in terms of the physical structure of acts. We can briefly describe three of the alternative approaches which have been advanced in the last few years—personalism, a relational and communitarian approach, a transcendental methodology. As mentioned above, these three approaches emerge within the context of a more historically conscious worldview and understand man and moral reality in a way that differs from the concept of man and moral reality proposed by the classical methodology. All these approaches would deny the absolute conclusion of the papal encyclical in condemning all means of artificial birth control.

A more personalist approach has characterized much of contemporary ethics. For the Christian, the biblical revelation contributes to such an understanding of reality. A personalist approach cannot be something merely added on to another theory. A personalist perspective will definitely affect moral conclusions, especially when such conclusions have been based on the physical structure of the act itself. Personalism always sees the act in terms of the person placing the act. The Pastoral Constitution on the Church in the Modern World realized that objective standards in the matter of sexual morality are "based on the nature of the human person and his acts" (n. 51). An essay by Bernard Häring shows how a personalist perspective would not condemn artificial contraception as being always immoral.[56]

Classical ethical theory embraces two types or models of ethical method: the teleological and the deontological. H. Richard Niebuhr has added a third ethical model—the model of responsibility. Man is not primarily a maker or a citizen but a responder. There are various relationships within which the responsible self exists. "The responsible self is driven as it were by the movement of the social process to respond and be accountable in nothing less than a universal community."[57] Robert Johann in developing his understanding of man acknowledges a great debt to Niebuhr.[58]

In the particular question of contraception, a more relational approach would not view the person or a particular faculty as something existing in itself. Each faculty exists in relationship with the total person and other persons within a universal community. Morality cannot merely be determined by examining a particular faculty and its physical structure or a particular act in itself. The changed ethical evaluation of lying well illustrates the point. Both Johann and William H. van der Marck (who embraces a more phenomenological starting point) have employed a more relational approach to argue for the licitness of contraception in certain circumstances.[59]

A third philosophical approach to man espoused by a growing number of Catholic thinkers today is a theory of transcendental method. Transcendental methodology owes much to the neo-Thomist Joseph Marechal and is espoused today in different forms by Bernard Lonergan, Karl Rahner, and Emerich Coreth.[60] In general, transcendental method goes beyond the object known to the structures of the human knowing process itself. According to Lonergan, "the intrinsic objectivity of human cognitional activity is its intentionality."[61] Lonergan's ethics is an extension of his theory of knowing. Moral value is not an intrinsic property of external acts or objects; it is an aspect of certain consciously free acts in relation to my knowledge of the world. Man must come to examine the structures of his knowing and deciding process.[62]

Lonergan uses as a tool the notion of horizon analysis. Basic horizon is the maximum field of vision from a determined standpoint. This basic horizon is open to development and even conversion. Lonergan posits four conversions which should transpire from the understanding of the structures of human knowing and deciding—the intellectual, the moral, the religious, and the Christian. Ethics must bring people to this Christian conversion so that they can become aware of their knowing and doing and flee from inauthenticity, unreasonableness, and the surd of sin. Thus Christian ethics is primarily concerned with the manner in which an authentic Christian person makes his ethical decisions and carries them out. However, such a meta-ethics must then enter into the realm of the normative, all the time realizing the provisional value of its precepts which are limited by the data at hand.[63] One commentator has said of Lonergan's ethic as applied to moral theology: "The distinct contribution of the moral theologian to philosophical ethics would consist in clarifying the attitudes which are involved in man's responding in faith to the initiative of a loving God who has redeemed man in Christ."[64] Thus a transcendental method would put greater stress on the knowing and deciding structures of the authentic Christian subject. Such a theory would also tend to reject the encyclical's view of man and his generative faculties.

There has been even among Catholic theologians a sharp, negative response to the practical conclusions of the papal encyclical on the regulation of birth. This essay has tried to explain the reason for the negative response. The concept of natural law employed in the encyclical tends to define the moral act merely in terms of the physical structure of the act. In contemporary theology such an understanding of natural law has been severely criticized. Newer philosophical approaches to the understanding of man have been accepted by many Catholic thinkers. Such approaches logically lead to the conclusion that artificial contraception can be a permissible and even necessary means for the regulation of birth within the context of responsible parenthood.

V. APPLICATION TO THE SITUATION ETHICS DEBATE

In the last few years moral theology and Christian ethics have been immersed in a controversy over situation ethics. The controversy tends to polarize opinions and fails to show the huge areas of agreement existing among Christian moralists. There are, nevertheless, many real differences in approaches and in some practical conclusions. The principal areas of practical differences between some situationists and the teaching found in the manuals of moral theology are the following: medical ethics, particularly in the area of reproduction; conflict situations solved by the principle of the indirect voluntary, especially conflicts involving life and death, e.g., killing, abortion; sexuality; euthanasia; and divorce.

These major points of disagreement have one thing in common. In these cases, the manuals of Catholic moral theology have tended to define the moral action in terms of the physical structure of the act considered in itself apart from the person placing the act and the community of persons within which he lives. A certain action defined in terms of its physical structure or consequences (e.g., euthanasia as the positive interference in the life of the person; masturbation as the ejaculation of semen) is considered to be always wrong. I have used the term "negative, moral absolutes" to refer to such actions described in their physical structure which are always wrong from a moral viewpoint. Thus the central point of disagreement in moral theology today centers on these prohibited actions which are described primarily in terms of their physical structure.

In the area of medical ethics certain actions described in terms of the physical structure of the act are never permitted or other such actions are always required. Artificial insemination with the husband's semen is never permitted because insemination cannot occur except through the act of sexual intercourse.[65] Contraception as direct interference with the act of sexual intercourse is wrong. Direct sterilization is always wrong. Masturbation as the ejaculation of semen is always wrong even as a way of procuring semen for semen analysis.[66] Frequently in such literature the axiom is cited that the end does not justify the means. However, in all these cases the means is defined in terms of the physical structure of the act. I believe in all the areas mentioned above there are circumstances in which such actions would be morally permissible and even necessary.

Catholic moral theology decides most conflict situations by an application of the principle of the indirect voluntary. Direct killing, direct taking of one's life, direct abortion, direct sterilization are always wrong. However, the manuals of theology usually define direct in terms of the physical structure of the act itself. Direct killing according to one author "may be defined as the performance (or the omission of) an act, the primary and natural result of which is to bring about death."[67] According to the same author "direct abortion is the performance of an act, the primary and natural effect of which is to expel a nonviable fetus from its mother's womb." In these cases direct refers to the physical structure and consequences of the act itself. One exception in the manuals of theology to the solution of conflict situations in terms of the principle of the indirect voluntary is the case of unjust aggression. The physical structure of the act is not the determining factor in such a conflict situation.

In general a Christian ethicist might be somewhat suspicious of conflict situations solved in terms of the physical structure of the act itself. Such a solution seems too facile and too easily does away with the agonizing problems raised by the conflict. Likewise, such an approach has tended to minimalize what is only an indirect effect, but the Christian can never have an easy conscience about taking the life of another even if it is only an indirect effect.

The case of "assisted abortion" seems to illustrate the inherent difficulties in the manualistic concept of direct and indirect. For example, the best available medical knowledge indicates that the woman cannot bring a living child to term. If the doctor can abort the fetus now, he can avert very probable physical and psychological harm to the mother from the pregnancy which cannot eventually come to term. The manuals indicate that such an abortion would be direct and therefore immoral. However, in the total context of the situation, it does not seem that such an abortion would be immoral. The example of assisted abortion illustrates the impossibility of establishing an absolute moral norm based on the physical description of the action considered only in itself apart from the person placing the action and the entire community. It seems that the older notion of direct enshrines a prescientific worldview which is somewhat inadequate in our technological age. Why should the doctor sit back and wait for nature to take its course when by interfering now he can avoid great harm to the mother? In general, I do not think that conflict situations can be solved merely in terms of the physical structure and consequences of the act.

Perhaps the approach used in conflict situations of unjust aggression would serve as a better model for the solution of other conflict situations. In unjust aggression the various values at stake are weighed, and the person is permitted to kill an unjust aggressor not only to save his life but also to protect other goods of comparable value, such as a serious threat to health, honor, chastity, or even material goods of great importance.[68] (I believe that in some cases the older theologians went too far in equating the defense of these values and the life of the aggressor.) Thus in the question of abortion there seem to be cases when it is moral to abort to save the life of the mother or to preserve other very important values. I am not proposing that the fetus is an unjust aggressor but rather that the ethical model employed in solving problems of unjust aggression avoids some of the problems created by the model of direct and indirect effects when the direct effect is determined by the physical structure of the act itself.

The present discussion about the beginning of human life centers on the criteria for identifying human life. Are the physical criteria of genetics and embryology sufficient? Or must other criteria of a more psychological and personalistic nature be employed for discerning the existence of human life? What then would be the difference between the fetus in the womb and the newborn babe who is now existing outside his mother's womb? There are many complicated problems in such a discussion. For many, the biological and genetic criteria are the only practical way of resolving the problem.[69] I am merely pointing out that the problem exists precisely because some people will not accept the biological and genetic considerations as establishing an adequate criterion for determining the beginning of human life.

Chapter Three will consider the question of sexuality which has been distorted in the Catholic theological tradition for many reasons including an overemphasis on the physical structure of sexual actuation. In the question of euthanasia, Catholic and other theistic ethicists generally approach the problem in terms of the limited dominion which man has over his own life. Today even the Christian claims a greater power over his own existence both because of scientific advances and because of better understanding of his participation in the Lordship of Jesus. However, in one important aspect in the area of euthanasia the question of dominion over one's life is not primary. Catholic thinking has maintained that the patient does not have to use extraordinary means to preserve his life. In more positive terms, there is a right to die. Many Catholic theologians remind doctors they have no obligation to give intravenous feeding to a dying cancer patient. Likewise, a doctor may discontinue such feeding with the intent that the person will thus die. But the manuals of theology would condemn any positive action on the part of the doctor—e.g., injection of air into the blood-stream—under the same circumstances.[70]

At the particular time when death is fast approaching, the primary moral question does not seem to revolve explicitly around the notion of man's dominion over his life. The problem centers on the difference between not giving something or the withdrawal of something necessary for life and the positive giving of something to bring about death. Is the difference between the two types of action enough to warrant the total condemnation of positively interfering? I do not think so; Catholic theologians should explore the possibility of interfering to hasten the dying process, a notion similar to the concept of assisted abortion mentioned above. But the theologian would also have to consider the possibility of a general prohibition based on the societal effects of such interference.

The problem of describing moral reality in terms of the physical description of an act viewed in itself apart from the person also manifests itself in the question of divorce. According to Catholic teaching a consummated marriage between two baptized persons is indissoluble. But consummation is defined in solely physical terms. Thus the notion of consummation as found in the present law of the Church is inadequate.[71] Moreover, divorce in general qualifies as a negative, moral absolute in the sense described above. A particular action described in nonmoral terms (remarriage after a valid first marriage) is always wrong. The entire question of divorce is too complex to be considered adequately in the present context since it involves biblical, historical, conciliar, and magisterial aspects. But the concept of "the bond of marriage" adds weight to the arguments against divorce. The bond becomes objectivized as a reality existing apart from the relationship of the persons which is brought into being by their marriage vows. All Christians, I believe, should hold some element transcending the two persons and their union here and now. But can this bond always be considered totally apart from the ongoing relationship between the two who exchanged the marital promises?

Thus a quick overview shows that the critical, practical areas of discussion in contemporary moral theology and Christian ethics center on the absolute moral prohibition of certain actions which are defined primarily in terms of the physical structure of the act. Moral meaning is not necessarily identical with the physical description of an act. Modern man is in a much better position than medieval man to realize that fact. The underlying problem is common to every human science—the need to clearly differentiate the category of meaning as the specific data of any science involving human reality. Historians of ideas would be familiar with this problem from the nineteenth century differentiation of Dilthey between the *Geisteswissenchaften* and *Naturwissenchaften*.[72] In the Anglo-American context, Matson has recently published an informative survey of the present status of this same differentiation involving the notion of human behavior.[73]

A word of caution is in order. It appears that some proponents of situation ethics have not given enough importance to the bodily, the material, the external, and the physical aspects of reality. On the other hand, contemporary man is less prone to accept the physical and the biological aspects of reality as morally normative. An analysis of the current scene in moral theology and Christian ethics in a broad ecumenical view indicates that the primary point of dispute centers on the existence of negative moral absolutes in which the moral action is described in physical terms. It would be unwarranted to conclude that the moral act is never identified with the physical structure and description of the act. However, one can conclude that an ethical theory which begins with the assumption that the moral act is identified with the physical structure and consequences of the act will find little acceptance by contemporary theologians.

NOTES

1.
E.g., *Light on the Natural Law*, ed. Illtud Evans, O.P. (Baltimore: Helicon Press, 1965); *Das Naturrecht im Disput*, ed. Franz Böckle (Dusseldorf: Patmos, 1966); "La Nature fondement de la morale?" *Supplément de la Vie Spirituelle*, 81 (mai 1967), 187-324; *Absolutes in Moral Theology?* ed. Charles E. Curran (Washington: Corpus Books, 1968).
2.
Edward LeRoy Long Jr., *A Survey of Christian Ethics* (New York: Oxford University Press, 1967); Thomas G. Sanders, *Protestant Concepts of Church and State* (Garden City, N.Y.: Doubleday Anchor Books, 1965).

3.
Such emphases can still be found, although not in an absolute sense, in the writings of Niels H. Söe. See Söe, "Natural Law and Social Ethics," in *Christian Social Ethics in a Changing World*, ed. John C. Bennett (New York: Association Press, 1966), pp. 289-309. The same article with a response by Paul Ramsey appeared in *Zeitschrift für Evangelische Ethik*, 12 (März 1968), 65-98.

4.
John C. Bennett, "Issues for the Ecumenical Dialogue," in *Christian Social Ethics in a Changing World*, pp. 377, 378.

5.
H. Richard Niebuhr, *Christ and Culture* (New York: Harper Torchbook, 1956).

6.
Niebuhr actually describes the Thomistic approach as "Christ above culture." He goes on to explain that "Thomas also answers the question about Christ and culture with a 'both-and'; yet his Christ is far above culture, and he does not try to disguise the gulf that lies between them" (p. 129).

7.
One cannot simplistically condemn the nature-grace and natural-supernatural distinctions. In their original historical contexts such distinctions tried with considerable success to describe and synthesize this complex reality. Although such distinctions do have some meaning today; nevertheless, many Catholic theologians realize the need to reinterpret such distinctions in the light of different metaphysical approaches. See the three articles by Bernard Lonergan, S.J., which appeared in *Theological Studies*, 2 (1941), 307-324; 3 (1942), 69-88; 375-402. For an exposition of the thought of Karl Rahner on this subject, see Carl J. Peter, "The Position of Karl Rahner Regarding the Supernatural," *Proceedings of the Catholic Theological Society of America*, 20 (1965), 81-94.

8.
A wire release of N. C. News Service with a Vatican City dateline published in Catholic papers in this country during the week of August 4.

9.
Bernard Häring, "The Encyclical Crisis," *Commonweal*, 88 (September 6, 1968), 588-594.

10.
Joseph Fuchs, S.J., *Natural Law*, tr. Helmut Reckter, S.J., and John Dowling (New York: Sheed and Ward, 1965).

11.
Christian Duquoc, O.P., *L'Eglise et le progrès* (Paris: Editions du Cerf, 1964), pp. 68-117. The author considers the past teaching in the Church on slavery, the freedom of nations, the dignity of women, Church and State, torture, and questions of war and peace.

12.
"Dialogue with Joseph Fletcher," *Homiletic and Pastoral Review*, 67 (1967), 828, 829.

13.
Helmut Thielicke, *Theological Ethics I: Foundations*, ed. William Lazerath (Philadelphia: Fortress Press, 1966), 622ff.

14.
Pope Leo XIII, *Rerum Novarum*, n. 7-14; Pope Pius XI, *Quadregesimo Anno*, n. 44-52.

15.
Thomas explicitly cites Isidore in *I-II*, q. 94, a. 2, ob. 1. In *II-II*, q. 66, a. 2, Thomas gives the opinion proposed by Isidore without a direct reference. Thomas explains that reason has called for the right of private property not as something against natural law, but as something added to natural law.

16.
The reasons adduced by Thomas in *II-II*, q. 66, a. 2, indicate

that human sinfulness is a very important factor in the argument for the right of private property.

17.
Rerum Novarum, n. 22.

18.
Hermenegildus Lio, O.F.M., "Estne obligatio justitiae subvenire pauperibus?" *Apollinaris,* 29 (1956), 124-231; 30 (1957), 99-201.

19.
Leo XIII was conscious of the social aspect of property (*Rerum Novarum,* n. 22), but he did not emphasize it. The subsequent Popes down to Paul VI have put increasingly more emphasis on the social aspects of property. The concentration on such social aspects explains the many discussions about the notion of socialization in the encyclicals of Pope John XXIII.

20.
See note 1; also my treatment of this precise question in *A New Look at Christian Morality* (Notre Dame, Ind.: Fides Publishers, 1968), pp. 74-89.

21.
Jean Marie Aubert, "Le Droit Naturel: ses avatars historiques et son avenir," *Supplément de la Vie Spirituelle,* 81 (1967), especially 298 ff.

22.
The Digest or *Pandects of Justinian,* Book 1, t. 1, n. 1-4.

23.
Odon Lottin, *Le Droit Naturel chez Saint Thomas d'Aquin et ses prédécesseurs,* 2nd ed. (Bruges: Charles Beyaert, 1931), p. 62.

24.
In IV Sent. d. 33, q.1, a.l, ad 4.

25.
In V Ethic., lect. 12.

26.
I-II, q.90, a.1, ob.3; q.96, a.5, ob.3; q.97, a.2; *II-II*, q.57, a.3, ob.1 and *in corp.*

27.
I-II, q.95, a.4.

28.
II-II, q.57, a.3.

29.
E.g., H. Noldin et al., *Summa Theologiae Moralis: De Castitate*, 36th ed. (Oeniponte: F. Rauch, 1958), pp. 21-43.

30.
Decree of the Holy Office on the ends of marriage, April 1, 1944, *AAS*, 36 (1944), 103. Also various addresses of Pius XII: *AAS*, 33 (1941), 422; 43 (1951), 835-854.

31.
Regis Araud, S.J., "Évolution de la Théologie du Marriage," *Cahiers Laënnec*, 27 (1967), 56-71; W. van der Marck, O.P., "De recente ontwikkelingen in de theologie van het huwelijk," *Tijdschrift voor Theologie*, 7 (1967), 127-140. English summary on page 140.

32.
Gerard Watson, "The Early History of Natural Law," *The Irish Theological Quarterly*, 33 (1966), 65-74.

33.
John L. Russell, S.J., "The Concept of Natural Law," *The Heythrop Journal*, 6 (1965), 434-438; Pierre Colin, "Ambiguïtés du mot nature," *Supplément de la Vie Spirituelle*, 81 (1967), 253-255.

34.
Charles E. Curran, "Masturbation and Objectively Grave Matter: An Exploratory Discussion," *Proceedings of the*

Catholic Theological Society of America, 21 (1966), 95-109; also Chapter Three.

35.
H. Noldin et al., *Summa Theologiae Moralis,* Vol. II: *De Praeceptis* (Oeniponte: F. Rauch, 1959), pp. 553-560; E. F. Regatillo, S.J., and M. Zalba, S.J., *Theologiae Moralis Summa,* Vol. II (Matriti: Biblioteca de Autores Cristianos, 1953), 1000-1018.

36.
J. A. Dorszynski, *Catholic Teaching about the Morality of Falsehood* (Washington: Catholic University of America Press, 1949); Francis J. Connell, C.SS.R., *More Answers to Today's Moral Problems,* ed. Eugene J. Weitzel, C.S.V. (Washington: Catholic University of America Press, 1965), p. 123, 124. Augustine had at one time accepted the distinction between falsehood and lying, but he later changed his opinion.

37.
Bernard Lonergan, S.J., *Collection* (New York: Herder and Herder, 1967), pp. 252-267; Lonergan, "A Transition from a Classicist Worldview to Historical Mindedness," in *Law for Liberty: The Role of Law in the Church Today,* ed. James E. Biecher (Baltimore: Helicon Press, 1967). Lonergan along with other theologians such as Marechal, Rahner, and Metz maintains that although Thomas Aquinas reflected a classical worldview, the followers of Thomas distorted his teaching especially in such areas as the emphasis on a deductive methodology and a nonrelational understanding of being.

38.
John Courtney Murray, S.J., "The Declaration on Religious Freedom," *Concilium,* 15 (May 1966), 3-16.

39.
Eulalio R. Baltazar, *Teilhard and the Supernatural* (Baltimore: Helicon Press, 1966); Leslie Dewart, *The Future of*

Belief (New York: Herder and Herder, 1966). Lonergan espouses historical mindedness but strenuously opposes the approach of Dewart. See Lonergan, "The Dehellenization of Dogma," *Theological Studies,* 28 (1967), 336-351.

40.
Murray, *Concilium,* 15 (May 1966), 11-16.

41.
John Courtney Murray, S.J., *The Problem of Religious Freedom* (Westminster, Md.: Newman, 1965).

42.
John Courtney Murray, S.J., "Freedom, Authority, Community," *America* (December 3, 1966), 735.

43.
Gaudium et Spes (The Pastoral Constitution on the Church in the Modern World), n. 44. For a competent one-volume translation of the documents of Vatican II, see *The Documents of Vatican II,* ed. Walter M. Abbot, S.J. (New York: America Press and Association Press, 1966).

44.
Karl Rahner, S.J., *The Dynamic Element in the Church* (New York: Herder and Herder, 1964).

45.
Daniel C. Maguire, "Moral Absolutes and the Magisterium," *Absolutes in Moral Theology?,* pp. 57-107.

46.
Herbert Butterfield, *The Origins of Modern Science, 1300-1800* (New York: Macmillan, 1951); Lonergan, *Collection,* p. 259 ff.

47.
Andreas van Melsen, "Natural Law and Evolution," *Concilium,* 26 (June, 1967), 49-59.

48.
Law for Liberty: The Role of Law in the Church Today, *passim.*
49.
Documents of Vatican II, p. 686, n. 20. The footnote on the role of civil law was written by John Courtney Murray.
50.
Thomas B. McDonough, "Distribution of Contraceptives by the Welfare Department: A Catholic Response," in *The Problem of Population,* Vol. II (Notre Dame: University of Notre Dame Press, 1964), pp. 94-118.
51.
Douglas Sturm, "Naturalism, Historicism, and Christian Ethics: Toward a Christian Doctrine of Natural Law," *The Journal of Religion,* 44 (1964), 40-51. Note again that some Catholic thinkers see in the excessive emphasis on *res in se* apart from any relational consideration a distortion of the understanding of St. Thomas.
52.
Russell, *The Heythrop Journal,* 6 (1965), 434-438.
53.
Karl Rahner, S.J., "Theology and Anthropology," in *The Word in History,* ed. T. Patrick Burke (New York: Sheed and Ward, 1966), pp. 1-23; Rahner, "Naturrecht," *Lexikon für Theologie und Kirche,* Vol. 7, 827-828.
54.
Lonergan, "Dimensions of Meaning," *Collection,* pp. 252-267.
55.
Lonergan, *Collection,* pp. 221-239; *Theological Studies,* 28 (1967), 337-351.
56.
Bernard Häring, "The Inseparability of the Unitive-Procrea-

tive Functions of the Marital Act," *Contraception: Authority and Dissent,* ed. Charles E. Curran (New York: Herder and Herder, 1969), pp. 176-192.

57.
H. Richard Niebuhr, *The Responsible Self* (New York: Harper and Row, 1963), p. 88.

58.
Robert O. Johann, S.J., *Building the Human* (New York: Herder and Herder, 1968), pp. 7-10.

59.
Robert O. Johann, S.J., "Responsible Parenthood: A Philosophical View," *Proceedings of the Catholic Theological Society of America,* 20 (1965), 115-128; William H. van der Marck, O.P., *Toward a Christian Ethic* (Westminster, Md.: Newman Press, 1967), pp. 48-60. Note that Germain G. Grisez in his *Contraception and the Natural Law* (Milwaukee: Bruce, 1964), argues against artificial contraception although he explicitly denies the "perverted faculty" argument. However, Grisez seems to accept too uncritically his basic premise that the malice of contraception "is in the will's direct violation of the procreative good as a value in itself, as an ideal which never may be submerged."

60.
For a succinct exposition of transcendental philosophy, see Kenneth Baker, S.J., *A Synopsis of the Transcendental Philosophy of Emerich Coreth and Karl Rahner* (Spokane: Gonzaga University, 1965).

61.
Bernard Lonergan, S.J., *Collection* (New York: Herder and Herder, 1967), p. 228.

62.
In addition to the bibliography of Lonergan's which has already been mentioned, see Bernard J. F. Lonergan, S.J.,

Insight (New York and London: Longmans, Green, and Co., 1964); also Donald H. Johnson, S.J., "Lonergan and the redoing of Ethics," *Continuum*, 5 (1967), 211-220.

63.
David W. Tracy, "Horizon Analysis and Eschatology," *Continuum*, 6 (1968), 166-179.

64.
Johnson, *loc cit.*, 219, 220.

65.
Pope Pius XII, Address to the Fourth World Congress of Catholic Doctors, Rome, September 29, 1949, A.A.S., 41 (1949), 560; Pope Pius XII, Address to the Italian Catholic Union of Midwives, October 29, 1951, A.A.S., 43 (1951), 850; Pope Pius XII, Address to the Second World Congress of Fertility and Sterility, May 19, 1956, A.A.S., 48 (1956), 472.

66.
Pope Pius XII, A.A.S., 48 (1956), 472; Pope Pius XII, Address to the Italian Urologists, October 8, 1953, A.A.S., 45 (1953), 678; Decree of the Holy Office, August 2, 1929, A.A.S., 21 (1929), 490.

67.
John McCarthy, *Problems in Theology II: The Commandments* (Westminster, Md.: Newman Press, 1960), 159, 160. The author mentions other current definitions of direct killing (e.g., an act which aims, *ex fine operis,* at the destruction of life) earlier on pp. 119-122.

68.
Marcellinus Zalba, S.I., *Theologia Moralis Summa II; Theologia Moralis Specialis* (Madrid: Biblioteca de Autores Cristianos, 1953), 275-279.

69.
Such an approach is adopted by Paul Ramsey who claims

that at least from blastocyst the fetus must be considered as a human being. Ramsey's paper, which was delivered at the International Conference on Abortion sponsored by the Harvard Divinity School and the Joseph P. Kennedy Jr. Foundation, will be published as part of the proceedings of the conference by the Harvard University Press. I have not seen a response to Ramsey's argument which is totally convincing even though I remain somewhat uneasy with his position.

70.
Gerald Kelly, S.J., *Medico-Moral Problems* (St. Louis: Catholic Hospital Association, 1957), pp. 128-141.

71.
For a fuller critique of the notion of consummation, see Dennis Doherty, "Consummation and the Indissolubility of Marriage," *Absolutes in Moral Theology?*, pp. 211-231.

72.
Wilhelm Dilthey, *Pattern and Meaning in History* (New York; Harper Torchbook, 1967).

73.
Floyd W. Matson, *The Broken Image* (Garden City, N.Y.: Doubleday Anchor Books, 1966).

3

Sexuality and Sin:
A Current Appraisal

The Roman Catholic theology of sexuality has been frequently criticized in the past because it was too negative
and gave an undue importance to sexuality. In the last few
years the renewal in moral theology has stressed the primacy
of love and service of the neighbor and not sexuality as the
hallmark of Christian life. An appreciation of human sexuality based on the theology of creation, incarnation and bodily
resurrection at the end of time has replaced the antimaterial
and antisexual prejudices of an older theology. A total Christian view of sexuality also sees the limitations of human sexuality: the imperfections involved in time and space, the
fact that sexuality is just one aspect of human life, and the
reality of human sinfulness which affects sexuality and all
human life.[1]

However, there remain many questions about sexual ethics.
One very important obstacle in the attempt to arrive at a
more balanced view of human sexuality and its role in the
life of the Christian is the teaching that all sins against sexuality involve grave matter. Is that statement true? What

was the reasoning process that led to such a conclusion? Will a changed understanding of the gravity of sins against chastity change any of our other teaching on sins against sexuality? This article will attempt to explain the older approach in Catholic theology to sins against chastity and their gravity. The older approach will be criticized, and then the final section will survey some general and particular guidelines for an understanding of sins against sexuality in contemporary Catholic moral theology. There remain many other even more important aspects of human sexuality which Catholic theology must consider, but first of all it is necessary to show the inadequacies in the older way of understanding sins against sexuality and their gravity and to point out newer approaches.

I. THE OLDER TEACHING AND ITS DEVELOPMENT

In general, Catholic moral theology has approached the question of sexuality in the light of a natural law methodology. Such a methodology recognizes that there exists a source of ethical wisdom and knowledge apart from the explicit revelation of God in the Scriptures. Whereas individual texts from the Scriptures were used by the theologians in pointing out the malice of certain actions, Catholic theology realized the insufficiency of the revealed Scriptures for furnishing a complete and adequate understanding of the way in which the Christian should view human sexuality. Natural law methodology as such does not necessarily imply the existence of any absolute norms. Since natural law in its best understanding is right reason, such a methodology is deliberative rather than prescriptive.[2] Unfortunately, the natural law approach to sexuality in Catholic theology illustrates the problems developed at great length in Chapter Two including the ambiguity in the very concept of natural law.

In the natural law understanding of sins against chastity, nature does not mean right reason. In this context nature means the physical, biological, or natural processes which are common to man and all the animals. Theology textbooks from Thomas Aquinas until a very few years ago divided the sins against sexuality into two classes—sins against nature (*peccata contra naturam*) and sins according to nature (*peccata iuxta naturam*).[3] Nature in this distinction refers to the physical, biological process common to man and all the animals in which male semen is deposited in the vas of the female. Sins against nature are those in which this natural process does not take place and are generally listed as masturbation, sodomy, homosexuality, bestiality, and contraception. Sins according to nature are sexual actuations in which the biological or "natural" structure is observed, but they are opposed to the distinctively human aspects of sexuality. These sins include fornication, adultery, incest, rape, and sacrilege.[4] Chapter Two has shown that this understanding is logically and historically influenced by the ideas of Ulpian.[5]

A second inadequacy in the textbook natural law approach to sexuality is the over-emphasis on procreation as the primary end of marriage and also of sexuality.[6] Such an understanding of the primary end of marriage theoretically follows from the natural law understanding of Ulpian. Ulpian himself gives the example of procreation and education of offspring as the classical example of natural law as that which is common to man and all the animals.[7] Ulpian's theory would of necessity relegate the love union aspect of marriage and sexuality to a secondary end. The primary or fundamental in man is what he shares with the other animals. The human aspect is something which is another layer merely placed on top of the primary layer of animality. Since relationality and love union do not enter into animal sexuality, these aspects are relegated to secondary ends of sexuality and marriage.

The emphasis on procreation and education shows through in the arguments proposed for the malice of certain sexual sins. Sins against nature are wrong because they violate the order of nature and thus impede the procreation of offspring.[8] However, even the sins according to nature are wrong primarily because they are against the primary end of procreation and education. Even though there may be no other circumstances present, such as the injustice to another marriage in adultery or the lack of consent in rape, all sins according to nature partake in the basic malice of fornication. Simple fornication is a grave sin because both parents are needed to provide for the proper education and upbringing of the child who might be born as a result of such an act.[9]

Imperfect medical and biological knowledge merely heightened the importance attached by the older theologians to the physical and procreational aspects of sexuality. Contemporary Catholic theologians too often forget the recent and rapid advances in scientific knowledge about human reproduction and sexuality. The very word "semen," taken from the agricultural metaphor of seed, indicates that the male semen merely had to be put in the fertile spot provided by the female. The classical authors in moral theology knew nothing of the exact contribution of the female to the human reproduction process. Very little progress in any type of anatomic knowledge was made until the sixteenth century because of the difficulty in obtaining corpses. In the sixteenth century, Gabriele Falloppio discovered the fallopian tubes in the woman, but he did not understand their true purpose.[10] In 1672 De Graaf described the female ovaries and the follicle which bears his name, but he made the mistake of identifying the ovum with the entire follicle. Only in the nineteenth century was the theory of De Graaf revived and corrected by the realization that the ovum is contained within the follicle.

In 1677, Van Leeuwenhoek, the great microscopist, discovered spermatozoa. Even after the discovery of spermatozoa a number of scientists thought that the male element was the only active element in reproduction. Some of Van Leeuwenhoek's over zealous followers even published pictures of the "homounculus" or little man which they found outlined in the spermatozoa![11] Obviously, such an understanding would attach great importance to human semen and spermatozoa.

Less than a century ago (1875), Oscar Hertwig showed that fertilization was effected by the union of the nuclei of ovum and sperm. Thus, only within the last hundred years or so has science realized that the woman is not fertile for the greater part of her menstrual cycle. Procreation is not possible after every act of sexual intercourse but only during a comparatively short time each month.[12] Thinkers like the classical moral theologians who lacked the knowledge of modern medicine necessarily would give too great a value to human semen and see too strong a connection between the individual sexual actuation and procreation.

Catholic theologians generally followed the teaching of St. Thomas that sins against sexuality are grave because they go against an important order of nature or because the absence of marriage between the parties fails to provide for the education of the child who might be born of such a union. Thomas also considered the question whether touches and kisses are grave sins. Thomas responded that an embrace, a kiss or a touch is not mortal *secundum speciem* because such actions can be done for some reasonable cause or necessity. However, something can be mortal because of its cause; and if these actions are done for a libidinous reason, they are mortal sins. Thomas had earlier argued that consent to the pleasure of a mortal sin is itself a mortal sin; therefore, if such actions are done from a libidinous intention, they are mortal sins.[13]

The commentators on St. Thomas approached the question of embraces, kisses, etc. in this Thomistic context. Martin Le

Maistre (1432-1481) disagreed with Thomas.[14] Martin denied that such actions *secundum quod libidinosa sunt* are mortal sins. If such a kiss is done for the pleasure involved in the kiss and is not ordered to fornication, such a kiss is not a mortal sin. There remains the problem of what is meant by libidinous. However, for the purpose of our present study, the stage is thus set for the famous question of the existence of parvity of matter in sins against sexuality. Martin of Azpilcueta, the famous Doctor Navarrus (1493-1586), was apparently the first theologian to affirm that in matters of sexuality there can be parvity of matter.[15] Navarrus proves his point by merely stating that the transgression of any precept is excused from grave sin because of parvity of matter and the precept governing chastity should be no different.[16] The opinion of Navarrus was accepted by Thomas Sanchez (1550-1610) who maintained there could be a slight venereal pleasure which would not involve lethal guilt provided there is no danger of pollution and no danger of consent to a carnal act.[17]

In 1612, the General of the Society of Jesus, Claudius Aquaviva forbade Jesuits to maintain the existence of parvity of matter in deliberately willed, imperfect sexual actuation or pleasure. This was later extended to imperfect sexual actuation which may have arisen indirectly but was later consented to. The opinion proposed by Sanchez was ordered to be changed in all the editions of his work.[18] (In 1659, the Revisores of the Society of Jesus did admit that the opinion affirming the existence of parvity of matter in questions of chastity was still extrinsically probable and penitents holding such a position could be validly absolved.)[19] The teaching denying the existence of parvity of matter in the sixth commandment gradually became so strong that contemporary theologians claim it is temerarious to deny it.[20] The ruling by Father Aquaviva has obviously prevented any true discussion of the question by the Jesuit theologians who have been most influential in the area of moral theology. Since the issue was not allowed to be discussed, one can and should seriously question the validity of the apparent consensus of Catholic theologians on this point.

Jose M. Diaz Moreno recently published a protracted historical study of eighty theologians from Cajetan to St. Alfonsus to determine if the opinion admitting parvity of matter ever enjoyed probability. Only nine of these authors affirmed that parvity of matter excuses from grave sin in matters of sexuality.[21] However, the author concludes his lengthy investigation by saying that the arguments advanced by the proponents of parvity of matter are so generic or open to other interpretations that they do and did not constitute a solidly probable opinion. Nor do the nine theologians who maintained such a teaching constitute an extrinsically probable opinion either because many of them do not enjoy great esteem or because the reasons proposed by some (e.g. Navarrus and Sanchez) are not convincing.[22]

There have been no definitive interventions of the hierarchical magisterium concerning the question of parvity of matter.[23] Some statements definitely indicate and even presuppose the teaching denying the existence of parvity of matter in sexual sins.[24] A number of statements have condemned those who would assert that kisses, embraces, and touches that are done for carnal pleasure are only venial sins.[25] Also one response of the Holy Office presupposes there is no parvity of matter in the sixth commandment.[26] All of these are comparatively minor statements and must be judged today in the light of many different circumstances.

Since the seventeenth century theologians have generally taught that even imperfect sexual actuation or pleasure outside marriage does not admit of parvity of matter. There was some dispute, but only concerning the ultimate reason for such a teaching. Was the teaching based on intrinsic and theoretical reasons or merely practical and moral reasons?[27] Just a decade ago theologians maintained that the teaching denying parvity of matter was so certain that the contrary opinion was temerarious.[28] The reasons proposed by theologians for their opinion denying parvity of matter in the sixth commandment have taken different forms. Diaz Moreno summarizes the two arguments proposed by the authors he studied from Cajetan to St. Alphonsus. The first argument is based on the fact that all these imperfect sexual actuations are ordered to sexual intercourse, and thus all venereal pleasure, even the smallest, is the beginning of copula or pollution. The second argument consists in the danger of consent to a complete act which is intimately connected with these previous acts.[29] Fuchs proposes what he considers to be the best intrinsic argument in this way: in incomplete sexual actuation outside marriage there is a substantial breaking of an order of great importance, insofar as the individual desires for himself that which was ordained by the creator for the good of the species.[30]

In fairness to the theologians one must carefully examine what is meant by the axiom that there is no parvity of matter in sexual matters. According to the best interpretations, the axiom means this: imperfect sexual actuation or pleasure outside marriage, which is directly willed, whether purposely procurred or consented to, is by reason of matter always a grave sin.[31] Note well that the axiom denying parvity of matter in the sixth commandment does not mean that every sin against the sixth commandment constitutes a mortal sin. Sexual actuation or pleasure within marriage and indirect sexual actuation outside marriage are not grave matter. Although the matter is always grave in the other cases, the theologians constantly taught that sufficient reflection and full consent of the will are necessary for mortal sin. St.

Thomas very wisely remarked that libido in the sensitive appetite diminishes sin because passion reduces culpability. Thomas admits that passion in sexual matters is very strong and difficult to overcome.[32]

II. EVALUATION OF THE OLDER TEACHING

What about the teaching of the theologians that complete sexual actuation outside marriage is always grave matter and that direct, imperfect sexual actuation or pleasure outside marriage is always grave matter? I believe that such opinions and axioms are not true.

Contemporary moral theology views mortal sin in the light of the theory of the fundamental option which has been developed at great length in Chapter One. The difference between mortal and venial sin does not reside primarily in the difference between grave and light matter. Mortal sin involves the core of the person in a fundamental choice or option, a basic orientation of his existence. Venial sin is an action which tends to be more peripheral and does not involve such a change in basic orientation. At best the distinction between grave matter and light matter is a presumption. The presumption is that grave matter will usually call for an involvement of the core of the person whereas light matter tends to call for only a peripheral response. If grave and light matter are at best presumptive guidelines, then such axioms as *ex toto genere suo gravis* or *non datur parvitas materiae* lose much of their rigidity.[33] However, my contention is that one cannot maintain the presumption that all complete sexual actuations outside marriage and all directly willed, imperfect sexual actuations outside marriage constitute grave matter. In the following arguments much of the attention will be directed to the case of complete sexual actuation outside marriage. However, if such complete sexual actuation outside marriage does not always involve grave matter, *a fortiori* directly willed, imperfect sexual actuation does not always involve grave matter.

The older view of the theologians rests upon a very inadequate notion of natural law which has exaggerated the importance attached to actions against sexuality. The Christian should be especially alert to a theological axiom which would seem to give primary importance to sexuality and chastity and not to the primary element of Christian love. Negative attitudes towards sexuality have definitely accented the over-emphasis on the importance of sexual sins. However, our discussion will center on the concept of natural law underlying the meaning and appreciation of sexuality and sexual sins in the teaching of the Catholic theologians before the last few years.

The manualistic concept of natural law applied to questions of sexuality distorts the meaning and importance of sexuality because it sees sexuality only in terms of the physical, biological process. No mention is made of the psychological which is just as objective an aspect of human sexuality as the physical. The older theologians can be excused because man has become aware of the psychological only within the last century. However, to deny the value and importance of the psychological distorts the meaning of human sexuality. For example, psychology reminds us that masturbation is not a very important matter in the life of some people such as the developing adolescent.[34]

The natural law concept underlying sexual morality in the manuals also fails to see the individual action in relation to the person. The Pastoral Constitution on the Church in the Modern World calls for theology to take into consideration the person and his acts.[35] The older approach viewed just the act in itself. There is a danger in some ethical thinking today which tends to give little or no importance to individual actions. However, it is equally fallacious to consider the act apart from the person placing the action. Masturbation may mean many different things depending on the person placing the action.

The exclusive emphasis on the physical aspect and the individual act apart from the person fails to do justice to the full meaning of human sexuality. One cannot brand all pre-marital sex under the same blanket condemnation of fornica-tion. There is quite a bit of difference between sexual rela-tions with a prostitute and with a spouse to be. Criteria which cannot come to grips with the differences involved in such cases do not seem to be adequate criteria. An emphasis on the physical and the natural, as opposed to the personal aspect of the action, also fails to see the need of growth and develop-ment as a person gradually strives to achieve a mature sexu-ality. Growth and development might even involve tem-porary problems along the way, but these are to be seen in view of the overall effort to reach the goal of an integrated human sexuality.

Perhaps the greatest error in the older approach is the close connection seen between every sexual actuation and procreation. Procreation is a very important human value. If every sexual actuation outside marriage involves a direct going against actual procreation, then there would be reason to assert the generic gravity of sins against sexuality. How-ever, Catholic theology now realizes the over-importance attached to the relationship between sexuality and procrea-tion in the past. The more recent statements of the hierarchi-cal magisterium no longer mention procreation and educa-tion of offspring as the primary end of marriage.[36] Even the acceptance of the rhythm system of responsible parenthood argues that not every sexual actuation is closely connected with possible procreation. Ironically, an approach to sexual-ity exclusively in terms of procreation could logically lead to interesting consequences. Thomas Aquinas saw the generic grave malice of fornication in the harm done to the child who might be born of that union. The use of contraception would destroy the primary argument of St. Thomas asserting the generic malice of fornication!

Older biological notions also exaggerated the importance attached by Catholic theologians to the connection between sexual actuation and procreation. Even from a physical viewpoint the vast majority of sexual acts will not result in procreation because the woman is sterile for the greater part of her period. Modern science with its knowledge of the prodigality of nature in giving spermatozoa and the realization that semen is not the only active element in procreation indicates that human semen is not as important as older theologians seemed to think. Contemporary medical knowledge thus argues against the reasons assigned for the generic importance attached to sins of sexuality in the past.

From the pastoral viewpoint, it is most important to discard the older view denying parvity of matter in sexual sins. Such a view gave an undue importance to sexuality in the overall view of the Christian life. In addition such a teaching tended to stifle a proper understanding of human sexuality and human sexual development. Sex was always connected with the fear of mortal sin. Such fear impeded the development of a proper attitude toward human sexuality on the part of many Catholics and even brought about grave repercussions in their adult attitude to sexuality.

III. CONTEMPORARY APPROACHES

It would be impossible to develop a coherent and systematic approach to the question of sexuality within the context of this study, even if there were such an approach. I will merely attempt to point out some of the problems involved, the generic approaches that are being taken, the important questions remaining, and the present state of the question on the morality of particular sexual acts as seen by some Roman Catholic theologians.

The question of sexual ethics raises again the problem of moral methodology which underlies most of the present discussions in Christian ethics and moral theology. The Christian ethicist certainly looks to the Scriptures for guidance. However, there is a realization today that the Scriptures cannot be used as proof texts to definitely indicate that one particular action is always wrong.[37] Scripture scholars remind us that the Scriptures are historically and culturally limited. Since the Scriptures reflect the historical conditions of their own times, they might not be applicable in changed circumstances. In some cases the words of Jesus may refer to an ideal of behavior rather than a norm required in all circumstances. The Scriptures tell us of the basic thrust of the Christian life and the attitudes that characterize such existence. The revelation of God in the Scriptures may also enunciate norms, and even particular norms for the Christian life. However, modern biblical scholarship does not permit the ethician to accept something as an absolute norm just because it is mentioned in the Scriptures. Chapter Five develops a more positive methodological approach to the use of the Scriptures in moral theology. The Christian theologian also pays great attention to tradition. Tradition records the experience of other men and women who have lived under the inspiration of the Spirit. One must give serious attention to such experience and reflection. However, historical changes, sociological developments, and increased knowledge brought to light through the recent knowledge explosion caution the ethician against a mere repetition of the traditional formulae and an unquestioning acceptance of the teaching of the past.

Chapter Two has given a detailed critique of the natural law approach of the manuals of theology and pointed out some of the contemporary approaches. Contemporary theological notions stress the personal rather than the natural, the human rather than the physical, the relational rather than the substantial. Moral theology is also more conscious of the historical and cultural relativism that is a part of our evolving human existence. A more *a posteriori* approach gives more importance to what the other sciences tell us about man and his actions. Likewise, more importance is given to the experience of Christian people and all men of good will in determining the morality of particular actions.

Moral theology views sexuality in the light of the full Christian message. Sexuality reflects the goodness of God since it is part of his creation and is destined to share in the resurrection of the body. Human sexuality shares not only the goodness of all creation but also the inherent limitations of human existence here and now—the limitations of time and space as well as human sinfulness. Revelation and personal reflection remind us of the tragic aspect which is present in the human story of sexuality and marriage. Sexuality forms an important aspect of human existence, but not the only or most important aspect of human existence.

All must admit the negative and even unhuman approach to sexuality which existed in the past both in Catholic theory and practice, but fortunately a much more positive approach is beginning to prevail. However, there lurks the danger of becoming so lyrical about sexuality that one forgets the imperfections, limitations and tragedy that mark sexuality, as well as everything human. An overly optimistic theology which has flourished in the last few years has tended in general to forget the aspect of the total Christian vision which reminds us of imperfection, sin and death. That is why one must insist today on the total vision. The imperfections of human sexuality stem from the creaturely limitations of space and time; the full sexual union lasts but a fleeting moment and cannot overcome the limitations of space and time. There is a rhythm of life and death in sexual actuation itself which is a constant reminder of limitation and incompleteness. Pierre Grelot devotes eight pages to the tragic aspects of the couple in the Old Testament literature and concludes: "All these facts show what is the real situation of sexuality and the human couple in a sinful world: a frail thing, constantly threatened and far removed from its original ideal."[38] But the Christian does not despair, for sexuality and marriage, again like all human reality, share in the redemption and the promise of the future. This study is considering the comparatively narrow aspect of what has been called the sins against sexuality, but it is helpful to present a brief overall view of sexuality that should be the starting point for any more particular consideration.

Christian ethics has traditionally seen the meaning of human sexuality in terms of love and procreation although too great an importance was attached to procreation at the expense of the unitive purpose of sexuality. Generally all Christian ethicists today, Protestant and Roman Catholic, view human sexuality in terms of a personal relationship between man and woman. Sexuality is not a mere object or even a faculty divorced from the person, but a very personal and intimate way of man and woman giving themselves to one another in a relationship of love. There are some non-Catholic theologians who argue that sexual intercourse as a personal act of loving does not always demand the binding and total commitment of man and woman. However, Catholic theologians generally and most Protestant theologians still hold to the principle that the union of two bodies *generally* calls for the total and complete union of two hearts which is the commitment of marriage.[39]

What about the relationship between sexuality and pro-creation? In the past, Catholic theology seems to have erred by seeing a connection between every act of sexual inter-course and procreation. Those who would argue for extra-marital or premarital sex would naturally deny any necessary connection between sexuality and procreation. It is obvious that there is some connection between sexuality and procrea-tion. The creation story in Genesis bears witness to this rela-tionship. But even the approval of rhythm, to say nothing of the widespread rejection of the ethical conclusion of *Humanae Vitae*, indicates that not every act of sexual inter-course has to be open to procreation. Catholic theologians generally speak now of a connection between procreation and sexuality to the extent that sexual intercourse has mean-ing only within a realm of procreative acts or with a person with whom one is joined in a procreative union; in other words, in marriage. Sexuality as an expression of love also calls for some real connection with openness to procreation. Love itself is creative. The covenanted love of husband and wife tends to procreation just as the covenant of Yahweh with his people and Christ with his Church is a life-giving covenant of love. A problem arises in those cases in which even a married couple should not have children (e.g., be-cause of a genetic problem or even societal reasons), for even their marital sexuality should not be procreative. Paul Ram-sey answers this objection by saying that such married part-ners would still be saying that *if* either has a child it would come about only through their one flesh unity.[40]

Another aspect that is too often left out of consideration by some extreme contextualists is the effect on society of such behavior. The societal aspect could call for the fact that certain practices are always observed even though in a par-ticular case an individual might be greatly inconvenienced or even harmed to some degree. Catholic theology holds that the seal of the confessional is always binding because of this societal factor. Without such absolute assurances some Catholics might have difficulty in confessing their sins in the sacrament of penance. At least this societal aspect must be considered in the question of human sexuality, since marriage and sexuality affect many people and the entire society.

In the light of the inadequacies of the past approaches and the newer considerations a brief survey of the questions of masturbation, homosexuality, and premarital intercourse will follow. However, it will first be useful to call to mind an important distinction—the distinction between sin and right or wrong. In the theory of the fundamental option mortal sin is seen as the change of the basic orientation of the person. Sin thus considers the action in relationship to the responsibility and personal involvement of the one placing such an action. But the human act is complex. The human act must also be considered in relationship to the development of the person himself and in relationship with other acts and other persons. Right or wrong can be used to designate the human act under this aspect. Thus an action may be wrong, but not sinful; e.g., the act of becoming drunk is wrong, but for this particular person because of his personal make-up this might not be gravely sinful. Too often even professional ethicians seem to confuse the two different aspects which I have designated in terms of sin or right and wrong.

Masturbation. The blanket and sinful gravity of masturbation in the older teaching was derived from the one-sidedly physical approach, the emphasis on the connection of each sexual act with procreation, and the erroneous importance attached to male semen. A more personal approach and better psychological as well as physical knowledge point out that masturbation is ordinarily not that important a matter. There is no blanket gravity that can be assigned to every act of masturbation. Masturbatory activity is generally symptomatic; it can be symptomatic of many different things. Masturbation might be expressive of a deep-seated inversion or just an adolescent growing-up process.[41] Generally speaking, I believe masturbation is wrong since it fails to integrate sexuality into the service of love. Masturbation indicates a failure at a total integration of sexuality in the person. This wrongness is not always grave; in fact, most times it is not. In the developing adolescent individual acts of masturbation are definitely not that important at all provided the individual is trying to develop his personality and enter into healthy relationships with others and the world around him.

Catholic educators should openly teach that masturbation is not always grave matter and most times, especially for adolescents, is not that important. Thus, masturbatory activity should not be a reason preventing an adolescent from full participation in the Eucharist. Also such a teaching would remove the fear so often induced by the inadequate teaching that masturbation always involves grave matter. However, the teacher should not leave the adolescent with the impression that there is absolutely nothing wrong with masturbation. Mature sexuality has meaning only in terms of a relationship of life-giving love to another. Sexuality should develop in this direction. Individual masturbatory actions are not that important provided there is a general growth toward communion with others and interpersonal relationships.

Homosexuality. It would be impossible even to summarize the recent literature on the subject of homosexuality.[42] I believe that homosexual actions are wrong. Sexuality seems to have its meaning in terms of a life-giving love union of male and female. The priest as counselor must not speak primarily in terms of grave sinfulness. The theology of sin in terms of the fundamental option and modern psychological knowledge indicates that most often homosexual actions do not involve the person in grave or mortal sin. Help should be available to the homosexual so that he can come to a better development of his sexuality. What about the cases in which modern medical science cannot help the homosexual? In these cases it seems to me that for such a person homosexual acts might not even be wrong. I am not saying that such acts are ever a goal or an ideal that should be held up to others to imitate. Homosexual acts for such a person, provided there is no harm to other persons, might be the only way in which some degree of humanity and stability can be achieved. This would be a practical application of the theology of compromise. Compromise maintains that because of the existence of sin in the world a person might be forced to accept some behavior which under ordinary circumstances he would not want to choose.[43] Since many experts trace homosexuality to psychological roots springing from the lack of love in early development, the application of compromise because of the existence of sin seems most appropriate in these cases.

Premarital sexuality. The older approach with its naturalistic criterion grouped all premarital or extramarital sexuality under the same generic gravity and wrongness. A more personalist approach realizes that there is quite a difference between sexual relations with a prostitute and sexual relations between an engaged couple. The gravity is inversely proportionate to the degree of personal commitment involved. The gambit of personal relationship can run all the way from prostitutional to playboy, to casual, to friendly, to committed. The same generic degree of wrongness cannot apply to all these different sexual relationships short of the commitment of marriage. However, the degree of personal commitment cannot be the sole criterion of the moral judgment in these cases, for other aspects must also be considered.

Catholic theologians generally uphold the teaching that sexuality outside marriage is wrong. Even the extreme situationists admit that sexuality calls for some degree of personal relationship and commitment. The position affirming that sexual relations outside marriage is wrong employs different arguments. Sexual relationships are a personal giving of one to another as persons. They are more than just chance encounters. In a sexual encounter one accepts responsibility for another; to accept full responsibility means that the persons are totally committed to one another. The biblical understanding sees two in one flesh as the sign of the total giving of one to another in marriage. Such a union of two in one flesh becomes the analogue of the covenant that God has made with man. Just as fidelity marks the covenant of God with his people, so personal fidelity must characterize the union of two in one flesh. This is the fidelity of the marriage commitment. A similar argument views the sexual union as the language of total commitment. The union of two bodies in one flesh is the sign and the symbol of the union of two hearts. The union of bodies is a lie and a false sign unless it bespeaks a total union of two hearts. Likewise the defenders of the traditional Christian teaching against premarital sexuality point to the connection between sexuality and procreation. (Even the small failure rate in contraception is a reminder that sexuality has a relationship with procreation.)[44]

There also seem to be lacunae in some of the arguments proposed in defense of the theory that premarital sexuality is sometimes right. The societal dimension is often forgotten. In fact, frequently the situation is reduced to the very immediate and does not extend beyond the present moment. The fact that under the emotional impact of the present moment other important values might be forgotten does not enter into the argument. James Gustafson, himself a moderate contextualist, complains that the ethics of Fletcher often restricts the situation much too narrowly.[45] Premarital and extramarital sexuality could have grave repercussions on the very important social realities of marriage and the family. Also, it is extremely difficult to know one's true motives and feelings. Can one be sure he is not taking advantage of another? Does the boy particularly realize the different psychological attitude of the girl and her different reactions? As in many emotional situations, for example, war and sex, there is always the danger of escalation!

Underlying many of the arguments in favor of premarital sexuality seems to be a false dualism. How often does one hear the argument: as long as both parties agree, there is nothing wrong with it. However, in the phrase of Paul Ramsey, man is the soul of his body just as much as he is the body of his soul.[46] To say that one can sin only against man's soul (his freedom) and not against his body appears to presuppose an inadequate anthropology. This false dualism will be discussed at greater length in the essay on genetics.

However, some contemporary Catholic theologians are aware of the difficulty of stating that sexual relationships outside marriage are always and everywhere wrong. The more historical and relational approach that characterizes contemporary moral theology is more willing to see exceptions in absolute norms. I personally do see occasions where sexual intercourse outside marriage would not be wrong, but the exceptions are quite limited. Others have argued that sometimes sexual relations for the engaged couple would not be wrong, but it seems to me that such people may already have made the total commitment to one another even though they have not publicly expressed this commitment in the marriage ceremony.[47] In the theory of compromise one could imagine certain situations in which sexual relationships outside marriage would not be wrong. Also in view of proper medical experimentation and knowledge, sexual intercourse outside marriage would not seem always wrong (although by no means do I intend to justify all that is presently being done along these lines).

The theologian is also aware that many young people have a difficult time in seeing generally accepted teaching on premarital sexuality. Perhaps they are blinded by the immediacy of their own situation. Or could it be that they are saying something to the professional theologian? Theologians will have to continue grappling with these questions.

This essay has attempted to show the inadequacies of the older approaches to sexual sins and their gravity and also to indicate some of the current approaches to sexuality in general and to particular sexual problems. Although these inadequacies do not necessarily call for a total rejection of the older teaching, many aspects of the older approach must be rejected. The very fact that theologians are more certain about the insufficiencies of the past than the approaches of the present is most revealing. Although uncertainty and greater hesitation will characterize the theological approach of the future, the moral theologians must continue their consideration of ethical methodology and its bearing in the area of sexuality.

NOTES

1.

For a non-technical but well-balanced approach to sexuality from within a Catholic context, see Sidney Cornelia Callahan, *Beyond Birth Control* (New York: Sheed & Ward, 1968).

2.

Thomas Aquinas, *Summa Theologiae, Ia Ilae,* q. 91, q. 94. Josef Fuchs, *Natural Law,* tr. Helmut Reckter and John A.

Dowling (New York: Sheed & Ward, 1965), distinguishes both an ontological and a noetic element in the Thomistic concept of natural law. For a description of natural law ethics and Thomistic ethics as deliberative rather than prescriptive, see Edward LeRoy Long, Jr., *A Survey of Christian Ethics* (New York: Oxford University Press, 1967), pp. 45-52.

3.
IIa IIae, q. 154, introduction and a. 11. E.g., H. Noldin et al., *Summa Theologiae Moralis: De Castitate,* 36th ed. (Innsbruck: Rauch, 1958), pp. 21-40.

4.
Thomas Aquinas has practically the same enumeration as found in the more recent manuals of moral theology.

5.
Ulpian's definition and theory is briefly cited in Justinian's *Digest,* 1. I, tit. I, I.

6.
For a survey of the teaching on procreation as the primary end of marriage and sexuality, see John C. Ford, S.J., and Gerald Kelly, S.J., *Contemporary Moral Theology:* Vol. II: *Marriage Questions* (Westminster, Maryland: Newman Press, 1963), 1-127.

7.
Ulpian, *loc. cit.*

8.
IIa IIae, q. 154, a. 1, *in corp.;* a. 11, *in corp.* Note that Thomas does speak about such actions as also being against right reason, but Ulpian's notion of natural law appears to have been the determining factor of what Thomas considered against right reason in this area. Lottin admits that Thomas in his attitude toward earlier definitions of natural law definitely "shows a sympathy for the formulae of Roman Law."

Odon Lottin, *Le Droit Naturel chez Saint Thomas d'Aquin et ses prédécesseurs*, 2nd ed. (Bruges: Charles Beyaert, 1931), p. 67.

9.

IIa IIae, q. 154, a. 2, *in corp*. Noldin, p. 23, like Thomas, mentions that fornication is wrong because it is against the good of offspring and the propagation of the human race. No mention is made of the unitive or love union aspect of sexuality.

10.

The historical information on the development of knowledge of human reproduction is taken from the following sources: George Washington Corner, "Discovery of the Mammalian Ovum," *Publications from the Department of Anatomy, School of Medicine and Dentistry, University of Rochester*, II (1930-33), No. 38, 401-423; Richard A. Leonardo, *A History of Gynecology* (New York: Forben Press, 1944); Harvey Graham, *Eternal Eve: The History of Obstetrics and Gynecology* (Garden City, N.Y.: Doubleday, 1955); Harold Speert, *Obstetric and Gynecologic Milestones* (New York: Macmillan, 1958).

11.

Leonardo, p. 202.

12.

The rhythm method of family planning, which is based on this comparatively recent information, only became scientifically acceptable through the independent work of Ogino and Knaus in the late 1920's.

13.

IIa IIae, q. 154, a. 4, *in corp*.

14.

Martinus DeMagistris, *Quaestiones Morales*, Vol. II (Paris, 1511), *De temperantia, Quaest. de luxuria*, fol. 54.

15.
In the historical development of the question of parvity of matter in the sixth commandment, I am following quite closely the work of Jose M. Diaz Moreno, S.I., "La doctrina moral sobre la parvedad de materia 'in re venerea' desde Cayetano hasta S. Alfonso," *Archivo Teologico Granadino,* 23 (1960), 5-138.

16.
Operum Martini ab Azpilcueta (Doct. Navarri), Vol. II (Rome: 1590), *Commentaria in Septem Distinctiones de Poenitentia,* d. 1, cap. *si cui,* n. 17. Navarrus here admits that he has found no other theologians who admit "a small venereal pleasure."

17.
Thomas Sanchez, *Disputationum de Sancto Matrimonii Sacramento,* Vol. III (Venice, 1606), lib. 9, dis. 46. n. 9. Compare this with the change made in the later editions of his work in accord with the order of Father Aquaviva—e.g., the Antwerp edition of 1626.

18.
Josephus Fuchs, S.I., *De Castitate et Ordine Sexuali,* 3rd ed. (Rome: Gregorian University Press, 1963), p. 139; Diaz Moreno, 42-47.

19.
Arthurus Vermeersch, S.I., *De Castitate et De Vitiis Contrariis* (Bruges: Charles Beyaert, 1919), n. 352, p. 357.

20.
Marcellino Zalba, S.I., *Theologiae Moralis Summa,* Vol. II: *De Mandatis Dei et Ecclesiae* (Madrid: Biblioteca de Autores Cristianos, 1953), pp. 340, 341.

21.
Diaz Moreno lists the following as arguing in favor of parvity of matter in the sixth commandment: Navarrus, Thomas

Sanchez, Cunhafreytas, John Sanchez, Marchant, Caramuel, Bassaeus, Hurtado and Verde. However, four of these authors treated the question only indirectly in the context of the question of sollicitation in confession.

22.
Diaz Moreno, 135.

23.
This statement is made by the contemporary manualist M. Zalba, p. 340. Waffelaert maintains that the opinion admitting parvity of matter was not condemned by the Pope or rejected as improbable. G. J. Waffelaert, *De Virtutibus Cardinalibus: De Prudentia, Fortitudine et Temperantia* (Bruges, 1889), n. 188, p. 303. Obviously this statement is limited to the time before Wafflelaert wrote his manual.

24.
Response of the Holy Office of February 11, 1661, concerning the denunciation of sollicitation in confession: "Cum in rebus venereis non detur parvitas materiae, et, si daretur, in re praesenti non dari (detur?), censuerunt esse denuntiandum, et opinionem contrariam non esse probabilem." *DS, 2013.*

25.
One of 45 propositions condemned by decree of the Holy Office, March 18, 1666, as at least scandalous. *D.S.* 2060. For the order issued under Clement VIII and Paul V to denounce to the inquisitors those who assert that a kiss, an embrace, or a touch done for carnal pleasure is not a mortal sin, see Zalba, p. 340.

26.
A decree of the Holy Office of May 1, 1929, withdrew from commerce the book of P.A. Laarakkers, *Quaedam moralia quae ex doctrina Divi Thomae Aquinatis selegit P.A. Laarakkers* (Cuyk aan de Maas, 1928) in which the author argued in favor of parvity of matter in the sixth commandment. For

details, see Benedictus Merkelbach, *Questiones de Castitate et Luxuria* (Liege, 1936), pp. 28-31.

27.
Fuchs, p. 139.

28.
Fuchs, p. 139; Zalba, p. 341. Bernard Häring, *The Law of Christ*, III, (Westminster, Maryland: Newman Press, 1966), p. 291, says that it would be presumptuous to place the traditional thesis in doubt.

29.
Diaz Moreno, pp. 135-137.

30.
Fuchs, p. 141. Note the emphasis here on procreation and the good of the species. The same explanation with the same emphasis is found in Noldin, pp. 16, 17 and Zalba, pp. 342, 343.

31.
The authors mentioned in note 30 all agree with this interpretation.

32.
IIa IIae, q. 154, a. 3, ad. 1.

33.
Anton Meinrad Meier, *Des Peccatum Mortale Ex Toto Genere Suo* (Regensburg: Verlag Friedrich Pustet, 1966).

34.
As an example of such assertions made by Catholic psychologists, see Frederick von Gagern, *The Problem of Onanism* (Cork: Mercier Press, 1955), p. 95; George Hagmaier, C.S.P., and Robert Gleason, S.J., *Counseling the Catholic* (New York: Sheed and Ward, 1959), p. 81.

35.
n. 51.

36.
The Pastoral Constitution on the Church in the Modern World does not mention the question of the ends of marriage and their mutual relationship in its consideration of marriage, sexuality and responsible parenthood. The addresses of Paul VI on the precise question of responsible parenthood (June 23, 1964; March 27, 1965; October 29, 1966) seem to studiously avoid the question of the relationship between the ends of marriage. Even the encyclical *Humanae Vitae* does not speak of procreation as the primary end of marriage.

37.
For one approach to the methodological question of the role of the Scriptures in moral theology from a Catholic viewpoint, see E. Hamel, S.J., "L'usage de l'Écrite Sainte en théologie morale," *Gregorianum,* 47 (1966), 53-85. For a fine summary of the use of Scripture in recent Protestant ethics, see James M. Gustafson, "Christian Ethics," in *Religion,* ed. Paul Ramsey (Englewood Cliffs, N.J.: Prentice-Hall, 1965), pp. 309-320.

38.
Pierre Grelot, *Man and Wife in Scripture* (New York: Herder and Herder, 1964), pp. 54-55.

39.
For a review of some of the moral literature on the question, consult the "Notes on Moral Theology" which generally appear every June and December in *Theological Studies.* Joseph L. Walsh, C.S.P., "Sex on Campus," *Commonweal,* Feb. 24, 1967, 590 ff., raises questions and doubts about the traditional teaching against premarital intercourse. A good summary of three different methodological approaches now current in Christian ethics to the question of premarital sexuality is found in *Sex and Morality: A Report of the British Council of Churches* October 1966 (Philadelphia: Fortress

Press, 1966), pp. 25-31. A more contextualist approach to morality would tend to be against absolute norms although not all contextualists would permit sexual intercourse outside marriage.

40.
Paul Ramsey, "A Christian Approach to the Question of Sexual Relations Outside Marriage," *The Journal of Religion*, 45 (1965), 100-113.

41.
A. Plé, O.P., "La Masturbation: Réflexions théologiques et pastorales," *Supplément de la Vie Spirituelle*, 77 (1966), 258-292.

42.
As examples of the abundant literature on homosexuality, see from a Catholic perspective: John Harvey, O.S.F.S., "Morality and Pastoral Treatment of Homosexuality," *Continuum*, 5 (1967), 279-297; Henri J. M. Nouwen, "Homosexuality: Prejudice or Mental Illness?" *National Catholic Reporter*, Nov. 29, 1967; John G. Milhaven, S.J., "Homosexuality and the Christian," *Homiletic and Pastoral Review*, 68 (May, 1968), 663-669. From other Christian perspectives: Canon D. A. Rhymes, "The Church's Responsibility Towards the Homosexual," *Dublin Review*, 241 (1967), 83-95; Morton T. Kelsey, "The Church and the Homosexual," *Journal of Religion and Health*, 7 (1968), 61-78. These more recent articles contain ample bibliography.

43.
See my article, "Dialogue with Joseph Fletcher," *Homiletic and Pastoral Review* 67 (1967), 828, 829.

44.
The crucial theological problem is if these reasons plus the question of societal needs and practices mentioned above warrant the conclusion that premarital intercourse is always

wrong. Richard F. Hettlinger accepts the arguments based on personal commitment and a connection of sexuality with procreation, but he does not conclude that premarital intercourse is always and under all circumstances wrong. However, he does not give enough attention to the question if there is a need for rules and practices because of the good of society. In general, Hettlinger exemplifies a "summary rule approach" which sees a great and important value in such rules but does not categorically state that such rules are always to be followed. Hettlinger, *Living with Sex: The Student's Dilemma* (New York: Seabury Press, 1966). See also note 39.

45.

James M. Gustafson, "Love Monism," in *Storm Over Ethics* (No place given: United Church Press, 1967), pp. 31, 32. For a summary of different opinions expressed about situation ethics which is frequently illustrated by questions of sexuality, read *The Situation Ethics Debate,* ed. Harvey Cox (Philadelphia: Westminster Press, 1968).

46.

Paul Ramsey in one of the papers in *The Vatican Council and the World of Today,* a collection of papers read at Brown University, March 15, 1966, and prepared for publication by the Secretary of the University.

47.

Dennis Doherty, "Sexual Morality: Absolute or Situational?" *Continuum,* 5 (1967), 235-253. The author tries to show in continuity with the manualist theology that voluntary insemination apart from marital intercourse is not always evil. In the question of premarital sexuality, the author limits himself to the problem of sexual relations between engaged couples.

4

Moral Theology and Genetics: A Dialogue

Through technology and science man has been able to improve his lot in this world. In the last decade science has acquired an almost undreamed of knowledge about genetics and man's genetic development. There is the definite possibility that in the future, and to some extent even now, man can eliminate deleterious genes from the human gene pool and add desirable genes which will improve human individuals and the human species. Thus there arise the ethical problems concerned with man's interference in his own evolutionary development to better the individual and the human species. There is another aspect to the problem: man may very well have to interfere in his evolutionary future to prevent a gradual and perhaps even apocalyptic deterioration of the future of the human race. Conditions in modern civilization (e.g., exposure to radiation) bring about deleterious changes in man's genetic makeup, while advances in medical science now make it possible for many genetically deficient people to live and reproduce, whereas before modern medicine such people would die and not be able to reproduce. As a result, there are more and more deleterious genes present in the human gene pool. Man may have to intervene to change the human evolutionary process just to avoid possible extinction in the future.

From the outset of the discussion, one must realize that the relationship between the scientist and the ethician is not one of opposition or exclusion. The scientist in his own field and in his daily life is constantly making ethical decisions. Many conscientious scientists, perhaps influenced by the horrible use of nuclear power, believe they have a duty to make all of us cognizant of the possibilities that lie ahead in the area of human genetics. Man should be prepared for such possible developments so that all the people in our society can have a part in determining how man will handle the genetic powers that he has now and might have in the future. All of us humans should be grateful for such attitudes on the part of many scientists. The ethician or moral theologian, on the other hand, does not claim to be a more moral person than any other in society. The ethician tries to study the way in which men make their decisions and to point out those choices he believes to be right, good, or fitting. (It is difficult to choose a particular word, for different ethical systems would look at it differently). The Christian ethician looks at a particular problem in the light of the Christian understanding of man, his life and his world. All people are required to constantly make ethical judgments; the professional ethician tries to criticize and analyze human decisions. Although the ethicist and the scientist have different roles, their functions should be complementary and not antagonistic.

To discuss the problems raised by the possible genetic patterning of man, one must first know the scientific facts— the possibilities and the needs; but, unfortunately, many competent scientists disagree on a variety of issues. The theologian can only note such disagreement, since he is incompetent to judge the conflicting opinions. First, the actual situation. Is the genetic future of the human species in danger because of a deleterious gene load in our population? Hermann J. Muller, the late Nobel prize winner, takes a quite pessimistic view: "Thus it is evident that under modern conditions, so long as the dying out is seriously interfered with, human populations must become ever more defective in their genetic constitution, until at long last even the most sophisticated techniques available could no longer suffice to save men from their biological corruptions."[1]

The position advocated by Muller appears to be a minority opinion in the writings on the question. Theodosius Dobzhansky is not as pessimistic about the human future, even though he does admit the problem created by deleterious gene mutations coupled with the fact that modern medicine allows genetically deficient people to live and reproduce. The majority opinion believes that more positive factors, both of a cultural and even of a biological nature, will more than outbalance these negative considerations. "Man is a product of his cultural development as well as of his biological nature. The preponderance of cultural over biological evolution will continue or increase in the foreseeable future."[2] In the meantime, man does not have enough knowledge to act in the way envisioned by Muller.

Even if there is no need to intervene in human evolution in the very near future to divert a genetic apocalypse, the ethical problems raised by the fact that man can better the human species still remain. First, it is necessary to briefly summarize the ways in which modern science can now or might be able in the future to control and direct human evolution through genetics. Although various authors employ diverse terminology, we will speak of three generic types of approach: eugenics, genetic engineering and euphenics.[3]

Eugenics is simply described as good breeding. From a more technical viewpoint, eugenics is described as the selection and recombination of genes already existing in the human gene pool. Negative eugenics aims at removing the deleterious genes from the gene pool. Positive or progressive eugenics tries to improve the genes existing in the gene pool.

The biologists quite generally admit that negative eugenics will have little or no effect in reducing the load of genetic defects in the human species. Recessive genetic defects are generally carried in heterozygotes and thus escape detection. Even if one could detect such recessive genetic defects in heterozygotes, the very fact that most people have some such recessive genetic defects would make it practically impossible to eliminate them from the human population. Negative eugenics is a matter of real concern on a more personal basis in considering problems of the immediate family. Through genetic counselling, a couple may be provided with information which at times should convince them not to marry, or at least not to have children. If a couple knows that the chances are one out of four that their child will be mentally retarded and two out of four that the child will be a carrier of such retardation, there seems to be a strong moral argument not to have children. In addition to voluntary decisions, there could also be laws forbidding such people to marry or also laws requiring the sterilization of some genetically defective people. The compulsory aspect and the interference by the government in the reproductive lives of human beings, however, raise moral problems about such solutions in these cases.

Positive eugenics embraces a much more ambitious program for the betterment of the human species. Hermann J. Muller and Julian Huxley think that in the future there may be other means available, but at the present time man must use the means for improving and saving the human species which are already available. Muller proposes that sperm banks be established to store the frozen sperm of men of outstanding characteristics. A panel would decide, preferably after a waiting period of twenty years, which sperm should then be used. Women would then be artificially inseminated with this sperm, and the whole genetic future of man would improve. Muller even looks forward to a veritable utopia of never ending progress in the development of the human species. Although in his later writing he does still occasionally mention such wide scale utopian schemes and plans, he talks more of the small number who would voluntarily accept such a practice in the beginning. This small group would then serve as an experiment for future development.[4]

A more radical approach, which is not yet possible in men, has been suggested by Joshua Lederberg and others. Lederberg speaks of clonal reproduction which, like Muller's suggestion, would begin with the genetic types now known to be strong and make sure these types would be reproduced in great numbers in the future. Clonal reproduction would replicate in an a-sexual way already existing genotypes. Now science can remove the nucleus from a fertilized frog's egg and replace it with a nucleus from one of the cells of a developing embryo (part of the problem is that the genes must not be already differentiated as is the case in most cells). The fertilized egg thus develops into a frog which is the genetic twin of the frog from which the nucleus of the cell was taken. Cloning would thus be an even surer way than artificial insemination of insuring that genetically gifted people continue to exist and multiply in the future.[5]

A second generic type of approach has been called genetic engineering, genetic surgery, algeny, or transformationist eugenics as distinguished from selectionist eugenics.

The aim of genetic engineering is to change the genes in such a way as to eliminate a certain deleterious type (negative) or to improve the genotype (positive). Genetic engineering aims at changing a particular molecule in the complex structure of the gene. At the present time, science does not have the finesse necessary to change a very specific molecule in the complex structure without affecting other molecules. However, in the future, man may be able to direct genetic mutations. Genetic engineering also embraces the phenomena of transformation and transduction. In transformation scientists are now able to take a strain of bacteria not containing a certain genetic property and introduce this property with the DNA extracted from another strain. Transduction tries to transfer such properties through a virus. Such experiments have already been successful with bacteria. However, there are tremendous problems of specificity, directivity and efficiency which must be overcome before genetic engineering could be a possibility on human beings. Also, the fact that human traits have a polygenic base greatly complicates the problem. The individual diversity of every human being tends to make some scientists quite pessimistic about the future possibilities of genetic engineering. Others, however, think it remains a real possibility even though it might be many years away.

A third generic type of improving the human species has been called euphenics. Euphenics is somewhere between eugenics and euthenics or environmental engineering. In the past and probably even more so in the future human development occurs primarily because of man's intervention in and control over his environment. Lederberg has proposed euphenics as that part of euthenics concerned with human environment. Euphenics aims at the control and regulation of the phenotype rather than the genotype. This would involve all efforts at controlling gene expression in man without changing the genotype and thus would not involve hereditary changes. Eye glasses to correct poor vision is one example; insulin for diabetes sufferers is another. Lederberg believes there are a number of areas in which medical science should proceed: accelerated engineering in the development of artificial organs; development of industrial methodology for synthesis of specific proteins; eugenic experiments with animals to produce genetically homogeneous materials for spare parts in man. Lederberg was arguing in 1962 that priority should now be given to euphenics and then later to long-range eugenic concerns of the human genotype.[6] Also, there is the future possibility that man will know how to switch on and off different genes at specific periods of development and greatly change the individual.

In general, these are the various ways in which it might be scientifically possible for man to interfere in and direct his own human development. At the present time, the only available positive means which might be efficacious are the positive eugenics proposed by Muller. Many scientists would agree with Paul Ramsey, the Christian ethicist from Princeton, that the means that are now possible raise more moral problems than the forms of genetic engineering possible in the future.[7] Many scientists, in fact the majority writing on the subject, are also unwilling at the present time to accept the proposals of Muller on both scientific and moral grounds. The majority of scientists are raising these questions today primarily for discussion so that in the future man is not suddenly confronted with these problems without having thought of any way to cope with them.[8] This essay too will follow that general approach and consider primarily the various elements in the discussion which raise problems not only about the ethical use of this scientific power, but also raise methodological questions for moral theology itself. First, the area of moral theology.

II.

At first it might seem strange that possible advances in man's control over his heredity should raise problems for moral theology itself. History, however, reminds us of the dangers of a totally *a priori* theological approach to newer developments in science. Theology is not totally settled once and for all, but itself is in a continual process of growth and change. Moral theology as the study of Christian man and his actions is constantly in dialogue with the empirical and social sciences to try to understand better man and his actions. This section will develop three dangers that a theological methdology must avoid, or more positively, three emphases that must be present in any theological approach to the problems raised by man's possible power over his own future development.

The first emphasis that must be present in the approach of moral theology is a greater appreciation of historicity and historical consciousnes. Catholic theology, in many ways following the lead of Protestant theology, first adopted an historical perspective through the renewal of the study of Scripture. The Scriptures as the Word of God in the words of men are historically and culturally limited documents. Theology has also learned from the mistakes of the liberal Protestant movement in the nineteenth and twentieth centuries in assuming an overly simple identity between the historical experience of the contemporary interpreter and the first century biblical witness.[9]

The notion of historicity or historical development has been employed by some theologians to show that the teachings of Gregory XVI and Pius IX in the area of religious liberty were not contradicted by the later teachings of Vatican II. In the light of the historical contexts of the times, both teachings could be correct in their own circumstances.[10] John

Courtney Murray saw the primary reason for the different approaches to religious liberty in the different understanding of the role and function of the state in the nineteenth and twentieth centuries. Perhaps those theologians who have been defending the teaching of the nineteenth century popes on religious liberty have been somewhat too indulgent in explaining the total difference in terms of historicity.[11] But at least Catholic theology is realizing the need for an historical understanding in its approach.

The growth and progress of modern civilization in all areas, not only in science and technology, have made contemporary theology more aware of historical growth and change. Changes in politics, science, economics and sociology cannot remain unreflected in approaches to moral theology. Philosophy today illustrates the greater emphasis on historicity in many of its contemporary trends such as process philosophy. According to Rahner, theology's possibility of error is ultimately rooted in its historical character.[12] The very fact that contemporary advances in the science of genetics raise problems and dangers for moral theology is another indication of the historicity of theology itself.

A more historically conscious theology will tend to have a different concept of man himself—a concept that is more open than closed. Man is not totally determined by a fixed nature existing within him. The genius of modern man is his ability toward self-creation and self-direction. Man is constantly open to a tremendous variety of actions and options. Any theological position based on a closed concept of human nature as being something already within man to which he must conform himself and his actions will be an inaccurate understanding of the human reality and tend to result in unacceptable moral conclusions. Thus the predominant concept can no longer be an immutable and unchangeable nature, but rather the concept of historicity. Notice that historicity provides both for continuity and discontinuity, thus avoiding the extremes of an immobile classicism or the complete discontinuity of sheer existentialism.

In the area of questions raised by the possible drastic developments in genetics, the theologian must be ever mindful of the need for an historical approach; but he must also avoid the danger of uncritically accepting every new scientific possibility as being something necessarily human and good.

The progressive eugenics proposed by Muller would call for the separation of procreation and the love union aspect of sexuality. Christian ethics has generally maintained that these two aspects are joined by the design of the Creator and Redeemer, and man cannot separate what God has joined together. However, there is a methodological problem in proving such a fact by merely citing the first chapters of Genesis in which the unitive and procreative nature of human sexuality is taught. Obviously, the teaching of Genesis is quite historically conditioned. Can the theologian merely extrapolate from the circumstances of Genesis and make an absolute and universal norm for the understanding of human sexuality? There are definite dangers in that approach.

Paul Ramsey argues against the plan proposed by Muller precisely because it breaks the bond between the procreative and the love union aspects of sexuality. Ramsey, however, does not base his argument primarily on Genesis, or creation, or nature. Ramsey argues primarily from the "Second Article of the Creed" as specifying the Christian concept of creation and conjugal love in the Prologue of John's Gospel and the fifth chapter of the Letter to the Ephesians. Just as the creative and redeeming act of God is a life-giving act of love, so human sexuality is both procreative and loving. Ephesians 5 contains the ultimate reference for the meaning and nature of conjugal love.[13] It seems, nevertheless, that the teaching which Ramsey finds in Ephesians 5 might also be historically conditioned.

I do believe that at the present time in our circumstances sexuality has its proper expression, value and meaning in the marital realm within which the procreative and love union aspects of sexuality are joined together. However, one can envision a possibility in which greater values might be at stake and call for some type of altering the way in which Christian marriage now tries to preserve these important values. For example, if the dire predictions of Muller were universally accepted and mankind did face a genetic apocalypse in the near future, then the entire situation might be changed. It seems that even the Scriptures witness many cases in which the understanding of marriage had to be changed because of the conditions of the times (e.g., polygamy). Ramsey himself does admit some possible relativity in his teaching by saying that there might be some redeeming features in Muller's proposals, but this is not "sufficient to place the practice in the class of morally permitted actions."[14] I agree with Ramsey's understanding of things as they are at present, but his argumentation and his prospects in the future do not seem to give enough place to historicity.

A second danger in the approach of moral theology to genetics is the danger of an individualistic methodology and the failure to emphasize the communitarian and societal dimensions of reality. Christian thinking deserves much credit for upholding the dignity of the individual which in many ways is also the foundation of our modern society, although at times Christian practice has not always lived up to Christian theory. Today, however, man is much more conscious of his communitarian nature and his relationships with all other people and the world. The approach of moral theology will have to balance more adroitly the proper claims of the individual with the claims of society. The Christian notions of *agape, koinonia,* and the reign of God all seem to be more open to communitarian and social understandings. Problems facing contemporary man in politics, sociology and economics all show a greater role being given to the communitarian, the social and the cosmic. Moral theology cannot employ models that are exclusively individualistic or narrowly interpersonal.[15]

In the past, moral theology has been somewhat ambivalent about the tension between the individual and the community. In many areas the approach has been too individualistic; whereas there were other instances in which too much stress was placed on the power of the community over the rights of the individual. For example, theologians affirmed the obligation of the defendant to publicly admit his guilt which denied the right of the individual not to incriminate himself by admitting his own guilt.[16] Also, the failure to accept religious liberty shows an unwillingness to accept the total freedom and dignity of the individual.

The area of social ethics furnishes an example where Catholic theology was too individualistic in its approach. Perhaps such an emphasis can be explained in the light of a reaction to communism and socialism. Lately some Catholics have become upset at the papal call for socialization which they look upon as an invasion of the rights of the individual. Pope John, in his social encyclicals, emphasized the social aspect while still preserving the legitimate claims of the individual by basing his social ethics on the two principles of subsidiarity and socialization. These two principles try to keep in tension the legitimate demands of the individual and society.[17] The same danger of individualism can be seen in the overemphasis on private property in some Catholic teaching. The social teaching of Leo XIII acknowledged the social aspect of property, but it was not emphasized. Today, Catholic theology is stressing the social aspect of property because the goods of creation exist primarily for all mankind. *Progressio Populorum* of Paul VI well illustrates the more communal and social emphasis required today.[18]

Too individualistic a concept of man has also affected Catholic understandings of medical morality, especially as this was influenced by the principle of totality. Pope Pius XII developed the principle of totality in many of his discourses on medical matters. According to the principle of totality, the individual may dispose of the members or functions of his body for the good of the whole, but a part may be sacrificed "only when there is the subordination of part to whole that exists in the natural body."[19] Pius XII wrote in the context of totalitarian governments, and was very careful to deny that by virtue of the principle of totality the government had power over the life of the individual, for the individual is not merely a part of the totality which is the state. At times, Pius XII limited the application of totality to physical organisms with their physical unity or totality.[20] Thus the principle of totality cannot be used to justify the transplantation of organs or experimentation for the good of others, since in this case the strict relationship of part to physical whole does not exist. Some Catholic theologians went further and denied that organic transplantation or experimentation for the good of others was morally permitted.[21] Other theologians justified such practices, however, either by introducing other principles (e.g., charity) or by attempting to expand the principle of totality itself.[22] Thus the principle of totality, at least in its narrower understanding and application, apart from other considerations, can overly emphasize the individual at the expense of other aspects of reality.

Perhaps the area of greatest disagreement in the past between the medical ethics proposed by Catholics and other ethical theories concerns the generative organs. In accord with the understanding of the generative organs and functions of man as existing for the good of the species, as well as for the good of the individual, the principle of totality would not justify the direct suppression of the generative organs or functions for the good of the individual. This results in the condemnation, among other things, of direct sterilization. However, if the totality of the person is somewhat enlarged to consider "his relationship to his family, community and the larger society," then one could find a justification at times for direct sterilization.[23] Or one could justify direct sterilization by talking about the marital union and relationship itself as a whole or a totality. Again, notice the dangers of applying too individualistically the principle of totality without taking into account other important aspects.

The present historical situation calls for a greater understanding of man as existing in community with other persons intertwined with many different relationships. The task for moral theology is to develop a methodology which does justice to the communitarian, social and cosmic needs of the present without falling into a collectivism. The ever growing consciousness of the one world in which we all share has tended to underline the need for a more communitarian approach. The economic problems of England and the United States affect the whole world; the fashions of Paris become available all over the world; the political decisions in Moscow and Washington have repercussions around the world. Science through its many steps in controlling our environment has affected many people.

Precisely in the area of genetics and heredity the individual realizes the existence of other responsibilities which limit his own options and freedom. Traditional Catholic theology has recognized some limitations in this area. The older manuals of theology spoke of the primary end of marriage which included the procreation and education of offspring. Responsible parenthood is a moral imperative for couples, and responsible parenthood entails some responsibility for the children who will be born and to the race itself. Genetic reasons at times should compel a couple not to marry or not to bring children into the world. If offspring have a one out of four chance of being severely retarded and a two out of four chance of becoming carriers of severe retardation, it seems the couple have a moral obligation to refrain from having children.

What about the possibility that the community might positively intervene to prevent and prohibit such marriages? In the past, Catholic theology has been willing to accept like practices. The impediments to marriage in the Code of Canon Law include even impediments like consanguinity which may even have been based on some eugenic reasoning. Another question arises about the compulsory sterilization of certain classes of people. I believe that this interference with the individual person is not called for today, especially without a first attempt to employ genetic counseling on a wide scale. Most scientists writing in this area are also somewhat unwilling to propose such compulsory measures. There also looms in the minds of many the abuses of power to which such practices would be susceptible.

The very complexity of the problem will in the long run call for some community control. In other areas of human life the more power that an individual has and the more complex things become, the greater is the need for community intervention and control. Things from the right of people to fly their own airplanes to the rights of people to hunt and fish, to say nothing of the daily questions in the order of economics, politics and education, have required some type of community control. The very power which science and genetics can bring into existence must be under some greater control than the individual can provide. In the not-too-distant future, there may well be need for some type of community control in the area of genetics and heredity. What if man acquires the power to determine the sex of his children? Tremendous problems could very easily result for society if the proportion between the sexes was greatly affected. This would have ramifications in just about every other sector of human existence. The stability of families and the basic social structure of our society would be somewhat threatened. Society could not allow an unbalanced proportion of the sexes to exist for a long time. What could be done? Society could forbid its members to use such means of determining the sex of their children, or it could set up an elaborate system of control. Obviously there will be many problems no matter which choice is made. The point is that society may very well have to make such a choice. Nor can one avoid the problem by merely condemning the research that might lead to such power. I am not euphoric at the prospect of controlling such power, but it is man's creative challenge to use it for his betterment despite all the inherent human limitations.

My contention is that the complexity and interrelatedness of human existence, plus the tremendous power that science may put into the hands of men, are going to call for a more communitarian and social approach to the moral decisions facing our society.

A third required emphasis in the approach of moral theology to questions raised by man's control over his own hereditary future concerns the dominion and the power which man has over his own life. Christian thought has constantly emphasized that man does not have complete dominion over his own life. Man is the steward of the gift of life he has received from the Creator; man's final destiny lies outside and beyond this world. On the other hand, man is the glory of creation and the greatest sign of God's handiwork in this world.

Today more than ever in the past man is conscious of the power that he has over his own life and his own future. Catholic theologians do not hesitate to say that man today is his own self-creator, for in a sense man is unfinished and capable now of creating himself. The power of self-creation has always been rooted in the spiritual power of man himself —a truth recognized by Thomas Aquinas. Thomas does not hesitate to see man as an image of God precisely because he is "endowed with intelligence, free will, and a power of his actions which is proper to him . . . having dominion over his own activities."[24] Thanks to the marvels of science, man is now able to extend this dominion into many other facets of his existence.

The Christian attitude toward man tries to balance or even hold in dialectical tension the two aspects of man—his greatness precisely because he is free and the guide of his own development on the one hand, and his creatureliness and sinfulness on the other hand. Corresponding to these two aspects of human existence are what the older theological tradition has called the two capital sins of sloth and pride. Harvey Cox has pointed out that too frequently we forget that the great sin of man is sloth or the failure to take responsibility for the world which is his to make.[25] Although at times sloth has been an often neglected aspect of Christian life, Cox and others cannot forget the terrible evils connected with pride through which men have used all kinds of power —social, economic, political, military, and even religious—to pursue their own particular ends and gain advantage over others.[26] The proper Christian approach must be cognizant of both these aspects in man's use and abuse of the power and dominion which is his. Just as Cox has at times overemphasized sloth and neglected pride, Paul Ramsey, especially in his writing on genetics, seems to overemphasize *hubris* or pride. "In fact it may be said that the ethical violations we have noted on the *horizontal plane* (coercive breeding or nonbreeding, injustice done to individuals or to mishaps, the violation of the nature of human parenthood) are a function of a more fundamental happening in the *vertical* dimension, namely *hubris,* and playing God."[27] Certainly Ramsey is correct in seeing that some genetic proposals do fail to take account of the limitations and sinfulness of man; but one cannot deny that since man does have a greater dominion over his life and future today, there is the danger of man's not using responsibly the dominion or power he either has now or may possess in the future.

Although I agree with most of Ramsey's conclusions on the questions of genetics at the present time, I believe he does not give enough importance to the aspects of historicity and the greater dominion which man has today. Both of these differences stem from a basic theological stance because of which I would attribute greater importance to man's own efforts in cooperating with the building of the new heaven and the new earth. This difference raises the fundamental problem for the Christian ethicist of ethics and eschatology. Ramsey views eschatology primarily, and sometimes exclusively, in terms of apocalypse: "Religious people have never denied, indeed they affirm, that God means to kill us all in the end, and in the end He is going to succeed. Anyone who intends the world as a Jew or as a Christian—to the measure in which this is his mode of being in the world—goes forth to meet the collision of planets or the running down of suns, and he exists toward a future that may contain a genetic Apocalypse with his eyes fixed on another *eschaton.* . . ."[28] Ramsey rightly emphasizes the aspect of apocalypse or discontinuity between this world and the next against the naive progressivists who see the future age in perfect continuity with the present. However, it seems that Christian eschatology includes three aspects, all of which have to be retained if one is going to have a proper understanding of the relationship between this world and the next: the teleological, the apocalyptic, and the prophetic.[29] By stressing just the apocalyptic, Ramsey fails to give the due but limited importance to man's efforts in cooperating with God in bringing about the new heaven and the new earth. Although Ramsey may emphasize exclusively the apocalyptic aspect of eschatology because of his polemic with the humanistic, progressive mentality which sees man as bringing about the blessed future through his own efforts and technology, nevertheless, his entire ethical theory seems to rest on an eschatology which overly stresses the apocalyptic. Precisely because of such an eschatology, Ramsey sees Christian ethics based on the model of deontological ethics rather than the model of teleology or responsibility.[30]

Man does have more dominion over his life today than he has ever enjoyed in the past—a fact that has already had a great impact on Catholic moral theology. The dissatisfaction with some explanations of natural law theory, especially as illustrated by arguments against artificial contraception, stems from the fact that man now has the power and ability to interfere with the physical and biological laws of nature. Scientific and technological progress have given man a greater power over both his life and death so that today Catholic theologians even acknowledge "the right to die."[31] Obviously this approach raises questions about the argument against euthanasia which were discussed in Chapter Two. All these indications point out the need for theologians to be very precise and cautious in applying the notion of man's limited dominion over his life to the theological questions raised by advances in genetics. The contemporary Christian does have greater dominion and control over his life, although the creature will never have complete dominion over his life and future.

III.

This paper will now criticize from a viewpoint of Catholic moral theology some of the attitudes seen in various approaches of scientists. Especially in the proposals of Muller there is a utopian outlook on the future, although in his later writings, Muller appeared to be somewhat less utopian than in his earlier writings. His proposals were scaled down somewhat to an experimental nucleus, but his overall goal remained. "By these means the way can be opened up for unlimited progress in the genetic constitution of man to match and reinforce his cultural progress, and reciprocally to be reinforced by it, in a perhaps never-ending succession."[32] Muller advocates the use of sperm banks and artificial insemination of women with this superior semen because there are no other means available at present. He does not think other techniques of genetic surgery will be available until the twenty-first century, if then; but such genetic surgery may very well "do much better than nature has done."[33]

Muller does recognize an element of the tragic in man, but he believes many of the problems could be overcome by progressive eugenics. "Thus, men grievously need the Golden Rule, but the Golden Rule grievously needs men in whose very nature it is more deeply rooted than in ours. These men would not require the wills of saints, for their way of life would be normal to them. They would take it for granted, and could live full wholesome lives, joyously carrying out the ever greater enterprises made possible for their strengthened individual initiative, working hand in hand in free alliance with their enhanced cooperative functionings. At the same time their personal relationships would be warmer and more genuine, so that they could enjoy more of the love that gives itself away. Along with this, less forcing would be required of them in extending their feelings of kinship to those more remote from their contacts."[34]

The Christian vision of man and his world cannot accept any utopian schemes. Modern life and science do give man much greater dominion than he had before, but man remains a creature and a sinner. The final stage of the reign of God is in the future and not totally continuous with man's present existence. Although in the past, many Christians may have been guilty of what has been called "eschatological irresponsibility," since they forgot about the possibility of bringing about a relative justice here and now, contemporary Christians can never forget the transcendent aspect of the reign of God which is his gracious gift to us. Science and technology can do much to help man, but they cannot overcome the creatureliness and sinfulness which mark man in the Christian perspective.

Christian theology has also learned from its own history the dangers of utopian thinking and the temptations of a naively optimistic outlook on human growth and progress. Some Roman Catholics naively looked to the past and saw a romantic utopia in the thirteenth, the greatest of centuries. Liberal Protestantism less than a century ago made the mistake of thinking that man could bring about the kingdom of God in this world by his own work and effort. Christian theologians are chastened by the remark (in my judgment too negative and critical) of H. Richard Niebuhr about such attempts to bring about the reign of God in this world. "In this one-sided view of progress which saw the growth of the wheat, but not that of the tares, the gathering of the grain, but not the burning of the chaff, this liberalism was indeed naively optimistic. A God without wrath brought men without sin into a kingdom without judgment through the ministrations of a Christ without a cross."[35] Christians should realize the important contributions that science can make, but the Christian knows only one Lord and Messiah—Christ Jesus. Biology or genetics will never completely overcome man's inherent limitations.

The ambitious genetic proposals of Muller (sperm banks) and Lederberg (cloning) would call for large scale changes in our contemporary society if they are to be successful even from a biological viewpoint. Lederberg points out that a system of tempered clonality would be necessary to provide for the variety and adaptability necessary if the human gene pool is to progress. Thus some people would reproduce clonally and some sexually.[36] Among the many problems that would arise for both Muller and Lederberg would be the selection of the ideal types. Who is to decide? What criteria are to be employed? How do we know if a person will do as well in a different type of environment? Why is it that many children of geniuses have not made great contributions themselves? Even Muller agrees that men would have a difficult time selecting the ideal person and what characteristics he should have. Commentators occasionally note that Muller himself changed his opinion about who would be ideal types. In 1935 he claimed no woman would refuse to have a child by Lenin, but a later list leaves Lenin out of the acceptable "fathers."[37] All these problems are raised to illustrate the complexities that are often not given sufficient attention by the proponents of such approaches.

Human history seems to confirm the Christian understanding of human limitation and sinfulness. Even if man does acquire such tremendous power over genetics and his heredity, there is every indication that such power will not always be used for the good of all mankind. History shows that man uses his power for evil as well as for good: the horrible use of eugenics by totalitarian regimes still is a clear and horrendous memory in the minds of many people. Industrialization has brought about a tremendous increase in economic power, but such power probably has been used more often to exploit rather than to help poor people and poor nations. Scientists themselves frequently have pangs of conscience over the uses made of nuclear power. Even the seemingly neutral

accomplishments of technology reveal the ambiguity con-
comitant in human existence. The automobile has brought
with it many contributions to a more human life; but it has
also brought with it staggering accidental death tolls, air
pollution, the disruption of poor people from their homes
and the spoiling of natural beauty. A good number of people
in our country today, to say nothing of the total world, are
dissatisfied with both the foreign and domestic policies of the
government. Have dominance and self-interest not played
the greatest roles in the shaping of our foreign policy? Does
the priority of certain domestic programs indicate a true will-
ingness to share the goods of our society with others or rather
an attempt to make sure that the gulf widens between the
"haves" and the "have nots" in society? The very thought
that our genetic planners would be of the same type as our
domestic, economic, political, and foreign policy planners
does not augur for a utopia on the way.

Catholic theologians generally admit the axiom that abuse
does not take away the use. Preliminary discussion and
planning might help to eliminate some possible abuses, but
some will always remain. History again indicates that as
more solutions are found, further questions and problems
will also arise. Utopia will always be outside the reach of
man. It is important to note that the vast majority of the
scientists writing on this issue disavow the utopian proposals
put forth, for example, by Muller. Also in fairness to Lederberg, he has not to my knowledge advocated the proposal of
clonal reproduction although he does mention it as a very
likely possibility, if and when it is biologically possible.
Lederberg and others believe it is their obligation to inform
the general public about the problems all of us might be
facing in the not too distant future.

A second danger found in the writings of some scientists is
the identification of the scientific with the human, but the
human includes much more than just science and technology.

A fortiori a Christian view of man embraces more than the limited horizon of science and technology, for the scientific approach to a particular question is only a partial aspect of the whole reality. The scientific and the human do not necessarily coincide, thus there exists a potential source of conflict. This danger was pointed out by Pope Pius XII in an address to the First International Symposium on Genetics in 1953.[38] The very fact that man is scientifically capable of doing something does not mean that it should be done, for man must control the evolution and development of science. Too often one has the impression that it is science and technology that are going to control man. Men today are somewhat aware of the need to give human direction and guidance to technology. Just because our nation has the ability and knowledge to send a man to the moon does not mean that such projects should have priority over more pressing human needs. Just because science can keep a dying man alive for a few more hours, does not mean that such means should be employed. At times there are important human values involved which should not be sacrificed for the good of any science.

Such a narrowness of view does seem to color some of the writings of Muller. Muller argues that man should use the means now available, a progressive eugenic program through sperm banks and A.I.D. rather than wait for the genetic surgery which might be available in the next century. His argumentation is most revealing. "The obstacles to carrying out such an improvement by selection are psychological ones, based on antiquated traditions from which we can emancipate ourselves, but the obstacles to do so by treatment of the genetic materials are substantive ones rooted in the inherent difficulties of the physico-chemical situation."[39] Notice that the only substantive obstacles are those rooted in the biological order.

Muller dismisses the obstacles in the way of his progressive eugenics program as merely "psychological ones based on antiquated traditions." Thus there seem to be no obstacles that stand in the way of scientific development and scientific goals other than those things to which science has not as yet found a suitable answer. However, it does seem there can be and there are important human values which would stand in the way of the geneticist on some occasions. I am sure that not even Muller would allow the scientist to experiment on man the same way in which he experiments on bacteria. Elsewhere Muller refers to the primary obstacle standing in the way of the adoption of his eugenic program, as the attitude of "individual, genetic proprietorship, or pride of so-called blood."[40] But many people see in these obstacles very important human and moral values, since parenthood and family bonds are more than antiquated traditions. For the Christian, the bond between procreation and love union is more than a mere arbitrary arrangement even if one can envision certain historical situations in which it might be sacrificed for greater values.

The narrowness of vision of one who sees all reality through the eyes of an individual science can be illustrated by the consequences that such a program might have on many other facets of human existence. A sociologist, for example, would have some very significant aspects to add to the total human picture. Marriage and family serve important functions and roles in our contemporary society. If sexual behavior is separated from reproduction, why should there be any regulation of sexual behavior at all? Muller's plan would raise grave problems for the psychologist who would then have to try to find some substitute for the stability and deep personal relationships which are now provided for in marriage and the family. For the ethician all these things also constitute important moral values. To the extent that a scientist fails to see all these other aspects or dismisses them as antiquated traditions, the scientist shows the narrowness and the ultimate "a-humanness" of his own vision.

The third danger follows from what has been said about the difference between the scientific horizon and the ultimate human horizon. The scientific and technical world view reality primarily in terms of effects and performances; they are success oriented and thus totally interested in results and effects. Thus there arise several sources of conflict with the human and the Christian horizon. The first potential area of difference concerns the ultimate reason for the dignity of the human person which, from the Christian perspective, cannot be measured in terms of utility or performance. The greatness of human life stems from the free gift of the loving God of creation. The Christian notion of love modeled on the love of Yahweh for his people and Christ for his Church indicates that the ultimate reason for the lovability of a person does not depend on his qualities or deeds or successes or failures; in fact, the covenant commitment of God to his chosen people appears as a sheer gift, especially in the light of the constant infidelities of his people. The Christian view of man does not see his value primarily in terms of what he does or can do for himself or others, but in terms of what God has first done for him.

On the level of ethical theory, an overemphasis on the importance of effects leads to a theory of consequentialism. In such a theory there remains the difficulty of judging the hierarchy of the different consequences and also the difficulty in that man can never know all the consequences of his actions. But even more fundamental is the danger of seeing all moral values in terms of consequences so that the model of the means-end relationship becomes centrally normative. Our basic human intuitions reject the manipulative spirit that tries to use everything as a means for a further end; e.g., we react against people "using friends" or "using other human lives," etc. Thus, especially in the area of genetics Ramsey has pointed out the need for an ethic of means as well as an ethic of ends, since there are certain values that cannot be sacrificed as means for certain other ends.[41] Pius XII, in his 1953 address, likewise pointed out the danger of making a good end justify any means.[42] However, in Catholic moral theology there has been a tendency to view the means-end relationship in too physical a manner and to forget that on occasion the end truly specifies the means.[43]

Most scientists are aware of the possible collision of values and other problems arising from the difference between the human and the scientific horizons. Some scientists, for example, see no problem in performing certain experiments on plants or animals, but they would not do such experimentation on man. Lederberg himself has brought up the problem of the first experiment in genetic surgery and especially the first attempts to clone a man.[44] One cannot experiment on human beings in the same way that one experiments on bacteria. This problem of experimentation will become even more acute in the future. This problem will be faced long before the problems created by the use of new techniques for directing the human evolutionary process.

The same problem has another face. The scientists I have read readily admit the dignity of man, and they constantly emphasize that nothing should be done to man without his consent. This respect for human dignity is admirable. Again, however, I would agree with Ramsey in pointing out that man is the body of his soul just as much as he is the soul of his body.[45] In more modern terms, man is not merely his freedom but also his corporality. One can offend against man not only by violating his spirituality, but also his corporality. There is the danger of a neodualism that sees man only as spirit. The very fact that a man consents to something does not mean that the act is thus necessarily right. Such a principle is rejected in our jurisprudence which holds that a man cannot give up his inalienable rights even if he consents to do it. Too often today in many ethical problems one hears the saying that there is nothing wrong with it provided that everybody agrees and consents. Unfortunately, the Catholic tradition has tended to make the biological normative, but the opposite extreme of paying no attention to man's corporality also goes against human dignity precisely insofar as it is human

IV.

This paper has tried to raise some of the dangers both from the viewpoint of theology and the viewpoint of biology which will be present in the future discussions about man's control of his evolution. Since the scientists themselves and especially Ramsey have given extensive ethical criticisms of some of the genetic proposals, this paper concentrated more on the problems such genetic questions raise for moral theology or Christian ethics.[46] I agree with most scientists that now is the time to begin discussing these important issues. In the meantime, it seems that voluntary negative eugenics should be encouraged through a more widespread use of genetic counseling. The majority of the scientists themselves who have written in this area do not believe that the program proposed by Muller should be put into practice even from the limited viewpoint of biology. From the moral viewpoint, I agree that such a program should not be adopted now. In my view, whatever the future brings, it will not be a utopia. Scientific advances will also bring problems and difficulties especially in the control of such great power that man will have. However, these problems are not sufficient reason to stop all experimentation and work toward acquiring a greater power over man's heredity and genes. In the experimentation and continual probing, it will be necessary to respect human dignity and not totally subordinate the individual to the goals of scientific advancement. Since man may have such power within a century, it is not too early to continue in a more structured way the dialogue which has already been initiated.

NOTES

1.
Hermann J. Muller, "Better Genes for Tomorrow," *The Population Crisis and the Use of World Resources,* ed. Stuart Mudd (The Hague: Dr. W. Junk Publishers, 1964), 315. For most of Muller's articles and addresses in the field of genetics before 1961, see *Studies in Genetics: The Selected Papers of H. J. Muller* (Bloomington, Ind.: Indiana University Press, 1962).

2.
Theodosius Dobzhansky, "Changing Man" *Science* 155 (1967), 409. Dobzhansky (411) maintains that we do not have enough knowledge to be sure of the value, even from the biological perspective, of mankind freed from all genetic loads. For a fuller explanation of his thought, see Dobzhansky, *Mankind Evolving* (New Haven: Yale University Press, 1962). Others who also are not as pessimistic as Muller and maintain the need to wait for more knowledge include: S. E. Lurie, "Directed Genetic Change: Perspectives from Molecular Genetics," *The Control of Human Heredity and Evolution,* ed. T. M. Sonneborn (New York: Macmillan, 1965); John Maynard Smith, "Eugenics and Utopia," *Daedalus* 94 (1965), 487-505; Curt Stern, "Genes and People," *Perspectives in Biology and Medicine* 10 (1966-67), 500-523; and many others.

3.

In the preparation of this paper, in addition to the bibliography already mentioned, the following studies from the scientific viewpoint were helpful:—E. Shils, et al., *Life or Death: Ethics and Options* (Seattle: University of Washington Press, 1968); Frederick Osborne, *The Future of Human Heredity* (New York: Weybright and Talley, 1968); John D. Roslansky, ed., *Genetics and the Future of Man* (New York: Appleton-Century-Crofts, 1966): T. M. Sonneborn, ed., *The Control of Human Heredity and Evolution* (New York: Macmillan, 1965); Gordon Wolstenholme, ed., *Man and His Future* (Boston: Little, Brown, and Co., 1963). Also, Leonard Ornstein, "The Population Explosion, Conservative Eugenics, and Human Evolution," *Bulletin of the Atomic Scientists* 23 (June 1967), 57-60; Joshua Lederberg, "Experimental Genetics and Human Evolution," *Bulletin of the Atomic Scientists* 22 (Oct. 1966), 4-11; James F. Crowe "The Quality of People: Human Evolutionary Changes," *Bioscience* 16 (1966), 863-867; N. H. Horowitz, "Perspectives in Medical Genetics," *Perspectives in Biology and Medicine* 9 (1965/66), 349-357; Roland D. Hotchkiss, "Portents for a Genetic Engineering," *Journal of Heredity* 56 (1965), 197-202; T. M. Sonneborn, "Genetics and Man's Vision," *Proceedings of the American Philosophical Society* 109 (August 1965), 237-241; Sonneborn, "Implications of the New Genetics for Biology and Man," *A.I.B.S. Bulletin* 13 (April 1963), 22-26. (A.I.B.S. is the American Institute of Biological Sciences).

4.

Later articles by Muller include: "Genetic Progress by Voluntarily Conducted Germinal Choice," *Man and His Future*, 247-262: "Means and Aims in Human Genetic Betterment," *The Control of Human Heredity and Evolution*, 100-123. Julian Huxley, *The Humanist Frame* (London: Allen and

Unwin, 1961): *Eugenics in Evolutionary Perspective* (London: Eugenics Society, 1962); *Essays of a Humanist* (New York: Harper and Row, 1964).

5.
Lederberg, *Bulletin of the Atomic Scientists* 22 (Oct. 1966), 4-11.

6.
Joshua Lederberg, "Biological Future of Man," *Man and His Future*, 263-273.

7.
Paul Ramsey, "Moral and Religious Implications in Genetic Control," *Genetics and the Future of Man*, 153.

8.
This conclusion is based on the works cited above and is the same conclusion reached by James M. Gustafson in reviewing *Life or Death: Ethics and Options* in *Commonweal* 89 (4 Oct. 1968), 28.

9.
Lloyd J. Averill, *American Theology in the Liberal Tradition* (Philadelphia: Westminster Press, 1967), 125-127.

10.
Roger Aubert, "La liberté religieuse du Syllabus de 1864 a nos jours," *Recherches et Débats* 50 (1965), 13-25. Among Murray's many writings, see especially for this aspect, John Courtney Murray, S.J., *The Problem of Religious Freedom* (Westminster, Md.: Newman Press, 1965).

11.
Etienne Borne, "Le problème majeur du Syllabus: vérité et liberté," *Recherches et Débats* 50 (1965), 26-42.

12.
Karl Rahner, S.J., "The Historical Dimension in Theology," *Theology Digest*, Sesquicentennial Issue (1968), 30-42.

13.
Ramsey, *Genetics and the Future of Man*, 145-147.
14.
Ibid., 159.
15.
Johannes B. Metz, "Relationship of Church and World in the Light of a Political Theology," *Theology of Renewal* II, ed. L. K. Shook, C.S.B. (New York: Herder and Herder, 1968), 255-270; Metz, "The Church's Social Function in the Light of a Political Theology," *Concilium* 36 (June 1968), 2-18.
16.
Patrick Granfield, O.S.B., "The Right to Silence," *Theological Studies* 26 (1965), 280-298; 27 (1966) 401-420.
17.
John F. Cronin, S.S., *The Social Teaching of Pope John XXIII* (Milwaukee: Bruce Publishing Co., 1963).
18.
For a fine summary of this changing emphasis, see Edward Duff, S.J., "Property, Private," *New Catholic Encyclopedia* 11, 849-855.
19.
Gerald Kelly, S.J., *Medico-Moral Problems* (St. Louis: Catholic Hospital Association, 1958), 247.
20.
Acta Apostolicae Sedis 44 (1952), 786; 48 (1956), 461.
21.
Gerald Kelly, S.J., "Pope Pius XII and the Principle of Totality," *Theological Studies* 16 (1955), 373-396. A summary and applications of the principle of totality are found in Kelly, *Medico-Moral Problems*, 8-11; 245-269. Kelly on the basis of other moral principles would allow organic transplants and experimentation for the good of others. Note that Kelly

wrote before the address of Pius XII in 1958 in which Pius developed and extended the principle of totality: "To the subordination, however, of the particular organs to the organism and its own finality, one must add the subordination of the organism to the spiritual finality of the person himself." *A.A.S.* 50 (1958), 693, 694.

22.
For an interpretation which broadens the notion of totality in the light of Pius' 1958 discourse, see Martin Nolan, O.S.A., *The Principle of Totality in the Writings of Pope Pius XII* (Rome: Pontifical Gregorian University, 1960).

23.
Martin Nolan, O.S.A., "The Principle of Totality in Moral Theology," *Absolutes in Moral Theology?*, ed. Charles E. Curran (Washington: Corpus Books, 1968), 244.

24.
*I*ª*II*ᵃᵉ, Prologue.

25.
Harvey G. Cox, *On Not Leaving It to the Snake* (New York: Macmillan, 1967), "Introduction: Faith and Decision" and throughout the book.

26.
E.g., Reinhold Niebuhr, *Moral Man and Immoral Society* (New York: Charles Scribner's Sons, 1933 and 1960); *Love and Justice: Selections from the Shorter Writings of Reinhold Niebuhr*, ed. D. B. Robertson (Cleveland: Meridian Books, 1967), especially 46-54.

27.
Paul Ramsey, "Shall We Clone a Man?" an address given at a conference on "Ethics in Medicine and Technology" sponsored by the Institute of Religion at the Texas Medical Center and by Rice University, Houston, Texas, March 25-28,

1968. Professor Ramsey kindly sent me a copy of his address. This problem of the greater dominion possessed by modern man who still remains a sinful creature is recognized by Leroy Augenstein, *Come, Let Us Play God* (New York: Harper and Row, 1969).

28.
Ramsey, *Genetics and the Future of Man*, 136.

29.
Harvey Cox, "Evolutionary Progress and Christian Promise," *Concilium* 26 (June 1967), 35-47; M. C. Vanhengal, O.P., and J. Peters, "Death and Afterlife," *Concilium* 26 (June 1967), 161-181.

30.
Paul Ramsey, *Deeds and Rules in Christian Ethics* (New York: Charles Scribner's Sons, 1967), 108-109.

31.
John R. Cavanagh, "*Bene Mori:* The Right of the Patient to Die with Dignity," *Linacre Quarterly* 30 (May 1963), 60-68. This right follows from the traditionally accepted principle that man does not have to use extraordinary means to preserve his life.

32.
Muller, *Studies in Genetics*, 590.

33.
Muller, *The Control of Human Heredity and Evolution*, 109.

34.
Muller, *The Population Crisis and the Use of World Resources*, 332.

35.
H. Richard Niebuhr, *The Kingdom of God in America* (New York: Harper and Row, 1937; Torchback, 1959), 193.

36.
Lederberg, *Bulletin of the Atomic Scientists* 22 (Oct. 1966), 9-10.

37.
E.g., M. Klein, *Man and His Future*, 280.

38.
A.A.S. 45 (1953), 602, 603.

39.
Muller, *The Control of Human Heredity and Evolution*, 100.

40.
Muller, *The Population Crisis and the Use of World Resources*, 323.

41.
Most of the points briefly mentioned in this third danger have been developed at greater length by Ramsey in various articles and books, although I would again disagree with the eschatology sometimes expressed in these contexts. On consequentialism in general, see *Deeds and Rules in Christian Ethics*, especially 176-225. His two essays on genetics develop the need for an ethic of means.

42.
A.A.S. 45 (1953), 605, 606.

43.
William H. van der Marck, O.P., *Toward a Christian Ethic* (Westminster, Md.: Newman Press, 1967), 48-69.

44.
Lederberg, *Bulletin of the Atomic Scientists* 22 (Oct. 1966), 10. Ramsey develops the point at great length in his paper on cloning.

45.
Ramsey, *Genetics and the Future of Man*, 155-157.

46.
Since this paper was first presented, two other ethical studies of the question have appeared. Edward Manier, "Genetics and the Future of Man: Scientific and Ethical Possibilities," *Proceedings of the American Catholic Philosophical Association* 42 (1968), 183-192, develops mostly the scientific aspect with just a brief summary of Waddington's and Ramsey's positions without any critical analysis. Roger Shinn in a paper read at the January 1969 meeting of the American Society of Christian ethics did raise some of the methodological questions treated at greater length in this essay.

5

Social Ethics
and Method
in Moral Theology

Social ethics raises important methodological questions for moral theology or Christian ethics. This study will consider two such questions: What is the source or what are the sources of ethical wisdom for the Christian ethicist? How does the moral theologian use the Scriptures?

I.

The first question has generally been phrased in this way: Is there a source of ethical wisdom existing apart from the explicit revelation of God in Christ in the Scriptures? Catholic moral theology has answered the question in the affirmative with its teaching on natural law. However, the distinction between nature and supernature as found in most Catholic theological manuals appears today to be woefully inadequate. Nature and supernature are not two layers that can be totally separated from one another. The inadequate and misleading distinction between nature and supernature calls for a theological recasting of the natural law theory as mentioned in Chapter Two. But such a theory did have the merit of recognizing the existence of ethical wisdom apart from the explicit revelation of God in the Scriptures.

Some forms of Protestant ethics have denied the existence of ethical wisdom and knowledge apart from the Scriptures. Traditional emphases in Protestant theology tend in that direction. The *sola Scriptura* notion if pushed to an extreme denies the existence of ethical wisdom apart from the Scriptures. Stress on sin and corruption of sin leaves little or no room for a source of ethical wisdom existing outside the Scriptures. Without the saving intervention of God in Christ man is totally under the corrupting force of sin. The Protestant emphasis on justification by faith alone also tends to play down the activity and the work of man.[1]

These and other themes have led especially in the Lutheran tradition to such ethical teachings as the distinction between law and gospel and the two realms or two kingdoms theory. Law has the primary function of revealing to man his own sinful state. Law also has the function of trying to keep sin in check. The corruption of sin is ever present and law serves as a dike trying by coercion to keep sinful man in check. But law or justice in no way points out how the Christian is to act in his daily life.[2] The two realms or the two kingdoms theory separates man's inner relationship with God from all other political and social relationships in which he is involved. Man's relationship with God is a question of gospel under the Church. All other social relationships are governed by the law and have no relationship to the gospel and God. The two realm theory thus separates man's daily life in the world from the gospel and man's relationship to God in Christ.[3] Reinhold Niebuhr has sharply criticized such an ethical approach.

"By thus transposing an 'inner ethic' into a private one and making the 'outer' or 'earthly' ethic authoritative for government, Luther achieves a curiously perverse social morality. . . . He demands that the state maintain order without too scrupulous a regard for justice; yet he asks suffering and nonresistant love of the individual without allowing him to participate in the claims and counter-claims which constitute the stuff of social justice."[4]

Today the older Protestant positions are being abandoned and there seems to be a growing consensus favoring the existence of what John C. Bennett has called "common ground morality."[5] Both practical and theoretical reasons arising from social ethics have shown the need for a common ground morality existing apart from the explicit revelation of God in the Scriptures. In a pluralistic society Christians must act with others for the good of society and of the entire human race even though these others do not share Christian beliefs. The race and the peace movements in the United States have shown that Christians and non-Christians share very similar viewpoints on many important social questions. The very fact that Christians constitute a minority of the world's population calls for the need for cooperation with others if conditions in our modern world are to be changed. Christians share with many non-Christians identical views on the need to overcome world poverty, the elimination of discrimination, the protection of the rights of individuals. Life in a pluralistic society shows both the need and the possibility of a source of ethical wisdom existing outside the explicit revelation of the Scriptures.

Theoretical reasons for the existence of a source of ethical wisdom outside the explicit revelation of God in the Scriptures stem from the insufficiencies of the Scriptures, the realization that Christianity must have positive meaning for man and the world, and the very complexity of modern social problems. The Scriptures themselves are limited in many ways. The historical and cultural circumstances reflected in the Scriptures differ considerably from contemporary circumstances. Occasionally the scriptural teaching is now seen to be merely the incorporation of a very culturally determined concept—e.g., the inferiority of women. The prohibition of oath taking, the prohibition of interest taking, the relationship of master to slave all raise important questions about the understanding of these things in our contemporary society. The moral teaching of the Scriptures frequently is seen primarily in the light of individual relationships. However, social ethics raises vexing problems of a very complicated nature which require more than general admonitions. The Scriptures give little concrete help for the contemporary problems of sharing the wealth of creation in a more equitable manner, creating a community of nations, the control of populations, adequate medical care for all men, the right of man to make genetic mutations, etc. Thus the insufficiencies of the Scriptures in the area of social ethics are apparent. The Christian ethicist finds a theological basis for such ethical wisdom existing apart from the Scriptures especially in the notions of creation, incarnation, and cosmic redemption.

There is a source of ethical wisdom which is shared by all men. This fact has important ramifications for methodology in moral theology. There are a plurality of ways into the ethical problem, and all of Christian morality can not be reduced to merely a specifically Christian concept. In the terminology employed by Frankena and followed by Paul Ramsey any form of mere agapism is not sufficient.[6] *Agape* or whatever is chosen as the distinctive aspect of Christian ethics is not the only source of ethical wisdom for the Christian. Mixed agapism realizes there is another way into the ethical problem for the Christian other than the distinctively Christian aspect found in the Scriptures whether this aspect is referred to as *agape* or *koinonia*. Social ethics thus points up the insufficiencies of any love monism, for one cannot reduce all moral theology to one distinctively Christian aspect.

The complexity of problems in social ethics not only calls for a source of ethical wisdom apart from the revelation of the Scriptures, but also argues for the need of different starting points in ethics. In this context James Gustafson has pointed out the danger in speaking of principles vs. context since Christian ethics embraces four different approaches— perceptive analysis of the social situation, theological affirmations, moral principles, and a conception of Christian existence. Although different approaches to Christian ethics will emphasize one of these aspects more than the others all four approaches need to be present in any adequate Christian ethical methodology.[7]

Perhaps today the statement of the question is significantly shifting. Especially within the context of Protestant theology the question was: Is there a source of ethical wisdom existing apart from the explicit revelation of the Scriptures? Today theologians are more often proposing the following question: What distinctive element does Christian ethics bring to bear on the social problems facing contemporary man? The question becomes even more acute when one realizes from history that the Roman Catholic Church, for instance, has often seemed to impede true human development and growth.

Christians find themselves frequently agreeing with many non-Christians and disagreeing with fellow Christians on many of the major issues of the day. On particular issues and problems there may be no appreciably different Christian approach. The distinctively Christian aspect above all appears to be a viewpoint or horizon with which the Christian views reality. Creation, sin, incarnation, redemption, and resurrection destiny made proleptically present in the resurrection of Jesus characterize the Christian view of reality. Human history is viewed in some relationship with the reign of God in Christ. Human history derives its ultimate meaning from such a relationship.

The Christian vision criticizes present reality and the social structures of society in the light of the reality of human sinfulness and the resurrection destiny accomplished first in Christ Jesus. Contemporary theology again stresses eschatology, and realizes that the Christian is now striving to cooperate in the building of the new heaven and the new earth which is ultimately the gift of the Lord of history at the end of time. In the past, Christian theology has used eschatology and its view of the future in such a manner as to deserve the charge of "eschatological irresponsibility." In the light of future existence little or no attention was given to the present. However, the reign of God as his eschatological activity is already operative in human existence and going forward to its final stage at the end of time. A proper understanding of eschatology serves as a criterion by which the Christian realizes the insufficiencies and shortcomings of every human and social structure. Sin and lack of fullness will always mar any human structure. The Christian vision thus makes the Christian sensitive to the shortcomings and sinfulness of the present structures and urges him to change those structures. The Christian can never be content with the present. The present always manifests the sinfulness and the limitations of the times in between the two comings of Christ. Thus the Christian is constantly conscious of the need for social reform and never willing to absolutize any structure or institution existing in the present.

The "eschaton" is here now and pressing forward to the new heaven and new earth, which is God's gift fully to be realized at the end of history. Emphasis on eschatology has been accompanied by an emphasis on hope and a stress on the future. The God of Israel and the God of the Christians is an Advent God—one who comes. The Christian God is the God of presence and promise. The Christian lives sustained by the hope and the promise of the resurrection. Christians involved in the struggle for social justice and the shaping of a better world will experience suffering, frustration, and perhaps even death itself. But his resurrection is our hope. The Christian commitment to the world is sustained and carried forward by the hope that despite sin, suffering, and death itself God will bring to completion the work of building the new heaven and the new earth.

The Christian should view the present social structures of society with an uneasy conscience and realize the need to work to reform them. In hope he commits himself to this task with all the problems inherent in it. Does the Christian vision exhaust itself in this form of negative criticism and in supplying a firm commitment to the work of renewal of social structures? Does Christian ethics have any uniquely positive contribution to make in the constant reform of social structures? I believe that Christian ethics can in a positive way add to the content of social ethics. A Christian will formulate social goals which will definitely differ from approaches of those who have a mechanistic view of man. Likewise the Christian vision stresses certain fundamental dispositions which should characterize the person himself. Different norms and directives for action could result from such a different view of man and his goals in society. However, theory and practice indicate that very often the non-Christian and the Christian will come to the same ethical conclusions in questions of social morality.

How can one explain this very frequent agreement between Christians and non-Christians on matters of social ethics? An older theology saw the area of nature as the common ground with non-Christians, whereas scriptural revela-

tion added the distinctively Christian element. Since social
ethics pertain to the area of justice which in the Thomistic
scheme refers primarily to the reality of things (*medium rei*),
there should be vast areas of agreement between Christians
and non-Christians. There is an aspect of truth in this approach, but contemporary theology realizes there is no such
thing as the natural, for the world and all mankind participate in the mystery of Christ. In one way or another all men
are offered the gift of salvation which the Christian finds in
the mystery of Jesus the Christ; therefore, it is possible for
the "anonymous Christian" or the "implicit Christian" (in
the terminology of some theologians) who has never heard
of Christ Jesus to come to a knowledge of God's loving gift
and the response required of him. For the Christian, however, the Scriptures and Christ Jesus remain the privileged,
but by no means the only way, in which God reveals himself
to us.

The realization that the Christian shares a great deal of
ethical wisdom with all men raises questions not only for the
methodology of Christian ethics but also for the approaches
of Christian Churches to problems of social ethics. If the
Christian Churches merely adhere to the biblical message,
then they can say nothing meaningful and relevant to a particular moral problem of great import. On the other hand, if
the Christian Churches become too specific and too doctri-
naire or authoritative on a particular approach to a moral
question, then they risk separating a member from the Christian community because of reasons that are not peculiarly
Christian.[8] It would seem that the Christian Churches must
speak out on particular moral problems facing society, but
with the realization that a detailed approach is one Christian
approach to the question and appears to be the solution most
in keeping with the contemporary understanding of the

Christian message without claiming any absolute certitude about such specific problems. The Christian Churches thus have a two-fold mission: to preach the basic moral message of change of heart and also to advocate those changes of structure in society which enable men to live a more human life in this world. In tension-filled times there is a danger that the Christian Churches might forget one of the two functions that they should serve today. The central moral message of conversion embraces not only the need to change men's hearts but also the need to change the structures of society.

II.

Social ethics also raises for moral theology the methodological question of the role and function of the Scriptures. In general, Catholic theology has justly been criticized for not emphasizing enough the scriptural aspect in its moral theology. The Pastoral Constitution on the Church in the Modern World tries to give a specifically Christian approach to the various questions treated and constantly emphasizes cosmic redemption as well as creation. William Lazareth is grateful for such an attempt but still faults the Pastoral Constitution for not always employing such an approach.[9] However, the question is far from solved by merely saying that Catholic moral theology must be more biblically oriented.

One of the major theological problems today is the question of biblical hermeneutics.[10] How does the Word of God in the Scriptures become meaningful and directive for contemporary man living in such diverse historical and cultural circumstances? In addition to the general hermeneutical problem there is a specific hermeneutical problem in moral theology. How does the Christian ethicist look at the moral teaching of the Scriptures? In general, I believe that the ethical theory employed by the ethicist definitely colors his view of the moral teaching of the Scriptures.

Philosophical ethics has frequently been divided into the two categories of teleological or deontological ethics. H. Richard Niebuhr has employed the two symbols of man the maker and man the citizen which coincide somewhat with the more technical philosophical distinctions.[11] The image of man the maker stresses the goal or the end which man strives to achieve by his actions. Man the maker discovers what is the good and then acts to achieve it. Other philosophers reject such an image precisely because man does not really have the control and the ability to dispose of the ends and means as he sees fit. Thus the political image of man the citizen is more accurate in their estimation than the technical image of man the artisan. The primary question for man is: To what laws should I assent and against which laws should I rebel? The image of man the maker emphasizes the good and what man must do to obtain it. The image of man the citizen emphasizes obedience, law, and duty, for the good is subordinate to the right.

Both models of ethical methodology have been used by Christian ethicians in their approach to the Scriptures. The model of man the maker tends to see in the Scriptures the plan of God for man and the world and how man is to act in achieving his goal and destiny. The Sermon on the Mount, for example, becomes the plan that points out the good for the Christian who strives to incorporate the ethical directives of the Sermon in his daily life. The Social Gospel School employed such an approach and the same general theme is present in the biblical ethic proposed by Reinhold Niebuhr.

The model of man the citizen adopts a more prescriptive form of ethics with emphasis on duty, right and obligation. Existentialist ethics with an emphasis on decision furnishes a good example of an act-deontological theory.[12] The ethics of Rudolf Bultmann well illustrate the model of man the citizen or the deontological approach. Bultmann sees the Scriptures as calling the Christian to make a decision in radical obedience to God.[13] Some of the neo-Orthodox approaches to ethics with their stress on the transcendence of God also emphasize man's obligation to obey the divine imperative.[14] However, the approach of some neo-Orthodox theologians also shows the presence of a different ethical model.

H. Richard Niebuhr argues for a third ethical model with the emphasis on responsibility. Man the responder, man in dialogue with other men, with his environment, with his world, and with the One, corresponds to a more modern view of man as constantly in interaction with others and the world.[15] H. Richard Niebuhr has had a great impact upon Christian ethics in the United States.[16] Niebuhr adopted the image of man the responder for philosophical reasons, but there are other reasons for adopting such an approach in interpreting the ethical teaching of the Scriptures.

The neo-Orthodox approach to the Scriptures contains important elements that favor the ethical image of man the responder. Karl Barth reacted against religion as a creation of man's own needs and desires. Christianity begins not from man's thoughts about God but rather from the revelation of God in the Scriptures. The Scriptures do not reveal a morality but rather speak about the activity of God in Christ. The Scriptures are not a source book of moral propositions and rules but rather the revelation of the activity of the living God. Thus the moral life of man is his response to the person of Jesus and the activity of the living God.[17]

Perhaps Paul Lehmann best illustrates the approach to the Scriptures in terms of the ethical model of man the responder. Lehmann begins his work by realizing the problem created by the hermeneutical question. Lehmann cannot accept a concept of the good as the starting point of Christian ethical reflection. "To put it somewhat too sharply: Christian ethics is not concerned with *the good,* but with what I as a believer in Jesus Christ and as a member of his Church, am to do. *Christian ethics, in other words, is oriented toward revelation and not toward morality.*"[18] The author of *Ethics in a Christian Context* also rejects the will of God as the starting point of Christian ethics. "In short, what God requires is meaningless apart from the dynamics of the divine activity, and the dynamics of the divine activity define the context within which 'all this commandment' is to 'be righteousness for us,' indeed, is to be carefully done" (p. 78). The Scriptures tell us what God is doing in the world to make and keep human life more human. The primary question is not: "what does God command?" but, "what does God do?" Christian ethics is concerned with revelation rather than morality. Christian ethics considers the indicative and not the imperative. In a Christological ethics of messianism the important question is what God is doing in the world to make and keep human life more human. It is in the *koinonia,* the fellowship of the Church, that the individual learns what God is doing to make and keep human life more human. Lehmann thus never develops a biblical ethic as such.

How should moral theology approach the Scriptures? The model of man the responder does seem to be a more congenial approach. The complexity of social ethics argues against the seemingly more simplistic approach to man the maker or man the citizen. Since the cultural and historical circumstances of the Scriptures differ so much from the contemporary situation, it is difficult to see in the light of the Scriptures the good which man should strive for in contemporary social ethics and how he can best achieve his goals today. The same complexity argues against the use of the model of man the citizen. In addition a deontological approach tends to downplay the creativity and initiative of man which are so characteristic of our ageric society.

However, there is a danger in insisting upon the model of man the responder to the exclusion of many valuable insights contained in the other models. It seems to me that Paul Lehmann is guilty of such an exclusive emphasis. Man the responder tries to do what is fitting, but such an approach must also see the good and the right in terms of the fitting. Christian ethics is concerned with the imperative as well as the indicative, with morality as well as maturity. In the past Christian ethicians perhaps did speak too easily and too quickly about the good or the right as it was found in the Scriptures. However, ethical discourse cannot continue speaking always and only in the indicative. The Christian is under the imperative to continue in time and space the creating, redeeming, and reconciling activity of God in Christ. Also the Scriptures do point out the general characteristics that mark the response of man in all the evolving moments of history. The ethical thrusts of the scriptural descriptions of the Christian life must be incorporated in any Christian ethic. The Christian ethician seems justified in approaching the Scriptures in terms of the model of man the responder provided that he does not entirely neglect the elements present in the models of man the maker and man the citizen.

The ultimate source of the differences I have with Lehmann is theological, for in the context of the Catholic tradition I believe more importance should be given to man the responder and to his reason in determining what that response should be.

The Scriptures cannot be used as proof texts to show that a particular action is always to be done. The complexity of social ethics militates against such a simplistic approach. If the Scriptures and man's understanding of contemporary reality do sensitize him to what God is doing in the world and what response man should make, there still remains the question of how the contemporary Christian knows precisely what God is doing in the world today. Lehmann emphasizes the *koinonia* as the context in which the Christian comes to know what God is doing in the world. However, Lehmann does not seem to show adequately how the Christian does determine what is the fitting response in this situation. Perhaps his promised second volume treating of specific issues will shed light on this problem. Another possible approach might be to develop the traditional notion of the discernment of spirits. How does the Christian know what the Spirit is calling him to do in a given situation? Perhaps there can be a fruitful ecumenical dialogue on how the Christian does discern the call of the Spirit in moral judgments.

The model of responsibility and of man the responder also seems to properly emphasize the fact that Christian ethics is a religious ethic. Man acts in response to and through the loving kindness of God in Christ. In the other ethical models there is the danger of forgetting that Christian ethics is ultimately a religious ethic and not just a pelagian effort at self-improvement. But the model of man the responder in interpreting the Biblical ethic is insufficient if it does not also consider the good and the right. Within the horizon of man responding to the creative, redeeming, and recreating activity of God in Christ, the Christian tries to understand the good and the right and tries to be more sensitized in his experience to the action of God in the world in the many complex ways in which such action takes place.

What are the criteria by which the Christian should judge his proper response in building the new heaven and the new earth? In establishing such criteria the ethicist needs the help of common ground morality and philosophical understandings of man and his world. This paper has already pointed out the impossibility of any love monism. The whole of the ethical question for the Christian cannot be reduced to the distinctively Christian aspect. The Scriptures retain a primary place for the Christian ethicist, but the Scriptures without other human wisdom remain inadequate for construing an adequate methodological approach to Christian ethics or moral theology.

NOTES

1.
For a critique of such themes by a Protestant ethician, see James Sellers, *Theological Ethics* (New York: Macmillan, 1968).

2.
Martin J. Heinecken, "Law and Gospel," *Dictionary of Christian Ethics,* ed. John Macquarrie (Philadelphia: Westminster Press, 1967), pp. 193-195.

3.
Roger Mehl, "The Basis of Christian Social Ethics," in *Christian Social Ethics in a Changing World,* ed. John C. Bennett (New York: Association Press, 1966), pp. 47-50.

4.
Reinhold Niebuhr, *The Nature and Destiny of Man, II* (New York: Scribner, 1964), pp. 194-195. Other Protestant ethicians are more positive in their interpretation of the two realm theory.

5.
John C. Bennett, "Issues for the Ecumenical Dialogue," *Christian Social Ethics in a Changing World* (New York: Association Press, 1966), p. 337.

6.

Paul Ramsey, *Deeds and Rules in Christian Ethics* (New York: Scribner, 1967), pp. 117-120. Ramsey maintains that natural law ethics or an ethics based on the orders of creation are the usual examples of mixed agapism although there may be other forms of mixed agapism in which some other type of revealed wisdom is joined with agape.

7.

James M. Gustafson, "Context versus Principles: A Misplaced Debate in Christian Ethics," *Harvard Theological Review*, 58 (1965) pp. 171-202.

8.

Paul Ramsey considers this problem confronting the Churches and their social teachings in *Who Speaks For the Church?* (New York and Nashville: Abingdon, 1967).

9.

John Reuman and William Lazareth, *Righteousness and Society: Ecumenical Dialog in a Revolutionary Age* (Philadelphia: Westminster Press, 1967), p. 196.

10.

For a fine summary of the debate in the present century on the hermeneutical problem, see Carl E. Braaten, *History and Hermeneutics, New Directions in Theology Today, II* (Philadelphia: Westminster Press, 1966).

11.

H. Richard Niebuhr, *The Responsible Self* (New York: Harper & Row, 1963), pp. 47-56.

12.

William K. Frankena, *Ethics* (Englewood Cliffs, N.J.: Prentice Hall, 1963), p. 21.

13.

Thomas C. Oden, *Radical Obedience: The Ethics of Rudolf Bultmann* (Philadelphia: Westminster Press, 1964).

14.
Emil Brunner, *The Divine Imperative* (Philadelphia: Westminster Press, 1947).

15.
Niebuhr, pp. 55ff.

16.
See *Faith and Ethics: The Theology of H. Richard Niebuhr,* ed. Paul Ramsey (New York: Peter Smith, 1957).

17.
In the exposition of such an approach to the Scriptures, I am following closely the excellent study of James M. Gustafson, "Christian Ethics," in *Religion,* ed. Paul Ramsey (Englewood Cliffs, N.J.: Prentice Hall, 1965), pp. 309-320. However, the criticisms mentioned in the following paragraphs are my own.

18.
Paul L. Lehmann, *Ethics in a Christian Context* (New York: Harper & Row, 1963), p. 45.

6

Afterword: Moral Theology Today

The strong negative reaction to the papal encyclical *Humanae Vitae* condemning artificial contraception brings to the fore the two major problems facing moral theology today: moral methodology and the teaching function of the Church in moral matters. The ecumenical aspect of all theological scholarship today is also emphasized by the fact that in the current literature these are the major problems facing Protestant ethicians.[1] Methodological problems are central in most sciences today because of the new and different circumstances in which we are existing. The first section on moral methodology will briefly summarize the positive approaches mentioned in the earlier essays and then criticize other approaches in moral theology which have appeared in the preceding studies or which are present in the contemporary literature.

MORAL METHODOLOGY

The methodological question in Christian theological ethics surfaces most perceptibly in the recent debate over situation ethics, but the same question lies behind the need to develop a Christian social ethic to come to grips with the problems confronting our society today. One of the difficulties in the recent situation ethics debate has been the predominant place given to more individualistic ethical problems with a resultant one-sided methodological approach which is not adequate in the area of social ethics. Methodological questions, especially in view of a more inductive approach in general, cannot be considered merely in an abstract and *a priori* fashion, for there exists a reciprocal relationship between ethical theory and the concrete problems of human existence.

The essays in this volume have argued for a more historically conscious methodology but have not fully developed any one particular methodological approach. These studies have shown the inadequacies of past approaches—especially the concept of natural law found in the manuals—and have indicated some ways (e.g., personalism, relationality, transcendental methodology) in which newer methodological approaches are being developed. This appears to indicate the state of the discipline of moral theology today. However, these essays have developed some more particular approaches to the problems arising in the contemporary debate, since theology is constantly confronted with these questions even while searching for more adequate overall methodological approaches. There are in my view three different and complementary ways of coming to grips with the problems raised in the debate over situation ethics. First, there remains a meaningful and important distinction between the objective and subjective aspects of morality, which results from the complex nature of the human act itself and its multiple relationships. This approach develops the concept of invincible ignorance proposed in the manuals and recognizes the need for a morality of growth according to which the person here and now for a number of reasons might not be able to do what the fullness of objective morality requires.[2] The greater complexity of human existence today and the increased realization of the many psychological and sociological factors limiting man argue for a greater use of this approach although realizing that other factors (e.g., the good of other persons, the good of society) must be taken into consideration. For example, in some countries polygamy has raised questions for missionaries. Should people be excluded from entry into the Church because they practice polygamy? It seems that in the world as we know it today the practice of polygamy does create a climate in which the equality and dignity of womanhood suffers. At the present time in these countries I believe that Christians can go along with the prevailing custom of polygamy while working for its ultimate change and abolition. In such an approach it is always necessary to keep in mind the existing tension, for otherwise there will be a tendency to accept the present polygamous situation as perfectly moral and normal. It appears that the early Christian Church adopted a somewhat similar approach to the question of slavery but unfortunately forgot the tension in the situation and too easily accepted slavery as a social reality.

A second distinct but complementary approach to some of the problems raised in the situation ethics debate is the theory of compromise which is based on the theological realization that sin continues to exist in man's heart and in the structures of society so that at times an individual will be prevented from doing what he would ordinarily do if it were not for the existence of sin. This theory thus takes into consideration the ambiguity and the tension which will always mark the human condition, but at the same time realizes there are certain values which cannot be sacrificed because of the existence of sin. The Christian can never rest content with the sin filled situation, for he is called through his participation in the redemption to overcome sin; but in this world the struggle against sin will never be completely successful so that a theory of compromise is necessary in Christian ethics.

A third way of approaching the problems often mentioned in the contemporary debate about ethics raises questions about and ultimately rejects the identification of the moral action with the physical structure of the act. Thus I would deny the existence of negative moral absolutes when the act is described only in terms of its physical structure.[3] As mentioned above, this calls for changes in the way in which Catholic theology has approached such problems as medical ethics, contraception, sterilization, conflict situations such as abortion solved by the principle of the double effect, euthanasia, divorce, and sexuality. The fact that it is easier to point out the deficiencies in the older approaches without being able to elaborate any systematic newer methodology remains symptomatic of the problems facing Christian ethical reflection today.

The moral methodology presented in the manuals in the Roman Catholic tradition is not the only source of difficulties in contemporary thinking in Christian ethics. I personally am in basic agreement with the thrust of the Catholic tradition which has constantly maintained that there is a source of ethical wisdom and knowledge existing apart from the explicit revelation of God in the Scriptures and that through reason man can come to some understanding of the destiny which is his in striving to build the new heaven and the new earth. But the older approach of the manuals did not properly understand the theological and philosophical limitations of human reason, did not properly relate the natural with the supernatural, and also fell into the "a-historical" error of identifying reason with just one philosophical understanding of man (the Thomist philosophy) which despite all its merits remains culturally and historically limited and unable in its totality to claim the title of the perennial philosophy. Many difficulties and errors have also surfaced in some of the contemporary responses and approaches to Christian ethics.

A first difficulty arises from a Christian vision or horizon which is too exclusive. The Christian posture or stance, a most important component in any theological ethics, as mentioned in the earlier essays, looks at reality in terms of the total Christian mystery of creation, sin, incarnation, redemption, and resurrection destiny. Christian thought in the past has frequently succumbed to extreme temptations of either an eschatological irresponsibility which has not given enough importance and value to the reality of the present or of an uncritical acceptance of the present and a naively optimistic feeling that man can bring about the new heaven and the new earth by his own efforts in the very near future. The eschatological aspect of Christianity confirms the incompleteness and limitations of the present; the Christian view of sin reminds man that sin affects all human reality.[4] Christian theological ethics must avoid the danger of a denial of transcendence resulting in an overly immanent approach. Transcendence reminds man that there is something beyond the present situation and the present life, but if properly understood in terms of eschatology also reminds the Christian of his call to cooperate in bringing about the new heaven and the new earth. Symptoms of this denial of transcendence can be illustrated by the failure of some contemporary theology to discuss certain topics; e.g., prayer, suffering, death.

Those who forget the transcendent aspect easily fall into a naive triumphalism which paradoxically shows itself in two almost diametrically opposed forms. On the one hand, there is a tendency to unquestionably and smugly accept the present and the social structures of the present as almost perfect mirrors of the reign of God and to resist and resent any efforts to change the present. On the other hand, those who rightly perceive the great limitations and sinfulness of the present sometimes live in the naive hope that by their efforts within a very short span of time they will usher in the new millennium. Both approaches suffer from the same basic triumphalism. The limitations and sinfulness of the present call for constant conversion which at times is truly revolution and rebellion against the present, but which will never perfectly succeed. The Christian living in the era of redemption and looking forward to the fullness of resurrection destiny knows that he is called upon to overcome the limitations and sinfulness of the present but with the realization that the final stage of the kingdom will come only at the end of time. The present efforts to change his heart and his world with its frustrations, setbacks, and sufferings make the Christian ever more conscious of belonging to a covenant people living in the hope of the promise that God in Christ will bring to completion the work he has begun.

A second source of erroneous approaches stems from a too exclusive emphasis on a particular aspect of what have been the traditional dichotomies or emphases in Roman Catholic and Protestant theologies. Today there is a general tendency toward convergence on these matters, but at times some of the older emphases appear in an exaggerated way.[5] Protestant theology has traditionally given more importance to faith, whereas Catholic theology has stressed the importance of works. Protestant theology has emphasized the transcendence of God and his freedom, whereas Catholic theology has upheld the goodness of natural man and his efforts. Protestant theology has underscored the freedom of the transcendent God and the Christian freedom of the believer, while Catholic theology has always admitted that man's reason is a source of truth. Catholic theology has thus developed a natural theology and a natural law, whereas Protestantism with its emphasis on the transcendence of God and the Scriptures as the sole norm of truth has downplayed and even opposed the rational and the philosophical. The earlier essays have pointed out the errors in the extreme emphasis in Catholic theology which too often has embraced Pelagianism, legalism, and an unwarranted trust in the goodness of man's reason especially as this was authoritatively interpreted by the Church.

In some contemporary Protestant ethical approaches, the traditional Protestant emphases lead to a dangerous theological actualism. This is true of the ethical theory of Barth and Bonhoeffer as well as Lehmann and Sittler in this country. In the Barthian tradition there is a severe critique of ethics as such, since ethics looks for goodness in man, his reason and his virtues; but James M. Gustafson points out that "the critique of ethics is never as drastic as the language in which it is made would sometimes lead one to think."[6] In theological ethics of this type there exists a tendency to play down the notion of obligation and the imperative as exemplified by Paul Lehmann, who speaks of the indicative rather than the imperative and phrases the ethical question in terms of what God is doing and not in terms of what man ought to do.[7] For Barth, command becomes permission because God enables us to do freely and thankfully what he requires us to do. Above all Barthian theology insists that the response of the Christian is always concrete and particular. Although the theological ethics of this approach are much more complex than some would believe, nonetheless, such ethics are ultimately too simplistic. This coincides with the judgment made on Barthian ethics by James Gustafson: "The moral actor faces exasperation if he turns to the ethics of Christ the Redeemer-Lord for some objective, authoritative answer to the question, 'What ought I to do in my situation.' "[8]

Ethicians must develop other criteria for trying to determine what God is doing in the world here and now. These other criteria developed through faith and reason will not usually furnish absolute certitude, but they should form part of the necessary process by which the ethician considers the way in which Christians make their ethical decisions. Thus in Barthian ethics, which is still present in some ethical approaches, there lurks the danger of a theological actualism which tries to perceive the concrete will of God here and now without giving enough importance to the other criteria, including those of a rational nature which the Christian must employ in trying to discern his response. As already pointed out, rational criteria in the form of norms will not often give that specific an ordering to our concrete actions, but such criteria at least can be helpful in eliminating some possibilities and establishing the area in which the concept of prudence and the role of the particular discernment of the Spirit begin to operate.

This theological actualism often brings with it an unwarranted specificity about the will of God in particular situations which reminds one of the Puritan spirit of old. Paul Ramsey has criticized statements of Protestant Churches and Protestant theologians especially in the area of social ethics for making too specific judgments about particular actions and not leaving enough room for prudence.[9] A theological actualism is logically connected with such a specific approach. This type of Protestant approach shares with an older Catholic approach the same triumphalistic spirit of claiming to know with too great a certitude what the precise will or design of God is in this particular situation. There are not only theological and philosophical problems but also ecclesiological problems connected with such specificity in the area of social ethics according to Ramsey, since there is the danger of saying that someone is acting in an unchristian way when there is no Christian criterion for making that judgment. Ramsey believes that the Churches instead of making such specific moral judgments on complex, particular problems—e.g., the war in Viet Nam—should rather concentrate on those criteria or norms, if you wish, on which all Christians can share agreement and leave the practical decisions in the area to the matter of prudence. A theological actualism easily leads to the conclusion that Christians and the Churches can easily arrive at the most complex moral decisions. Also the *ad hoc* problem-solving technique so often followed in statements by Church groups tends to concentrate on the need for very precise and particular solutions.

One can appreciate the problems connected with such a theological actualism without totally agreeing with the approach of Ramsey. Ramsey seems to argue for a distinction between "Christian moral judgments on the one hand and particular political, legal, and military judgments on the other";[10] but such a distinction is unacceptable. From a theological viewpoint all man's truly human decisions (not, for example, the purely mathematical decision) are ultimately moral and Christian decisions. Morality cannot be relegated to a limited sphere in man's life which does not include the political, legal, and military. From a practical viewpoint we have experienced the real problems created when the military or legal areas are withdrawn from the sphere of the moral.[11] Individual Christians must make very precise decisions in human life; nations and governments are called upon to make such choices. Christian theologians and the Churches should not shirk from making such judgments, but such judgments must be made in the light of more general criteria by which one moves from the very general notion to the particular decision and with the realization that such particular judgments may be wrong but seem to be the best possible response within the Christian perspective. The problem with theological actualism is the danger of coming to a very specific decision without the help of more general criteria which mediate the ultimate Christian understandings and of proclaiming such specific judgments with an unwarranted certitude which at times is reminiscent of the crusading spirit itself.

Consequentialism appears as another very real difficulty in some Christian ethics today. Paul Ramsey has accused Joseph Fletcher of being a consequentialist, for according to Fletcher morality is ultimately determined by weighing the consequences of our actions.[12] Two reasons have often been adduced in philosophical circles to show the inadequacies of pure consequentialism: no one can know beforehand all the consequences of his action, and there always remains the problem of appraising the hierarchical importance of the various consequences involved. Consequentialism appears to be a rather congenial approach in a highly technological society which is accustomed to measure success in the exclusive terms of results and consequences. Just as society must resist a purely technological approach, so too theological ethics must point out the shallowness and ultimate "a-human" character of consequentialism.

Consequentialism in an overly simplistic manner reduces all reality to the model of means and ends, but not all human reality can be made into mere means to be manipulated for various ends. Human persons, for example, cannot be treated as mere means employed and manipulated for the sake of other ends. For the Christian the thrust of consequentialism runs counter to certain basic Christian assumptions. The God-man relationship is revealed in the Scriptures in terms of the covenant, but the love of God for man depends only on God's goodness and faithfulness. Despite man's refusal and sins, Yahweh remains ever faithful to his commitment which is thus in no way dependent upon the consequent response of man. Likewise the value that Christianity attributes to man in no way depends upon his works, successes or failures. The fact that the privileged people in the reign of God are not the rich and the powerful but the poor, outcasts, children, and sinners emphasizes the fact that human worth and value do not ultimately depend on man's deeds and above all are independent of his successes. The technological and managerial spirit may judge man exclusively in terms of what he does or accomplishes, but such a judgment can never be the ultimate judgment for the Christian. Consequentialism as a success-oriented posture too easily forgets about the fact that frustration, suffering, tragedy, and ultimately death itself are important elements in the Christian understanding of human existence. The Paschal Mystery of Christ remains for the Christian the salutary reminder that immediately successful consequences are not the most important values in human existence. It is true that one could avoid the dangers of consequentialism mentioned in these paragraphs by emphasizing the Paschal Mystery and the Pauline strength in weakness, joy in sorrow, and life in death; but as a matter of fact consequentialist approaches in Christian ethics do not seem to follow such a course. There appears to be a real connection between the denial or underemphasis on the transcendent aspects of Christianity and an exclusive consequentialism.

Consequentialism accepts the fact that the end does justify the means, but the end cannot always justify the means precisely because all reality cannot be reduced to the one model of means-ends. Catholic theology, however, has erred in the past by defining the means in terms of the physical structure of the act itself and by failing to realize that in certain circumstances the end does specify the means. An example of such an erroneous approach on the part of consequentialism is the justification of the dropping of the atomic bomb as a means of bringing the war to a quicker conclusion.[13] Such problems raise the more basic question of the proper way of describing the human act. An older theology rightly stressed the importance of three elements: moral object, end, and circumstances. Consequentialism seems to forget about everything except the end. In somewhat the same way an extrinsicist or voluntaristic approach to ethics likewise overstresses the aspect of intention or end and fails to give enough importance especially to the moral object. Thus one may rightly point out that the dropping of the atomic bomb cannot be described in terms of an act of winning the war and reducing loss of life.

These considerations suggest another dangerous emphasis in some contemporary theological ethics of failing to give enough importance to the physical and material aspects of reality. It is true that an older Catholic theology erred by identifying the moral object with the physical structure of the act itself, but the opposite danger of not paying enough attention to the physical and the material aspects of reality appears in some approaches today. This contemporary neo-dualism or neo-angelism overlooks the importance of the physical and the material world, since all morality comes from outside the object itself. A Christian ethic, however, must stress more than just intention, for what we do, and not merely why we do it, remains a necessary ethical consideration. The Christian is called upon to build up the new heaven and the new earth by his actions which means that good intentions alone are not sufficient. The complex ethical problems facing our modern society such as the concept and use of power, redistribution of wealth, international trade relations, equality of educational opportunity for all the people in our own country and in the world cannot be solved merely by good intentions, since there are some ways more appropriate than others for solving these problems.

Many of these erroneous approaches illustrate the trend in some situation ethics (note the many different ways in which this term can be used) which fails to give enough importance to the societal aspect of reality. A narrow situationalism often fails to go beyond the two persons involved in a particular action and the very immediate consequences of their actions. Catholic theology has not given enough importance in the past to the human person and his subjective development, but a narrow personalism is really only an exaggerated individualism. The model of I-thou relationship has been emphasized with many important contributions in recent theological literature, but there remains a great danger in reducing all moral reality to the model of I-thou relationships. The model of ethical thinking must include all the aspects of reality including man's relationships to all other people, institutions, and the cosmos itself as well as his connections with the past and his responsibilities for the future.[14] It is interesting to note that the fascination with the situation ethics debate has waned in the last two years precisely because all today realize the greater importance attached to problems of social ethics, whereas situation ethics generally considered questions of an individual morality. Theological ethics needs a methodology which can deal effectively with both social and individual ethics.

Another danger existing today concerns the very concept of obligation and "ought" in moral theology. An older Catholic theology overemphasized obligation especially in the forms of Pelagianism and legalism which viewed the Christian life almost exclusively in terms of the model of obedience to the laws of God—the divine law, natural law, and positive law. In overreacting to the past there is a danger of completely forgetting the aspect of obligation which—although it can never be the cornerstone of all morality—remains an important element. The Christian has received the new life in Christ Jesus and has the obligation to grow in his understanding of the Christian life which is summarized in the death-to-life transition of the Paschal Mystery. There is truly no growth or development without implying the concept of obligation, for continual conversion remains both a gift and a demand for the Christian.

The essays in this volume have employed an historically conscious methodology in approaching moral problems which avoids the difficulties in the classicist approach, but there is an erroneous tendency today of adopting a sheer existentialism which is a philosophical actualism with some affinities to the theological actualism mentioned above. A sheer existentialism emphasizes the present moment with no connection to what has gone before and no connection with the future and without considering the horizontal relationships of the present that bind people to one another and to their commitments. Such an existentialism so highlights the singularity of the present that there are no adequate criteria for judging the present. Theological ethics has learned from its history the danger of uncritically accepting and baptizing the present moment, since everything in the present moment is not good. Theological ethics needs criteria by which it can judge and properly criticize the present. Any methodology which so concentrates on the present that it cannot stand back to critically judge the present cannot be an adequate approach. The classicist approach erred by establishing many universal norms to which the individual had to conform, but sheer existentialism errs by not being able, even in principle, to establish some criteria for judging the present.

Many of the erroneous approaches in theological ethics as in other sciences do not arise from positive error but rather from an overly simplistic approach which fails to take into consideration elements which are important and necessary. The danger of over-simplification can be seen in some contemporary stresses on the function of love in the life of the Christian. No one can deny the centrality and importance of love in the Christian life, but it is overly simplistic to go immediately from love to the solution of complex human problems. There appears again an unwillingness to grapple with the criteria by which one assesses the demands of love in concrete situations. H. Richard Niebuhr pointed out the impossibility of adequately describing Jesus and his ethics in terms of love or any other single virtue.[15] The critical reaction to Joseph Fletcher's insistence on love also illustrates the error in reducing all Christian ethics to love in an overly simplistic way. The late Bishop Pike criticized Fletcher's concept of love as *agape* precisely because it did not give enough importance to the notion of love as *eros. Agape* signifies a love for the other which is independent of the person's own merits or goodness, but Pike rightly points out that at times a person needs to be loved precisely for what he is in himself and not merely because of the love of God.[16] James Gustafson has criticized in Fletcher's work his confusing concept of love which takes on many different meanings: "It is the *only* thing which is intrinsically good; it *equals* justice; it is a formal *principle,* it is a *disposition,* it is a *predicate* and not a property, it is a ruling *norm.*"[17] Donald Evans has likewise pointed out the different and conflicting notions of love in the theory of Fletcher.[18] Since Fletcher reduces ethical theory only to love and the concrete situation, it is obvious that love must take on many different and ultimately conflicting meanings. Again the complex problems of social ethics argue against such an oversimplistic approach to Christian ethics.

A very unfortunate aspect of the situation ethics debate has been the tendency to view the Christian life almost exclusively in terms of law and its application, for the total moral phenomena include much more than just laws. Ethical considerations must also consider the person, the dispositions which characterize the person, and his multiple relationships. Also the goals and ideals of the Christian life are most important. As the role of law or norms rightly becomes less in the life of the Christian, these other aspects such as the dispositions and virtues, as well as the general horizon or outlook of the Christian on human reality, will take on even greater importance. There will always be some place for norms and principles in the Christian moral theory (although these essays have denied the existence of absolute norms in the form of negative, moral absolutes in which the moral act is described solely in terms of the physical structure of the act itself), but Christian thinkers have consistently emphasized that the primary "law" for the Christian is the internal "law of the Spirit." The external law remains always secondary and relative insofar as it points out some of the demands and criteria for recognizing the call of the Spirit.

THE TEACHING FUNCTION OF THE CHURCH

The most immediate problem raised by the widespread negative reaction to the papal encyclical on birth control obviously concerns the function and role of the teaching office in the Church. The recent debate has brought to light the fact that theology and the hierarchical magisterium did recognize in the past that Catholics could dissent from authoritative, noninfallible papal teaching when there are sufficient reasons for such dissent.[19] Theologians today are also reconsidering the entire concept of infallibility, but this aspect of the question lies beyond the scope of the present consideration. There has never been an infallible pronouncement or teaching on a specific moral matter; the very nature of specific moral actions makes it impossible, in my judgment, to have any infallible pronouncements in this area. The hierarchical magisterium has taught in the area of specific moral questions with an authentic or authoritative non-infallible magisterium. Even the terminology "authentic" or "authoritative" must be properly understood, for authentic does not necessarily mean that this teaching is always true. Such terminology is of comparatively recent origin, appearing for the first time in documents of the hierarchical magisterium in 1863.[20] The very term "noninfallible," no matter how it is interpreted, still signifies that this particular teaching is fallible. In the light of these and other considerations, what is the future of the teaching office or function in the Roman Catholic Church?

Should the Roman Catholic Church and other Christian Churches speak out on the moral problems facing man and society today? I believe that the Christian Churches have a responsibility to speak out on the issues, for the Church cannot withdraw from the reality and complexity of daily life in the world. The Church exists today in the service of life in the world and can no longer exist merely in sacred times and sacred places. The basic insight behind the theological position affirming the existence of natural law was the fact that man's daily life in the world is somehow meaningful and important, but the older approach with its dichotomy between the natural and supernatural did not adequately express the relationship between man's daily life in the world and the kingdom of God. Also in an older theological pattern the Church was looked upon as more important than the world and as controlling the world in some way, but contemporary theology stresses the importance and independence of the world. The Church can no longer dominate the world, but it must respect the integrity of the world and try to be of service in the world, which is constantly marked by the struggle against human limitation and sinfulness, in trying to cooperate in bringing about the new heaven and the new earth which will be in some continuity with the present but also in some discontinuity with the world and history.

How does the Church carry out its teaching function and mission in the world today? First of all, it is important to point out that the teaching function and role of the Church belong to the whole Church and not just to the hierarchical and papal teaching office in the Church. A Roman Catholic admits the hierarchical and papal teaching office, but there has been a danger in the past of identifying the whole magisterial function of the Church with these offices. The ecclesiology ratified in Vatican II has pointed out that the Church is the whole People of God and not just the hierarchy; now ecclesiology is pushing forward with the realization that the teaching function of the Church, like the Church itself, cannot be restricted to and identical with the hierarchical teaching office. This realization appears in a seminal way in some of the emphases of Vatican II, which point out the many different ways in which the Church teaches and learns. There exists a prophetic voice in the Church which is not the same as the hierarchical teaching office (Constitution on the Church, n. 12). The Declaration on Religious Liberty in the opening paragraph recognizes a desire for religious liberty arising in the consciousness and experience of men and declares these desires "to be greatly in accord with truth and justice." The truth of religious liberty did not come into existence merely when the conciliar magisterium published a decree, but obviously had been true before that time. A familiarity with the many areas of change in Catholic teaching points out the importance of the prophetic voice in the Church and the role of the experience of men.[21] The emphasis on dialogue in Vatican II—dialogue with other Christians, with non-Christians, with atheists, with the world—reminds us that the Roman Catholic Church does not have all the answers to the problems facing contemporary man. Again history points out the many times in which the Church has learned from other Christians and non-Christians: for example, religious liberty, interest on loans, the needs of the working man, and lately in our own country the importance of peace and the rights of the poor.

Theologically, the fact that the teaching mission of the Church cannot be restricted to the hierarchical teaching office stems from a number of accepted teachings in the Catholic Church. The primary teacher in the Church remains the Holy Spirit who dwells in the hearts of the faithful and in all men of good will, so that no one person has a monopoly on the Spirit. The Spirit is well characterized by the biblical expression that he blows where he wills. A theology of baptism also illustrates that the whole Church is magisterial. The liturgical renewal in the Church is based on the fact that through baptism every Christian participates in the priestly office of Jesus Christ and thus all are called upon to actively participate in the eucharistic life and worship of the Church. However, through baptism the Christian not only participates in the priestly function of Jesus but also in his prophetic or teaching and ruling function.[22] Just as the priestly function of all believers is not incompatible with the ministerial priesthood, so too the magisterial character of all Christians is not irreconcilable with the hierarchical teaching office in the Church. Thus theology supports the contention that the whole Church is magisterial. Catholic theology and practice can no longer simply identify the magisterium of the Church with the hierarchical magisterium, for the hierarchical magisterium is just one aspect of the total teaching mission of the Church.

One of the primary difficulties with the encyclical *Humanae Vitae* is the insistence on identifying the teaching function of the Church with the hierarchical teaching office. With the exception of somewhat general citations from Sacred Scripture and one reference to Thomas Aquinas, all the references cited in this document are to previous statements of the hierarchical magisterium. In fact, the primary reason for not accepting a different approach to the practical question of contraception was the previous teaching of the hierarchical magisterium (*H.V.*, n. 6). This papal document like many others in the past relies almost totally on past teachings of the hierarchical magisterium, and thus is guilty of an intellectual incest. The "papal predecessors of happy memory" have made many important and correct statements in the past, but such teaching on these matters is subject to error and also needs to be relativized in the light of the full teaching function of the Church. A number of overly simplistic approaches should be avoided in this context. The magisterial function of the Church can never be reduced to a mere consensus or majority rule, since the criteria for discerning the Spirit are much more complex than that. Likewise, one cannot merely dismiss papal teaching, but religious assent is the technical term used by the theologians in the past to indicate the respect that must be given to such teaching with the realization, however, that such teaching could be wrong and not call for an intellectual assent. By objecting to papal teaching theologians are not setting themselves up as a new and separate hierarchical magisterium but are merely carrying out their interpretive role in and for the Church. Precisely because the teaching function of the Church is not perfectly identical with the hierarchical teaching office there will always remain this tension which cannot be resolved in an overly simplistic fashion either by maintaining that the pope can never be wrong or by saying that the pope is just another theological voice in the Church.

In the future, theological understanding of the relationship between the hierarchical teaching office in the Church and the whole Church as magisterial in a certain sense must change the methodological approach to the way in which papal teachings are studied and proposed. There was a tremendous difference between the methodological approach in the writing of the Pastoral Constitution on the Church in the Modern World and the methodological approach to *Humanae Vitae*. The Pastoral Constitution was written after consultations with leading experts, theologians, and only after years of debate and consultation with all the bishops of the world. A papal commission was called into existence to help the Pope on the matter of birth control, but obviously *Humanae* Vitae was not written with their help and collaboration. The noncollegial character of the methodology employed in writing *Humanae Vitae* is evidenced by the small and nonrepresentative group of theologians who actually worked on the composition of the encyclical.[23] Future papal teachings must realize better in practice the magisterial function of the whole Church and be elaborated in greater consultation and collegiality with the whole Church so that they speak in a more complete and adequate manner for the whole teaching Church, but even then such teachings on specific moral matters will never enjoy an absolute certitude.

Theology today is much more conscious than it was in the past that teachings on specific matters cannot enjoy an absolute certitude. In the past a number of factors contributed to a greater insistence on certitude in the teaching of the Church although the older theologians recognized in a somewhat guarded way that such noninfallible, authoritative teaching did not insure an absolute certitude which excluded the possibility of error. From a theological perspective, an authoritarian and overly hierarchical understanding of the Church together with a juridical understanding of teaching authority tended to give an authoritarian certitude to the pronouncements and teachings of the hierarchical magisterium. Better theological approaches in these areas obviously show the more conditional aspect of such hierarchical teaching, but even more importantly theologians and philosophers today are much more aware of human limitations in arriving at certitude than they were in the past. The more historically minded methodology calls for a more inductive approach which by its very nature can never achieve the certitude of a more deductive approach. All sciences today reflect the changed scientific ideal which no longer even strives for an absolute certitude which would in reality be the enemy of any true progress in knowledge and science. Thinkers today are aware of the imperfections of human language in attempting to articulate and express our understandings of reality. These three aspects which are intimately connected with a more historically conscious methodology show the impossibility of arriving at absolute certitude on specific moral matters especially those affecting complex social problems. Above we have discussed the reasons against the truth, let alone the certitude, of negative moral absolutes described as actions in which the moral act is considered solely in terms of the physical structure of the act itself.

The fact that the teaching of the Church on such specific matters cannot claim absolute certitude follows from the incarnational nature of the Church with all its inherent human limitations which are not overcome by its union with Christ. The pilgrim nature of the Church and the insistence on the dialogical quest for truth also argue against the possibility of such certitude. It seems to me that the very ideal or goal of such absolute certitude itself remains an obstacle in the Church's carrying out its prophetic and teaching mission. If one aspires to certitude in his statements and teaching, then he is condemned either to speaking in platitudes or to speaking long after the critical problems have arisen and been faced. If the teaching function of the Church—both in the eyes of its members and others—is freed from the shackles of absolute certitude in the area of specific moral problems, then it can raise its voice in a way to help the world as it faces so many complex problems today. The complexity of problems and the swiftly changing aspects of contemporary life show the impossibility of any absolute certitude in these matters. However, the Church cannot merely stand back and say nothing, since the Christian Church does have a function in assisting men to do their important but limited work in bringing about the new heaven and the new earth.

The Church must raise its voice on particular issues facing the world and society today with the understanding that it does not speak with an absolute certitude but proposes what it thinks to be the best possible Christian approach with the realization that it might be wrong. The Church should avoid the dangers of theological and philosophical actualism by showing the various criteria and principles which enter into its judgment in this particular case. Many times the Church with more certitude will be able to point out in a negative fashion approaches which should not be taken. As the Church or anyone else comes closer to concrete, particular decisions the danger of error becomes greater. The Church in its teaching must continue to do two things: to express constantly and continually develop the various criteria, principles, goals, and ideals which the Christian incorporates into his decision-making process and at the same time, but in a more hesitant manner, propose some concrete solutions for the manifold problems facing contemporary man.

In discussing the teaching mission of the Church it is most important to underscore the analogous concept of the very term "teaching." The dangers of understanding the teaching role in an overly authoritarian and juridical way have already been pointed out. The concept of teaching authority itself opens the door to a voluntaristic and extrinsic concept of teaching which downplays the fact that the truth is the ultimate authority of teaching. Today and in the future one cannot discuss the teaching and prophetic function of the Church without understanding the different interpretations of "teacher." In the past the teacher was the person who packaged knowledge and handed it over in easily digestible form to his students who tended in a passive way to absorb this data. The teacher today is not primarily the person who imparts knowledge in this way, but rather the one who stimulates others to grapple with the questions of the day and thus to develop themselves and their society. The teacher is not necessarily an answer man, but rather one who stimulates his students by asking the right questions and pointing out possible avenues of approach. Too often in the past the teaching or prophetic role of the Church has been seen in giving answers or pronouncements to particular questions. This approach wedded to a claim of absolute certitude actually hindered the Church from properly fulfilling its teaching and prophetic function. The Church at times is in the best position to raise the embarrassing questions and also to show other institutions and society by its own actions what type of approaches might be taken to the problems of contemporary life.

The understanding of the teaching function of the Church described above has many important implications. From an ecumenical viewpoint, such an understanding of the teaching mission of the Church in these specific moral questions should not be an obstacle to the union of Christians, for it closely resembles many of the theoretical approaches adopted in Protestant circles today. The most important implications for the present involve the need for the Roman Catholic Church to realize not only in theory but also in practice such an understanding. The Roman Catholic Church badly needs the structures by which the magisterial character of the whole Church as well as the special hierarchical teaching office will exercise their proper roles in the teaching of the Church, which roles can never be viewed primarily in terms of pronouncements but which must always include this aspect of teaching.

NOTES

1.

For a summary of some critical comments on situation ethics, see *The Situation Ethics Debate,* ed. Harvey Cox (Philadelphia: Westminster Press, 1968). On the question of the Church and social teaching, see Paul Ramsey, *Who Speaks for the Church?* (Nashville and New York: Abingdon Press, 1967).

2.

Louis Monden, *Sin, Liberty and Law* (New York: Sheed and Ward, 1965), pp. 136-145; Bernard Häring, "Dynamism and Continuity in a Personalistic Approach to Natural Law," in *Norm and Context in Christian Ethics,* ed. Gene H. Outka and Paul Ramsey (New York: Charles Scribner's Sons, 1968), pp. 216-218.

3.

Such an approach denies the validity of a theory that begins by describing the moral act in terms of the physical structure of the act, but it does not deny that for truly moral considerations the moral act may be identical with the physical structure of the act.

4.

This particular criticism applies, for example, to W. H. van der Marck, O.P., *Toward a Christian Ethic* (Westminster, Md.: Newman Press, 1967).

5.

For an example of a contemporary Protestant approach which departs from some of the theological bases proposed in orthodox Protestantism, see James Sellers, *Theological Ethics* (New York: Macmillan Co., 1966).

6.
James M. Gustafson, *Christ and the Moral Life* (New York: Harper and Row, 1968), p. 28. The brief description of Barthian ethics in this paragraph is based primarily on Gustafson's summary, pp. 13-60.

7.
Paul L. Lehmann, *Ethics in a Christian Context* (New York: Harper and Row, 1963), pp. 131 and 159-161.

8.
Gustafson, p. 59.

9.
Ramsey, *Who Speaks for the Church,* pp. 58-118.

10.
Ibid., pp. 118-147.

11.
Ibid., p. 53. Ramsey earlier acknowledged that some would wrongly brand him as "one who believes the church to be a spiritual cult with no pertinent social outlook" (p. 20), but the distinction made above seems unfortunate precisely because creation, nature, and history do have a relationship to the reign of God in Christ.

12.
Paul Ramsey, *Deeds and Rules in Christian Ethics* (New York: Charles Scribner's Sons, 1967), pp. 187ff.

13.
For apparent approval of the dropping of the atomic bomb, see Joseph Fletcher, *Situation Ethics* (Philadelphia: Westminster Press, 1966), pp. 167-168; W. van der Marck, O.P., *Love and Fertility* (London: Sheed and Ward, 1965), pp. 61-63.

14.
H. Richard Niebuhr, *The Responsible Self* (New York: Harper and Row, 1963), pp. 55ff.

15.
H. Richard Niebuhr, *Christ and Culture* (New York: Harper and Row, 1951; Torchback, 1956), pp. 15-19.
16.
James A. Pike, *You and the New Morality* (New York: Harper and Row, 1967), pp. 68-69.
17.
James M. Gustafson, "Love Monism," in *Storm over Ethics* (no place given: United Church Press, 1967), p. 33.
18.
Donald Evans, "Love, Situations, and Rules," in *Norm and Context in Christian Ethics*, pp. 369ff.
19.
Joseph A. Komonchak, "Ordinary Papal Magisterium and Religious Assent," in *Contraception: Authority and Dissent*, ed. Charles E. Curran (New York: Herder and Herder, 1969), pp. 101-126.
20.
Komonchak, p. 115.
21.
Daniel C. Maguire, "Moral Absolutes and the Magisterium," in *Absolutes in Moral Theology?*, ed. Charles E. Curran (Washington: Corpus Books, 1968), pp. 57-70.
22.
Yves M. J. Congar, O.P., *Lay People in the Church* (London: Geoffrey Chapman, 1959), basically develops the second part of this work, originally written before World War II, in accord with the threefold participation through baptism in the office and mission of Jesus.
23.
Bernard Häring, "The Encyclical Crisis," *Commonweal*, LXXXVIII (Sept. 6, 1968), pp. 588-594.

Index

Abelard, Peter, 31
Abortion, 143-145
Absolution, 2, 31f., 39, 45, 54f., 57, 59, 64
Actualism, theological, 248-251, 255, 264
Agapism, 228, 240n., 256
Albert the Great, 106
Alphonsus, St., 114, 165f., 183n.
Alszeghy, Zoltan, 41, 64, 82-83n., 87-88n., 93n.
Anciaux, Paul, 34, 81n., 87n., 89n., 92n.
Anselm, St., 51
Anthropology, 10, 30, 99, 109; see also person
Aquaviva, Claudius, 164
Aristotle, 106, 132f.
Artificial insemination, 193
Augustine, St., 63
Authentic magisterium, 258

Barth, Karl, 235, 248
Bennett, John C. 98, 149n., 227, 239n.
Binding and loosing, 38-42, 53, 61
Biological knowledge of reproduction, 161-163, 170, 182n.
Bonaventure, St., 42
Bonhoeffer, Dietrich, 98, 248
Brunner, Emil, 98, 241n.
Bultmann, Rudolf, 235

Cajetan, Cardinal, 70, 79, 165f.
Carra de Vaux Saint Cyr, Bruno, 77, 85n., 94n., 97n.
Celebration of penance, 2, 26, 44, 59f., 73-79
Charles, P. 54f., 91n.
Church and state, 119-121, 127
Classicist methodology, 119-121, 124, 126, 129, 136, 255; see also worldview
Clonal reproduction, 193, 210, 215, 221n.

Collegiality and methodology, 261f.
Communitarian ethics, 139, 199-203, see also social ethics
Compromise, theology of 102, 244f.
Confession, 60-68; age for, 2, 80n., of devotion, 74f., experimentation with, 75-79; plurality of forms for, 61, 68, 73f., 92n., to others, 61f., wider use of term, 62-64; see also Integrity requirement, Penance
Confiteri, meaning of, 62f.
Consequentialism, 214f., 250-253
Contraception, 142, 144, 146, 207, 268
Contrition, 30f.
Conversion, 14, 26-30, 60f., 72-74, 84n., 233, 255; see also metanoia.
Coreth, Emerich, 140, 156n.
Cosmic redemption, 233
Cox, Harvey, 205, 222n., 226

DeGraaf, 162
DeLetter, P., 34, 86n.
Deontological ethics, 234-237
Didache, 37
Dilthey, Wilhelm, 147, 158n.
Discernment of spirits, 238
Divorce, 147, 244
Dobzhansky, Theodosius, 191, 21n.
Dualist views of man, of natural and supernatural, 99-102, 109, 215, 225-227n., 244f., 258

Ecclesial aspect of penance, 4, 31, 35-47, 58
Empirical approach, 128-130
End and means, 252f.
Epikeia, 78
Eschatology, 206f., 209, 230f., 245
Ethical methodology, see methodology
Eugenics, 192f., 208, 212f., negative, 192; positive, 192f.
Euphenics, 194f.
Euthanasia, 142, 146, 207, 244

Evans, Donald, 256
Existentialism in ethics, 255
Experimentation, medical and scientific, 179, 189f., 201 215-217
Ezekiel, 51

Faith & works dichotomy, 247f.
Falloppio, Gabriele, 162
First International Symposium on Genetics, 212
Fisher, John, 70
Fletcher, Joseph, 178, 251, 256, 267
Frankena, William, 228, 240n.
Fransen, Pierre, 67, 83n.
Fuchs, Josef, 166, 180n., 188n.
Fundamental option, 15, 19f., 50, 83n., 167, 175; *see also* sin

Genesis, 10-13, 198
Genetic engineering, 193f.
Genetics, 189-217; competence of ethicians on, 190f., morality, 196-217; scientific facts of, 191-195, 218n., *see also* eugenics, genetic engineering, euphenics
Gregory XVI, Pope, 196
Guzzetti, G. B., 55, 88n., 91n.
Gustafson, James, 178, 186n., 188n., 219n., 229, 240-241n., 248, 256, 267-268n.

Hadrian VI, Pope, 70
Häring, Bernard, 83n., 92n., 100, 140, 150n., 266n., 286n.
Heggen, F. J., 64, 80n., 92n.
Hermeneutic problem, 233, 240n.
Hertwig, Oscar, 163
Hesed, 51
Historical methodology, 5, 119-121, 126f., 130, 136, 243, 255, 263; *see also* worldview
Homosexuality, 176f., 187n.
Homounculus in spermatazoa, 163
Hope, 230f.
Hugh of St. Victor, 31
Humanae Vitae, 97-104, 116, 136-138, 174, 186n., 242, 260-262
Huxley, Julian, 192, 218n.

I-thou model, 257
Individualist methodology, 199-202, 254

Inductive methodology, *see* historical methodology
Infallibility, 257
Isidore of Seville, 103, 107
Instruction of March 25, 1944, 66, 78, 94n.
Integrity requirement for confession, 2, 26f., 65-68, 75-79, 92-93n.

James, St., 60
John, St., 18, 36, 41, 52, 198
John XXIII, Pope, 123, 151n., 200
Judgment in penance, 5, 47-60, 91n.

Kerygma, 9, 57

Lambruschini, Msgr., 100
Lazareth, William, 233, 240n.
Law, 130f., 226, 234, 256; *see also* natural law, obligation
Lederberg, Joshua, 193-195, 210f., 215, 218-219n., 223n.
Lehmann, Paul, 235-238, 241n., 248, 267n.
LeMaistre, Martin, 163f.
Lenin, N., 210
Leo XIII, Pope, 103f., 150-151n., 200
Libri Paenitentiales, 4
Ligier, Louis, 65, 94n.
Lombard, Peter, 30f.
Lonergan Bernard, 116f., 121, 134, 136, 140f., 149n., 153-156n.
Love monism, 229, 239, 268n.
Luke St., 36, 59
Lying and falsehood, 114-116

MacQuarrie, John, 135
Magisterium, *see* teaching role
Marechal, Joseph, 140, 153n.
Mark, St., 26
Masturbation, 114, 142, 152n., 161, 169, 175f., 187n.
Matson, Floyd, 147, 158n.
Matthew, St., 9, 18, 28, 39, 61
Metanoia, 26f., 29, 57, 59; *see also* conversion
Methodology in ethics, 119-136, 171f., 228f., 232, 242-257, 261-263; *see also* classicist methodology, historical methodology, etc.

Moreno, J. 165f., 183n., 185n.

Mortal sin, *see* sin, criteria for

Muller, Hermann, 191-195, 198f., 208, 210-213, 216, 216-218n., 222-223n.

Murray, John Courtney, 116f., 119-121, 127, 153-154n., 156n., 196f.

Natural law, 97-142, ambiguity of concept, 104f., 160; advantages of concept, 99, 101, 138f., 249, 258; alternatives to, 139-141; and common ground morality, 227, 238; and methodology, 97-99, 159, 168, 243; Protestant opposition to, 98, 226f., 248; and total Christian perspective, 98-104, 247f., Ulpian's view, 106-111, 161; and worldview, 116-138; *see also* cosmic redemption, dualist view of man, physicism

Nature, 99, 101, 111-113, 132f., 161, 244f., 258

Navarrus, Dr., 164f., 183n.

Niebuhr, H. Richard, 99, 140, 149n., 156n., 209, 221n., 234f., 240-241n., 256, 267-268n.

Niebuhr, Reinhold, 98, 221n., 226, 234, 239n.

Negative moral absolutes, 148, 245, 263

Obligation in morality, 254f.

Ogden, 136

Palmer, Paul, 77, 81n., 87-89n., 96n.

Parvity of matter in sexual sins, 160, 164-170, 183-184n.

Paschal mystery, 9, 25, 57, 71, 252, 255

Paul St. 52, 100, 198f.

Paul VI, Pope, 97, 110, 151n., 201

Pelagianism, 248

Penance, 1-7, 26-80; Aquinas on, 30-33; and Eucharist, 68-72; history of, 3-5, 30-35, 37, 49, 61-65, 69-71, 81n., magical approach to, 5, 34, 37, 72; matter and form of, 32, 60; necessity of, 35; renewal of, 2-6, 62, 66f., sacramentality of, 2, 30-35, 45, 76; Scriptures on,

Penance—(cont'd)
3, 5f., 26-30, 35-42; Thomist and Scotist positions, 33-35; worship aspect of, 59f., 92n. *see also* absolution, binding and loosing, celebration, confession, ecclesial aspect, integrity, judgment, *res et sacramentum*

Person, personalism, 15, 19f., 139, 172f., 214, 243, 254, 266

Peter, Carl, 67, 92n., 95n., 149

Physicism, 105-116, 141-144, 148, 161, 207, 216, 252f.

Pike, James, 256, 268n.

Pius IX, Pope, 196

Pius XII, Pope, 137, 157, 201, 212, 215, 220-221n.

Platonic worldview, 118

Polygamy, 244

Populorum Progressio, 201

Poschmann, Bernard, 81n., 83-85n., 87n.

Premarital sex, 169, 173, 177-180, 186n.

Primary and secondary ends of marriage, 110f., 161f., 169, 181n., 186n., 202f.

Property, 103f., 200f., 220n.

Psalms, Book of, 43, 63

Rahner, Karl, 6, 34, 39f., 42, 82n., 85n., 87n., 89n., 92n., 134, 136, 140, 149n., 153-156n., 197, 219n.

Ramsey, Paul, 98, 149n., 158n., 174, 186-188n., 195, 198n., 205-207, 215f., 219-224n., 228, 240-241n., 249-251, 266-267n.

Res et sacramentum, 42-44, 88n.

Responsibility ethic, 235-238

Salvation History, 13

Sanchez, Thomas, 164f., 183-184n.

Schillebeeckx, E., 34, 85n., 89n.

Scientific worldview, 214f.

Scotus, John Duns, 33

Scriptural methodology, 171, 186n., 227f., 233-238

Scrupulosity, 29

Sexual sins, 108, 168

Sexuality, 108-110, 142-145, 159-180, 198f., 213; broader aspects

Sexuality—(cont'd)
of, 160, 168-175; emphasis on physical, 168f., limitations of 172f., and love, 173f., 198f., 213; and procreation, 174, 198f., 213; societal aspect, 174f., *see also* biological knowledge, homosexuality, masturbation, primary ends, premarital sex.

Sin, 7-26; alienation of multiple relationships by, 7-15, 28f., 49-50n., 61, 73; and Church, offense against, 38, 40; community responsibility for, 8f., 82n., and corruption, 22; cosmic aspect of, 12f., criteria for distinguishing mortal and venial sin, 14-23, 50n., 167; and death, 57; external aspect emphasized, 10, 15-21, 49n., formal and material sin, 20; misuse of plural form of, 21; rarity of mortal sin, 16, 23, 75; reality of sin, 9f., 22-26, 101f., 172, 209f., 229f., 244f., reluctance to admit reality of sin, 7-10, 23f., 101; scriptures on, 10-15; *secundam naturam et contra naturam*, 108, 161f., *see also* fundamental option.

Sittler, J. 248

Situation ethics, 142-148, 243f., 254, 256

Social ethics, 225-233; Christian contribution to, 229-233, 253f., 256

Social Gospel, 254

Sterilization, 136f., 143, 192, 202, 244

Stoic philosophy, 111f.

Suarez, 42

Subjective and objective morality, 243f.

Teaching role of Church, 257-265; analogous meaning of teacher,

264f., and certitude, 262-264; role of whole Church as teacher, 259-262

Technology, 7f., 20, 112f., 136, 189, 207, 209, 211f.

Teleological ethics, 234

Tertullian, 37

Thomas, St., 31-35, 41, 56, 61, 85n., 93n., 103, 105-109, 113, 117, 135, 138, 150n., 153n., 161, 163f., 167, 170, 180-182n., 205, 260

Tillard, J.M.R., 71, 95-96n.

Totality, principle of, 201, 220-221n.

Transcendental methodology, 139-141, 243

Trent, Council of, 4, 30, 33, 35f., 47-49, 55, 58, 60-62, 64, 66f., 70f., 92n.

Triumphalism, 246f.

Two realm theory, 226f.

Ulpian, 106-111, 116, 161, 181n.

Utopian worldview, 208f., 211, 216

VanLeeuwenhoek, 162f.

Vatican II, *Constitution on the Church*, 44, 122f., 259; *Constitution on the Liturgy*, 2, 76; *Declaration on Religious Liberty*, 259; *Pastoral Constitution on the Church in the Modern World*, 5, 100, 110, 121, 139, 153n., 168, 186n., 233, 262; worldview of 121-123, 262

Venial sin, *see* sin, criteria for

Viet-Nam, 250

Vogel, Cyril, 69, 95n.

Voluntarist view, 33, 253

West, Charles, 8, 82n.

Worldviews, 116-119; classicist, 116-119, 124f., 131, 134, 136; historical, 116-119, 125, 132, 136, 196f., scientific, 214f.

Xiberta, B. 42-44, 88n.